GOING MISSING

LIVING AWAY FROM HOME: STUDIES IN RESIDENTIAL CARE

Other Titles in the Series

GOING MISSING

Young People Absent From Care

Jim Wade and Nina Biehal
with
Jasmine Clayden and Mike Stein

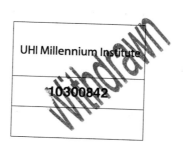
JOHN WILEY & SONS

Chichester · New York · Weinheim · Brisbane · Singapore · Toronto

National   01243 779777
International   (+44) 1243 779777
e-mail (for orders and customer service enquiries):
cs-books@wiley.co.uk
Visit our Home Page on http://www.wiley.co.uk
or http://www.wiley.com

Other Wiley Editorial Offices

John Wiley & Sons, Inc., 605 Third Avenue,
New York, NY 10158-0012, USA

WILEY-VCH Verlag GmbH, Pappelallee 3,
D-69469 Weinheim, Germany

Jacaranda Wiley Ltd, 33 Park Road, Milton,
Queensland 4064, Australia

John Wiley & Sons (Asia) Pte Ltd, 2 Clementi Loop #02-01,
Jin Xing Distripark, Singapore 129809

John Wiley & Sons (Canada) Ltd, 22 Worcester Road,
Rexdale, Ontario M9W 1L1, Canada

Library of Congress Cataloging-in-Publication Data

Wade, Jim.
    Going missing : young people absent from care / Jim Wade and Nina
Biehal with Jasmine Clayden and Mike Stein.
        p.   cm. — (Living away from home)
    Includes bibliographical references and index.
    ISBN 0-471-98476-0
    1. Runaway children—Great Britain.   2. Runaway children.
3. Runaway teenagers—Great Britain.   Runaway teenagers.
5. Social work with children—Great Britain.   6. Social work with
youth—Great Britain.   I. Biehal, Nina.   II. Title.   III. Series.
HV887.G7W33   1998
362.74—dc21   98-35151
                                                                                        CIP

British Library Cataloguing in Publication Data

A catalogue record for this book is available from the British Library

ISBN 0-471-98476-0

Typeset in 10/12pt Palatino by Dorwyn Ltd, Rowlands Castle, Hants
Printed and bound in Great Britain by Biddles Ltd, Guildford and King's Lynn
This book is printed on acid-free paper responsibly manufactured from sustainable forestry,
in which at least two trees are planted for each one used for paper production.

CONTENTS

ABOUT THE AUTHORS

Jim Wade has an extensive background in youth and community work and as a social worker with teenagers. Formerly a Research Fellow at the University of Leeds with a research interest in young people leaving care and youth transitions more generally, he is now a Senior Research Fellow at the Social Work Research and Development Unit, University of York.

Nina Biehal, a former social worker, has been involved in research on user involvement, leaving care and prevention. She is currently a Senior Research Fellow at the Social Work Research and Development Unit, University of York.

Jasmine Clayden formerly worked as a residential social worker and more recently has been involved in research on looked after young people at the Universities of Leeds and York. She is currently a Research Fellow at the Social Work Research and Development Unit, University of York.

Mike Stein is currently Professor of Social Policy and Social Work and Joint Director of the Social Work Research and Development Unit at the University of York. He has practised as a social worker and probation officer and has an extensive background of researching child care issues with a particular focus on leaving care.

The team has previously collaborated on a study of young people leaving care, published as: *Moving On: Young People and Leaving Care Schemes* (HMSO, 1995).

FOREWORD

We are pleased to have the opportunity to provide the foreword to this book, which is one of a series of publications that, we are sure, will prove to be a significant contribution to thinking in both the practice and management of the care of children who need to live away from home.

The group of studies about residential care was commissioned to address key concerns arising from public inquiries, such as the Utting (*Children in the Public Care*) and Pindown Inquiries, and to provide a balanced account of what life is like for children and staff in the majority of children's homes in the UK in the 1990s.

Twelve linked research studies were commissioned by the Department of Health in the period 1990–94: (a thirteenth – that of David Berridge and Isabelle Brodie – was not commissioned by the Department). These research studies came in the wake of the implementation of the Children Act 1989 and its Regulations and Guidance, which provided significant new safeguards for children living away from home. Additional government action to protect these children was taken following the publication of the reports *Children in the Public Care*, *Accommodating Children*, *Another Kind of Home* and *Choosing with Care*, notably through the publications of the Support Force for Children's Residential Care and circulars issued by the relevant Departments of State. However, as Sir William Utting tells us in his second report, *People Like Us*, published in 1997, providing safe and caring settings for children looked after away from home remains a significant challenge for the 1990s.

This book, taken together with the overview publication, and the others in the series contains lessons for all those concerned with children and young people living away from home, who are the responsibility of all of us.

Carolyn Davies, *Department of Health*
Lesley Archer, *University of York*
Leslie Hicks, *University of York*
Mike Little, *Dartington Social Research Unit*
—Editors

ACKNOWLEDGEMENTS

A great many people helped to make this study possible. We would like to thank the Department of Health for sponsoring the project and especially the members of our Advisory Group for their constructive help and support. Many thanks then to Dr Carolyn Davies, who chaired the group, to Chris Sealey and to our external advisers, Professors David Berridge and Jane Aldgate, for their helpful comments. We are extremely grateful to everyone in our participating local authorities who helped and advised us during the course of this study. In particular, we would like to acknowledge the members of our project groups and all the field social workers, residential social workers and foster carers who completed our questionnaires without complaint and gave their time for our interviews.

A special thanks goes to Gwyther Rees who acted as our statistical consultant. Despite taking on a group of unreconstructed qualitative researchers, he managed to guide us through the mysteries of statistical analysis with much patience and good humour. Also to Janet Barton, who provided secretarial support in the early stages of the project, and Sara Mason who organised our office and meticulously transcribed many hours of interviews for us. Thanks also to our colleagues in the Social Work Research and Development Unit at University of York; in particular to Professor Ian Sinclair and Lorraine Wallis whose detailed comments on earlier drafts were much appreciated.

Most of all we are indebted to the young people who participated in our study. Without their willingness to talk to us about quite painful aspects of their troubled lives, this book could not have been written. We hope that we have been able to do justice to their views.

The order in which the names of the two principal authors, Nina Biehal and Jim Wade, appear on the front cover is not intended to imply an unequal contribution to this work. Although by academic convention equal authorship is denoted by placing authors in alphabetical order, this can in itself be undemocratic when collaborative research is undertaken by the same team over time.

1

PERSPECTIVES ON RUNNING AWAY

WHY THE CONCERN?

Since the late 1980s there has been growing concern about young run-aways. A number of recent studies have not only pointed to the alarming number of runaways from home, but have also suggested that runaways from residential care are over-represented among young people who run away (Newman 1989; Abrahams and Mungall 1992; Rees 1993; Stein et al 1994; Barter 1996). These findings have been articulated with concerns about the risks faced by runaways from substitute care, particularly in the light of the West case, as a number of the victims had run away from home or care when they fell into the Wests' hands, and seven victims were either in care or had left care (Thompson 1995). The West case was significant in refocusing attention from a preoccupation with problem behaviour to a concern for the victim. In addition, revelations about abuse in care – at the Kincora Boys' Home in Northern Ireland, in Beck's establishments in Leicestershire, in the pindown regime in Staffordshire, and across children's homes in North and South Wales – have led to anxiety that running away may be symptomatic of fundamental problems within child care institutions. As a result of the emerging evidence on running away from residential care and the scandals involving children's homes, concern has focused more sharply in recent years on young people who go missing from placements in substitute care.

Yet it is interesting to note that running away by children in public care is not new. Running away has always been a problem for child care institutions. From the first Poor Law provision for destitute children in the sixteenth century, to the charity schools, workhouses and foster par-ents who cared for them in subsequent centuries, child care institutions have been disturbed by running away (Pinchbeck and Hewitt 1973). Indeed, at times this was a major problem: the Royal Philanthropic Society reported in 1796 that nearly a third of the 176 boys it had admitted up to that time had run away (Millham et al 1978). More recently, there was official concern about the dramatic post-war rise in absconding from community homes, which increased fourfold from 1951 to 1971, as well as the high rate of absconding from special schools, assessment centres and probation hostels, and this led to an earlier flurry of investigative studies during the 1970s (Millham et al 1977a).

However, if running away from substitute care is not a new phenomenon, it is clear that its contours have changed over time. The contexts from which looked after young people absent themselves today are very different from those studied less than thirty years ago and changes in policy have meant that, just as child care institutions have changed over the years, so, to some extent, have the populations admitted to them. This chapter therefore opens with a brief overview of changing patterns in residential and foster care and recent changes in the population of children looked after by local authorities.

We then move on to review recent studies of patterns of running away in Britain, together with earlier British and North American studies, which have variously examined the characteristics of runaways, their behaviour and motivations and the institutional responses to them. However, with the exception of the British research of the 1970s, the primary focus of the majority of studies has been on young people running away from home, with only limited attention to young people who go missing from substitute care. Where these studies have touched on the question of runaways from substitute care, the focus has been almost exclusively on residential care.

In contrast, this report differs from what has gone before in two ways. First, its aim is to understand more clearly why young people go missing from the contemporary context of substitute care and what happens when they do. By means of two surveys, in-depth interviews with 36 young people, their social workers and their carers, and a series of focus groups, we have attempted to map patterns, motivations and responses and have also examined the impact of the contexts from which young people go missing upon their behaviour. Second, unlike most previous studies, we have focused on young people missing from foster care as well as from residential care.

BACKGROUND TO THE STUDY

Changing Patterns of Child Care

Patterns of substitute care have changed markedly since research on young people running away from residential institutions was carried out in the 1970s. The looked after population has declined and patterns of residential and foster care have changed significantly. Since its peak in the late 1970s, the total number of children in care has fallen dramatically from around 101 000 in 1977 to 51 000 in 1996 (Department of Health 1997). Although demographic changes have accounted for some of this fall, the change has also been due to a substantial decrease in real terms in the proportion of children entering substitute care, as a result of changes in policy and practice.

The virtual ending of care orders in criminal proceedings was one reason for this decline, with the shift to a welfare model of intervention in youth crime following the Children and Young Persons Act 1969. This had a major impact on the care population, as the development of alternatives to custody schemes led to a reduction in the use of community homes with education (CHEs). Another reason was the growing emphasis on prevention deriving from the influence of the 'permanency planning' philosophy in the 1980s and the identification by a series of research studies of a lack of planning for children in care, which together led to a higher rate of discharges from care, shorter stays in care and so to a declining rate of children in care (Department of Health 1985; Thoburn et al 1986; Cliffe and Berridge 1991). This trend towards preventive work by social services departments, with the aim of maintaining more children at home with their families or rehabilitating them rapidly after a short admission to substitute care, was reinforced by the Children Act 1989.

Between the mid-1970s and mid-1980s, the fall in the number of children in care went hand in hand with a decline in the use of residential care for children. A number of explanations for this decline have been advanced, including concern about stigmatisation and the negative effects of institutionalisation, the view that family placements are better able to meet children's needs and concern about the expense of residential care (Cliffe and Berridge 1991). As a result, the proportion of looked after young people placed in local authority children's homes declined from 32% in 1978 to 21% in 1986, and by March 1996 only 11% of looked after children were in community homes (Department of Health 1991a, 1997). The number of both local authority and voluntary sector children's homes has shrunk considerably since the early 1980s (Berridge and Brodie 1998).

Although only a small proportion of the looked after population is in a residential placement on any one day, if we examine the succession of admissions to residential settings made during the course of a year it is clear that extensive use is made of residential care in accommodating teenagers. Studies of placement 'flow' over time have shown that over half of all placements made for older children and teenagers are in residential settings (Rowe et al 1989; Sinclair et al 1995).

Accompanying these changes in the scale of residential provision has been a change in the role of residential care, which now caters predominantly for older children whose needs cannot be met by foster care. In general, children in residential care are older than the looked after population as a whole, and the older a child is on admission to substitute care the more likely he or she is to be placed in a residential setting (Department of Health 1991b; Utting 1997). There is also greater emphasis on the use of smaller homes. Young people tend to remain in residential placements for a shorter period of time than in the past so there is a higher turnover (Department of Health 1996a, 1996b). This pattern of short term admissions has led to a situation where staff often have little knowledge of young people they are working with and little opportunity to build relationships with them. In these circumstances, it is also difficult to create a settled environment, which is particularly important for those young people who do remain in residential care in the longer term.

Although it is clear from this that residential care is a widely used resource for older children and teenagers, many in this age group are also cared for in foster placements. Two out of three children looked after are accommodated in foster placements and, although in overall terms children in foster placements tend to be younger than those in residential placements, over half of those in foster placements in March 1996 were age 10 or over (Department of Health 1997). Since, as previous research has shown, it is mostly older children and young people who go missing, the fact that a large proportion of this group are placed in foster care led us to investigate patterns of running away from foster care as well as from residential care.

Shifts in child care policy have not only contributed to the fall in the proportion of children accommodated in care placements, but have led to other changes in the nature of the looked after population. First, the emphasis on preventive work has raised the threshold for admission to care. The outcome of this is that children who cross that threshold are now likely to have a greater concentration of difficulties than their predecessors, and this poses new control problems for staff (Department of Health 1991b; Bullock et al 1993). Second, with the emphasis on finding family placements for as many children as possible, residential placements have increasingly come to be used for those with greater difficulties. As a result, children's homes now contain many young people with behavioural problems or long histories of neglect or disturbance (Rowe et al 1989; Department of Health 1991b, 1996b). Third, the contraction in the size of the residential sector and the financial pressures on social services have led to a situation where few choices are available to social workers seeking to accommodate children in residential settings, with the result that availability may be a more significant determinant of placement choice than appropriateness in meeting the child's needs (Utting 1997). Also, the lack of alternative specialist resources has had implications for the mix of young people in ordinary community homes, as smaller children's homes in the midst of communities are now dealing with a population that, a decade earlier, may have been accommodated in CHEs. A recent study has found that the proportion of entrants to residential care who posed behavioural problems had more than doubled since 1985 (Berridge and Brodie 1998). As we shall see, all of these developments have a bearing on this study.

Numbers of Runaways from Home and Care

Recent studies of running away have sought to establish the total number of young runaways on a national basis. In her nationwide survey of police missing persons statistics Newman estimated that there were 98 000 incidents of young people under 18 running away each year (Newman 1989). Abrahams and Mungall's study, also based on police missing persons statistics, estimated that there were 102 000 incidents of young people under 18 running away in England and Scotland in 1990, involving 43 000 young people (Abrahams and Mungall 1992). However, these are likely to be underestimates as they do not include running away incidents not reported to the police. On the basis of his schools survey of over 1200 young people in Leeds, Rees estimated that one in seven young people under the age of 16 had run away and stayed away overnight at least once (Rees 1993).

All of these studies indicated that young people looked after by local authorities were over-represented among the runaway population. While less than 1% of children and young people are looked after at any one time, Abrahams and Mungall found that 30% of young runaways were missing from substitute care, the vast majority (96% of them) from residential care (Abrahams and Mungall 1992). Similarly, in her study of Britain's first Safe House, Newman found that 29% of the young people using the project had run away from care placements (Newman 1989). Another recent study of 102 young people using streetwork projects, found that 70% had lived in substitute care of some form in the past and that a quarter of those under 16 had run away from residential care (Stein et al 1994). Rees, too, found a far higher rate of running away amongst young people from residential care than amongst young people living with their families and a study of Childline's Night Service found that 7% of young people contacting Childline about running away were from residential or foster placements (Rees 1993; Barter et al 1996). Barter's study of 200 young people using the Centrepoint/NSPCC refuge also found that young people from substitute care were over-represented among young runaways, making up a fifth of refuge users, the majority of them from residential care, while a Welsh study of juveniles missing over 12 hours found that 70% were absconders from care (Hutson and Liddiard 1989; Barter 1996). None of these studies are based on representative samples, as they refer only to samples of *reported* runaways, but taken together they give a strong indication that young people from care placements are indeed over-represented among runaways. As other studies all refer to 'running away' from care we shall use this term in discussing their findings, although in this study we prefer to use the term 'going missing', for reasons that we explain in the following chapter.

Comparing Young People Missing from Home and Care

A strength of these broadly based studies of running away from both home and substitute care is that they are able to identify some differences in patterns of running away between young people running from home and young people running from substitute care. First, there is evidence that individuals running from residential care were more likely to run away repeatedly than those from home (Abrahams and Mungall 1992; Rees 1993; Stein et al 1994). Second, repeat runaways from residential care were found, on average, to have stayed away longer than runaways from home or foster care (Abrahams and Mungall 1992; Rees 1993). Third, Rees found that young people running from residential care were likely to travel further afield, to stay away longer, to run away with someone else and be picked up by the police than young people running away from home. They were also more likely to have started running away at a younger age.

While these recent studies all point to the over-representation of young people from substitute care among young runaways, for many young people the roots of running away lie in the period when they were living with their families. Rees found that three-quarters of young people from residential care using the Leeds Safe House had first run away from their families, while Stein, Rees and Frost's study of streetwork projects found that most young people running from residential care had run away from their families before entering care (Rees 1993; Stein et al 1994).

Recent research on young people looked after by local authorities has also touched on the subject of running away. A study of young people accommodated under S20 of the Children Act identified running away as an area of concern in respect of seven out of ten 'difficult adolescents' who were accommodated, although it is unclear whether this refers to running away from home or care or both (Packman and Hall 1996). Another study of nearly 1100 young people in children's homes found high rates of running away from residential care and a strong association between criminal convictions and running away (Sinclair and Gibbs 1998). At the level of the individual, those who had previous convictions were far more likely to run away than those who had none. Also, those who ran away were far more likely to have been convicted while at the home than those who did not run away, and this association was particularly strong for those with no convictions prior to admission. Among those who had been in the home for no more than a month, 18% of those with no previous convictions and 71% who had previous convictions ran away, and these rates rose to 63% and 87% respectively for those who had been resident for six or more months. Running away rates in this study were high in comparison with rates of running away from approved schools or probation hostels studied thirty years earlier, but it is important to remember that, unlike those institutions, children's homes are open establishments in the sense that there is no legal requirement for young people to remain in them.

Theories of Running Away

Concern about the post-war rise in running away from residential institutions led to a cluster of studies published in the early 1970s which sought to establish the background characteristics of young people who absconded from approved schools, probation hostels, open borstals and secure units and to establish whether there were any differences between those who absconded and those who did not. Studies also examined the contexts from which young people ran, in order to discover whether particular institutional regimes encouraged or discouraged absconding, and highlighted the risks that young people faced while on the run. Although the institutional environments in which these young people found themselves were very different to contemporary children's homes, the findings of these studies provide valuable indicators for current research. Running away from these closed institutions was much easier for researchers to define and measure than is now the case, as the Home Office provided clear definitions of absconding and all absconding had to be reported to the police and officially recorded, whereas in the open establishments of today it is sometimes hard to identify a clear point at which going out or staying out without permission becomes defined as running away (Bullock 1997). Research interest in running away declined once approved schools moved into the child care system and became

CHEs in 1974. In the context of these open institutions running away was no longer an easily defined administrative problem (Bullock et al 1993).

Initially, researchers sought to establish whether absconding was caused by personal characteristics which might distinguish runaways from non-runaways. Clarke and Martin, who were clinical psychologists, investigated individual differences between absconders and non-absconders from approved schools in terms of age, IQ, education, family background, previous delinquency and many personality dimensions (Clarke and Martin 1971). However, in common with Sinclair in his study of probation hostels, they found that wide variations in absconding rates between different institutions could not be explained by differences in intake, a finding reiterated by Sinclair and Gibbs' recent study of children's homes referred to above (Sinclair 1971; Sinclair and Gibbs 1998).

The best predictor of running away appeared to be a history of previous absconding. A more delinquent history was also predictive (Brierley and Jones unpublished; Clarke and Martin 1971; Porteous and McLoughlin 1974). A habitual element was identified, with the length of time between each episode decreasing the more frequently a young person absconded, while a study of Aycliffe Assessment Centre suggested that previous residential experience could be influential (Porteous and McLoughlin 1974; Millham et al 1977a; Millham et al 1978). Other studies also found that previous offending and previous institutionalisation were associated with absconding (Brierley and Jones unpublished; Wilkins unpublished). In addition, researchers found that a sizeable minority ceased to abscond when moved to a different institution (Clarke and Martin 1971; Porteous and McLoughlin 1974).

Researchers therefore turned their attention to the environment from which young people absconded for an explanation of the wide variation in absconding rates between apparently similar institutions. Clarke and Martin moved from an internal causation theory towards an environmental learning perspective, shifting the focus of their attention from the individual to the environment (Clarke and Martin 1971). They proposed that young people feeling anxious or unhappy in institutions can respond to this in a number of ways, one of which is by absconding. From their experiences in the institution they learn to respond to internal cues, such as expectations about responses to them, and environmental cues including opportunities to run and the example or persuasion of other residents. Absconding was seen as a form of learned behaviour which could be reinforced by the responses of staff and peers. However, a weakness of this behaviourist model was that it was based entirely on observations of the boys' behaviour with no exploration of their motivations. Absconding was explained by a theory of individual learning which, while emphasising the importance of environmental factors, did not examine the nature of the regimes from which young people absconded and could not explain why some young people ceased to abscond when moved to a new unit.

Researchers at the Dartington Social Research Unit took a different approach, drawing on deviancy theory and the symbolic interactionist approach in sociology. Agreeing that environmental factors were of crucial importance, they discounted individual learning as an explanation and focused instead on the institutional process of ascribing deviance to absconders (Millham et al 1977b). This led them to examine the nature of institutional regimes and the way that they reacted to running away. In their studies of approved schools and secure units they argued that boys arriving in an institution were already 'labelled' by the contents of their files. As a result, difficult behaviour was expected and less serious forms of protest had little impact on staff, so the only way boys could get a reaction was through running away or violent behaviour. Although the boys themselves did not see absconding as a serious form of misbehaviour, it was defined as such by the institutions in which they were placed (Millham et al 1977a). Minor attention-seeking behaviour, such as absconding to test out how much staff cared about them, could quickly escalate as a result of the reaction that the initial absconding engendered. Although deep delinquency was also seen as influential, the crux of the argument was that 'it is the nature of the child's residential experience that makes him an absconder, that boys run because of the places they are in', so that the way in which institutions label and respond to deviant behaviour is a crucial element both in its development and in their success in dealing with it (Millham et al 1975, 1978:88).

While this scrutiny of environmental factors was important, its grounding in symbolic interactionist sociology leads to some problems with this perspective. First, runaways tend to be depicted as passive victims of the labelling process, implying that they have little autonomy or conscious choice. Second, it follows from this that analysis of young people's own motivations for running away is limited and the origins of their behaviour are not fully explored. Also, the work of Howard Becker and other labelling theorists of the 1960s suggested that researchers must take the side of the 'underdog', rejecting the perspectives of those with more power within institutions (Becker 1967). However, as others have pointed out, many of the problems which exist in institutions do not originate within them. Although professionals are more powerful within organisations than young people, this power may only be relative. It may be difficult to see, for example, how a residential worker trying to mobilise help for a young person can be defined as an 'oppressor' (Pitts 1991). The managers, practitioners and residents of institutions may, in fact, agree about what needs to change but feel powerless to effect that change, since institutions serve a variety of functions and social and political interests which are not determined by those who staff them (Pitts 1988, 1991).

Despite these problems with the labelling perspective, the Dartington studies were valuable in exploring the ways in which different institutions could make running away more or less likely. Drawing on evidence which indicated that there was a relationship between the nature of regimes in different institutions and their absconding rates, the Dartington researchers considered what made for effective regimes in child care institutions (Millham et al 1975). Disagreeing with behaviourist approaches, they dismissed the idea that institutional controls alone – such as sanctions, rewards and the limiting of opportunities to run – could reduce absconding. Instead, they argued that what was needed was a mix of firm institutional controls, providing order and security, and a high level of expressive controls, by which they meant a manifestly caring and moral environment which oriented young people towards a different set of expectations, aspirations and values (Millham et al 1977b). Their view was that effective regimes had good pastoral care and high expressive controls, which constantly stressed what behaviour was unacceptable and encouraged the internalisation of acceptable forms of behaviour (Millham et al 1975).

The Dartington team also turned their attention to the peer cultures among young people within institutions. They suggested that the relationship between the formal organisation of the unit and the informal world of the residents is crucial in determining the effectiveness of a regime, so that negative aspects of peer cultures are not allowed to dominate within an institution, which can lead to peer pressure on young people to run away (Millham et al 1975). Sinclair, too, was interested in the effect of the environment on behaviour within institutions, but he took the view that peer cultures were less influential on residents' behaviour than the way staff behaved towards them (Sinclair 1971).

Examining the impact of the behaviour of staff on the effectiveness of regimes in probation hostels, he found that institutions where managers were warm, where managers and staff were in agreement about how they should be run and where staff adopted a consistent approach towards residents were more successful in preventing absconding. Effective regimes were more successful in negotiating agreement with residents, irrespective of whether they were strict or not, although negotiating agreement was found to be easier in strict regimes. He found that institutions which had high levels of consistency between staff and were effective in negotiating agreement with residents had lower absconding rates.

Drawing on their studies of approved schools and probation hostels, Sinclair and Clarke recommended that not only should institutions provide a general therapeutic ambience to reduce motivation for deviant conduct within the institution, but they should also respond directly to behaviour such as absconding to prevent the reinforcement of learned deviant behaviour (Sinclair and Clarke 1973). In this, their recommendations bore some similarity to the Dartington researchers' view that a mix of expressive and institutional controls were needed within residential institutions for young people, although with a more behaviourist slant.

Ackland's study of absconding from a community home was atypical of the period in its focus upon girls but drew upon the same theoretical framework as the Dartington studies in its examination of the impact of regimes on young people's behaviour (Ackland 1981). He found that the most common reasons that residents offered for absconding related to their day-to-day experience of the institutional regime, followed by a cluster of reasons which related to their feelings about family separation and their desire to be with their families. Staff tended to view running away as an evasion of individual problems, whereas residents indicated that it was the regime in the home, together with bullying and peer conflict, which often prompted them to run away.

These British studies of the 1970s also considered whether there was a relationship between the responses to returning absconders and running away rates. Sinclair (1971) found that sanctions such as taking absconders from probation hostels to court did not have a deterrent effect, as the decision to abscond was not based on rational calculation. However, a willingness to accept back and work with absconders was influential. Those hostels which took back very few absconders had high running away rates, suggesting that the nature of the response to runaways can escalate the issue or diminish it. Clarke and Martin (1971) also suggested that absconding behaviour could be reinforced by a punitive response, as those absconders from approved schools who were punished or ridiculed by staff and other boys upon their return were more likely to abscond again.

More recently Payne has proposed the use of crisis theory to explain going missing in a variety of circumstances, including running away. He argues that for people in a vulnerable state the capacity to deal with problems is inhibited and a 'last straw' may prompt a person to go missing in an attempt to resolve the crisis. If this is perceived as successful in reducing distress, it becomes part of an individual's problem-solving repertoire (Payne 1995). However, this is only helpful in explaining running away in crisis situations but cannot account for the other circumstances in which young people go missing from substitute care.

There has also been extensive research on running away in North America and some in Australia, but much of this has limited relevance for our study as it has primarily been concerned with running away from home. Many of the earlier studies, from the 1930s–1970s, focused on a search for deviant personality characteristics among runaways (Nye 1980). In the 1960s and early 1970s much of the literature maintained this emphasis on personal pathology and was largely based on quantitative studies. More recently, qualitative research methods have been more widely used and there has been a greater interest in the family background of runaways.

Many of the North American studies have attempted to map the diversity of the runaway population through constructing taxonomies of runaways, in most cases on the basis of motives, behaviour or demographic characteristics. Studies of motivation employed have classified young people into reactive or spontaneous runaways or, alternatively, escapists or romantic adventurers (Berger and Schmidt 1958, cited in Brennan 1980; Tsunts 1966); and similarly into those 'running from' to escape unresolved problems or 'running to' for the purpose of pleasure seeking (Homer 1973). The Opinion Research Corporation of America shifted from an earlier focus on individual pathology to a categorisation of motivation into two types: 'parent-locus motivation', whereby reactive runaways are motivated by parental abuse or neglect or by authority struggles with parents, and 'child-locus motivation', whereby runaways are escaping from an institution or from the consequences of their own behaviour (Opinion Research Corporation 1976).

Shellow and colleagues' typology used the frequency and nature of runaway behaviour as a basis for classification and identified a 'multiple runaway' type with high levels of personal and family pathology and a high level of delinquent behaviour (Shellow et al 1967). Brennan's study of nearly 500 runaways employed a typology founded on social psychological theories of deviant behaviour, which involved a six part categorisation based on individual and family behaviour, peer relations, runaway behaviour and delinquency (Brennan 1980). This typology emphasised the dichotomy of delinquent/non-delinquent runaways, with delinquent runaways similar to Homer's classification of those 'running from', who were alienated from home and school and had low self-esteem.

From the late 1970s North American researchers started to turn their attention to the family backgrounds of runaways, suggesting that persistent runners, in particular, may have run away to escape severely abusive or rejecting parents (Brennan et al 1978; Simons and Whitbeck 1991). A history of sexual abuse has been associated with running away in a number of studies, although Stiffman warns that rates vary according to the definition of sexual abuse employed (Janus et al 1987; Stiffman 1989; Cohen et al 1991; Simons and Whitbeck 1991; Spatz et al 1994). Janus and colleagues found that 38% of youths in a Canadian home for runaways had experienced sexual abuse while Stiffman's study of 291 residents of an American home for runaway youths found that almost half had been abused by a family member, with just under 10% of the sample having been sexually abused and 44% physically abused.

Other studies have also identified physical abuse as a factor underlying the decision to run away, including Farber and colleagues' finding that three-quarters of the 199 young people in an American runaway shelter had been physically abused in the year before they ran away (Johnson and Carter 1980; Farber et al 1984; Simons and Whitbeck 1991). Many runaways were also found to have experienced parental rejection and Stiffman also cites two studies where half of the samples had parents with drug or alcohol problems (Brennan et al 1978; Johnson and Carter 1980; Stiffman 1989; Simons and Whitbeck 1991).

Some studies have touched on the importance of peer relationships and have described the friends of runaways as likely to be other young people in similar circumstances, who are themselves runaways and who may exert peer pressure on others to run away and to commit offences (Brennan et al 1978; Whitbeck and Simons 1990). Hier and colleagues' psychological study of 52 runaways and 'throwaways' (those abandoned or forced to leave home) in Australian shelters for homeless young people found that both groups had problems with social bonding and were likely to suffer from depression. Most tended to be socially isolated, but male runaways were found to be more socially isolated than female runaways (Hier et al 1990).

In reviewing the approaches taken by researchers on both sides of the Atlantic we can see that, just as British studies of running away shifted their focus from the individual to the environment during the course of the 1970s, during the same period researchers in North America became less preoccupied with discovering the psychological characteristics of those considered disordered or 'sick' and turned to an examination of family and other environmental factors. In Britain during the 1970s, researchers used psychological approaches, such as learning theory, or sociological approaches including labelling theory, to explain the processes of running away and returning (Clarke and Martin 1971; Sinclair 1971; Millham et al 1975, 1977a, 1977b, 1978). These studies were important in drawing attention to the contexts and processes involved in running away and to the effects of professional reactions when runaways return, as well as to the fact that young people who run away cannot easily be identified in terms of their psychological characteristics. However, as this research focused on (predominantly male) young people absconding from closed residential institutions, it cannot entirely explain why both female and male young people go missing from the very different contexts of contemporary children's homes and foster placements.

Caution is also needed in drawing on the findings of North American research as most samples were drawn from populations in runaway shelters, who may differ from the child care population in the UK and are in any case a highly specific group who are not representative of all runaways even in the United States and Canada. These studies nevertheless alert us to the range of motivations and behaviours that may be involved in running away, suggesting a need to map the diverse types of unauthorised absence from substitute care. They also remind us that, at least for some young people in substitute care, the origins of running away may lie in the period when they lived with their families.

As we have seen, more recent British research has also indicated that the roots of running away may lie in the family environment. In some respects it is also similar to the North American research in that some samples have been drawn from the populations of shelters for runaways and the young homeless or streetwork projects yet, just as in the American context, those runaways from substitute care who find their way to such hostels may not be representative of all those who go missing (Newman 1989; Stein et al 1994; Barter 1996). Recent British research has nevertheless been immensely valuable in providing information on rates and patterns of running away and in identifying some differences in patterns between those who run from home and those who run from substitute care. However, with the exception of Rees' analysis of a sub-sample of young people in residential care, there has been only limited attention paid to the individual histories and motivations of young people who go missing from substitute care.

Implications for this Study

This study aims to fill some of these gaps in the research. Teasing out the outcomes of interventions by substitute carers and social workers is a complex process (Biehal et al 1995). A number of factors, including young people's personal histories and experiences in their families, their experience of institutional regimes and substitute family care, their experiences in the education system, whether they have a history of offending and the influence of their peers may all have an impact on whether or not they go missing from substitute care and, if they do, what they do while they are away. How far the experience of substitute care itself makes young people more likely to go missing is therefore a complex question.

Our approach has been to take young people, rather than institutions, as our starting point, beginning with an examination of their diverse patterns of unauthorised absence from substitute care. Focusing on both the individual and the environment, we explore the interplay between young people's personal histories, their family and peer relationships, their placement contexts and the wider social context of contemporary child care. In doing so we have taken a life course analysis approach. This method was developed among family historians and sociologists who were dissatisfied with functionalist models of the life cycle. It explores the links and disjunctures between the experiences of individuals and families and the changing economic and social circumstances in which they find themselves in different historical periods. Life course analysts are concerned with the interaction between two chains of events, one belonging to the family and the other to the wider society (Cohen 1997). This approach, which has been usefully employed in recent research on youth transitions (Jones and Wallace 1992), explores the complex ways in which structural forces and personal biographies intersect to structure the life histories of individuals.

In the chapters that follow, we profile the young people in our study who went missing from care placements and outline key elements of their family backgrounds and care careers, as well as presenting initial evidence on patterns of school attendance, offending and substance misuse. We follow this with a mapping of the diverse patterns of going missing from care placements, and consider disturbing evidence of the risks that young people encounter while they are away. We then examine the circumstances in which young people first went missing, from home or substitute care, and chart their histories of going missing over time. The management of risk and the responses of caregivers and social workers to young people who go missing are explored, in an attempt to discover which strategies, if any, are likely to work, and in which circumstances.

We attempt to tease out the relative impact of individual motivations and the placement contexts in which young people find themselves, exploring the links between placement regimes, staff and peer cultures and going missing. We consider the interventions of social workers, in the context of their changing role, as well as the broader contextual issue of the effects of financial retrenchment on placement choice. Finally, we discuss the wider implications of our findings for services for young people who are looked after.

2

RESEARCH DESIGN

There were two stages to the research. First, in view of the limited data on running away from substitute care or accommodation, a mapping exercise was needed to clarify patterns of unauthorised absence. Two surveys of patterns of absence from substitute care or accommodation were carried out in four very different English local authorities: *City West*, a large city; *City East*, a smaller city; *County*, a Midlands county and *Borough*, an inner London borough. The surveys covered unauthorised absences during a one year period from July 1995 to July 1996.

Second, as we have seen, little is known about *why* young people go missing from substitute care, *what happens* when they do so, how professionals *respond* when they go missing and how young people and professionals view both the absences and the range of responses to them. In order to understand the meanings young people and professionals ascribed to patterns of absence, the impact of the contexts in which this behaviour occurred, the rationale for different professional responses and the perceived effectiveness of these interventions, qualitative methods were called for. The qualitative phase of our study was carried out in two of our authorities, City East and City West. Following an exploratory series of 14 focus groups with young people, social workers, residential and foster carers to elucidate the key issues, we carried out individual interviews with 36 young people, their social workers and their carers. This methodological triangulation enabled us to explore the research questions from different angles. We utilised quantitative methods in our surveys to identify patterns of behaviour and qualitative methods in our interviews to look at the social processes involved when young people go missing and the circumstances in which these processes occur (Denzin 1970; Hammersley and Atkinson 1983; Mason 1994).

PROBLEMS OF DEFINITION

As soon as the study began it became clear that running away was not an easy phenomenon to define – and if it could not be clearly defined, how could it be measured? Our early discussions with local authorities revealed a lack of clarity in definitions of unauthorised absence within and between agencies, which mirrored the variety of definitions used to measure running away in previous research (including self-definition, reported missing to the police, unauthorised absence overnight, and unofficial absence). The lack of clear agency definitions of running away was accompanied by a lack of comprehensive agency information about young people who were absent without permission. Where clear procedures existed for centrally recording information about young people missing from placements, in practice these only operated where young people had been missing for several days.

A further problem was the fact that a survey based on questionnaires completed by professionals cannot capture the *intentions* of young people when they go missing. We explored the circumstances in which young people see themselves as running away in the qualitative phase of the research, but our surveys were based upon professional understandings of running away, which may or may not coincide with the ways in which young people see their own behaviour. In view of these conceptual complexities, it seemed best to use a broad definition which would encompass a variety of types of absence, so for the purpose of this study we use the term *going missing* to cover all forms of unauthorised absence. Under this rubric, we identify different types of absence, *including* those that professionals or young people might define as 'running away'.

THE MAIN SURVEY

These problems of defining unauthorised absence and identifying missing young people meant that we needed a comprehensive and unambiguous definition of unauthorised absence which would trigger the completion of questionnaires in our survey. In our main survey we therefore asked staff to complete a questionnaire on the first occasion during the survey period when a young person was *either* missing overnight *or* was reported missing to the police. The advantage of this definition was that it was broad enough to encompass all types of unauthorised absence and that it would be able to gather information on young people not missing overnight but considered vulnerable enough to warrant reporting to the police.

The main survey collected information about young people going missing from all types of placements in our four local authorities over a 12 month period. For each young person identified, different questionnaires were completed by a social worker and a residential worker or foster carer following a single unauthorised absence. As well as information about the most recent incident of absence, information on the young people's history of going missing, their care careers, current placement, school attendance, offending and substance misuse was also collected. A total of 210 replies were received and the number of young people from each authority is shown in Table 2.1.

Table 2.1   Main survey sample by local authority

	Young people
County	64
City West	53
City East	42
Borough	51
Total	210

This included placements in foster homes, local authority children's homes, private or voluntary sector children's homes, residential special schools and secure units, as shown in Table 2.2.

Table 2.2   Placement at time of incident

	Placement	Young people	Percentage	Total (%)
Foster	Foster placement	69	32.9	
	Fostered with relatives	2	1.0	
	Remand foster	6	2.9	36.7
Residential	Local authority children's home	112	53.3	
	Private/voluntary children's home	11	5.2	
	Semi independence	2	1.0	
	Secure unit	2	1.0	
	Residential special school	2	1.0	61.5
	Placement with parents	4	1.9	1.9
Total		210	100.0	100.0

Our aim was to obtain a total sample of all young people missing from placements at least once during the survey period. However, since the local authorities' own information systems were unable to indicate the total number of young people who went missing, we were obliged to rely on individual staff and foster carers to notify us. As a result of these sampling difficulties, the above figures are certainly an underestimate of the true extent of the problem. The strength of our sample was that it was sufficiently large for us to identify a range of patterns of absence and to learn a great deal about young people who go missing. However, it is important to recognise that we cannot be sure how far this sample is representative of the total population of young people who go missing from substitute care, in respect of the *proportions* who have particular histories, characteristics or patterns of behaviour.

Also, since we gathered information on one absence *for each young person* in our sample rather than from a random sample of *all incidents* in the four authorities during the course of a year, it may not be representative of the patterns for all looked after young people. In particular, patterns associated with those missing often may be under-represented since they would account for a higher proportion of all incidents in a given year. However, as we will see below, given that for this sample we found little statistical evidence to support the contention that, for those missing more often, successive incidents necessarily become more protracted or riskier, it may be that the picture of incidents we present is reasonably accurate. The exceptions to this are likely to be in respect of the nature of the placements the young people were missing from and the nature of their absences.

THE COMMUNITY HOMES SURVEY

In order to obtain a more accurate picture of total numbers going missing than our main survey had been able to provide, we carried out an additional survey of all young people missing from local authority children's homes. It was only possible to do this in community homes as they all kept daily logs which included information on unauthorised absences, whereas data of this kind was not routinely collected by fostering staff. A small number of specialist units for severely disabled children were excluded, on the advice of agency staff, and young people in private and voluntary sector accommodation were not included in this survey.

The aim of this additional survey was to establish an accurate picture of the number of young people going missing from in-house residential units in a 12 month period and the number of incidents for which they were responsible. Each local authority children's home in our four local authorities was asked to complete a retrospective log sheet recording all unauthorised absences during the same 12 month period as the main survey. Information was also collected on the characteristics of the young people (age, gender and ethnic origin) and on the incidents during the course of the year (number and duration of absences). A total of 32 children's homes returned questionnaires, representing a 100% response rate.

Overall, 272 young people went missing in one year from 32 community homes in the four authorities. They were responsible for a total of 2227 instances of unauthorised absence. The breakdown by authority is given in Table 2.3.

Table 2.3   Community homes survey by local authority

	Young people
County	44
City West	96
City East	51
Borough	81
Total	272

THE FOCUS GROUPS

A series of 14 focus groups were carried out in 2 authorities, City East and City West. Focus groups were held with young people in 5 community homes as well as with a group of young people who had recently left care. Groups were also held with residential workers in 4 community homes, 2 groups of foster carers and 2 groups of social workers. The groups consisted of between 4 and 10 people. The young people's groups in community homes were usually smaller and the residential workers' and social workers' groups were larger.

The groups of foster carers and professionals generated lively and informative discussions but the groups held with young people in community homes were less successful. Although our prompts to discussion were couched in the most general terms, so that no one was required to reveal publicly any personal information, some of the young people clearly found it difficult to have a discussion of this kind in front of others living in the same unit. The pressures on young people to maintain a public persona and to 'perform' appropriately in front of their peers made it difficult to generate a productive discussion in a group context. Our focus group with care leavers was far more successful. Being older and no longer looked after, they were able to reflect thoughtfully on their experiences of going missing.

The focus group interviews were tape recorded and transcribed. As well as using the focus groups as an exploratory tool to assist us in designing the individual interviews, where appropriate we have added material from the focus groups to our discussion of issues arising in the individual interviews.

THE INTERVIEWS

Following our analysis of key issues emerging from the surveys and the focus groups, we carried out individual interviews with 36 young people in residential or foster placements who had recently gone missing overnight or had been reported missing to the police. Sixteen came from City East and 20 from City West.

As numbers in a qualitative sample are necessarily much smaller than in a survey sample, a random sample may not provide a sufficient spread of cases to be truly representative and may not offer the opportunity to explore all aspects of a social issue. We therefore decided upon purposive sampling, that is, where particular criteria are employed to stratify the sample in a systematic way (Bryman and Cramer 1990; Mason 1996). We wanted to ensure that our sample included a reasonable spread of males and females, black and white, in both residential and foster placements, over a broad age range and with varied histories of going missing, in order to deepen our knowledge of going missing in all its various manifestations. This means that although patterns *across* our interview sample cannot be seen as representative of all those who go missing from substitute care, the interviews can provide in-depth data about young people of both sexes, of various ages and in a variety of placements who go missing in a variety of circumstances. The qualitative interviews can also offer insights into the motivations and histories underlying the patterns identified in our quantitative surveys, and provide information on responses by carers, social workers and police to young people who go missing.

We identified our sample by contacting all fieldwork team managers, community homes and fostering officers in the two authorities. After an initial discussion with the relevant social workers to gather basic background information, we asked the caregivers or social workers to make an initial approach to the young people on our behalf. Only a very small number of young people refused to be interviewed, and there were a few instances where, because of social workers' concerns about the impact of our research, we did not interview young people.

It was not always easy to obtain the names of young people to interview from social workers as most were working under very pressurised conditions, so that helping researchers to identify a sample came fairly low on their list of priorities. As a result, the interview sample we obtained was inadvertently weighted in two ways. First, although we asked for the names of young people missing in a wide range of circumstances, it is possible that we were given the names of those causing the greatest concern, as our interview sample contains a high proportion of young people with more protracted or serious careers of going missing. Also, whereas we could contact children's homes directly in order to identify young people, for those in foster care we were entirely dependent on field social workers' and fostering officers' referrals. As a result, we were able to interview fewer young people in foster placements than we would have wished, so our interview sample contains more young people from residential placements. However, as many of those in residential care at the time of the interviews had had earlier placements in foster care, we were able to ask them about why they had, or had not, gone missing from past foster placements.

When we met the young people we explained how the research would be used and guaranteed that nothing they told us would be passed on, unless they revealed to us that they were being harmed in any way, in which case we would feel obliged to discuss with them who should be informed about this, for their own protection. At the end of interviews, we asked young people's permission to interview their current foster carers or residential workers and their social workers. None of them refused. All of the interviews were tape recorded and transcribed.

The interviews with young people, social workers and carers were semi-structured. We attempted to put young people at their ease as far as possible, adapting our style – and speed – of interviewing in response to their reactions to the interview process, and tried to be sensitive to any signs that certain questions distressed them. For example, if young people became withdrawn or restless when asked about family issues, we would move on to another area rather than probing further. Where appropriate there was some probing of responses in order to draw out the nuances and complexities in the accounts given. To enhance reliability, we also approached certain core issues from different angles at different stages in the interview – sometimes eliciting the response from the more perceptive young people, 'This is boring – I've already told you about that.'

DATA ANALYSIS

Statistical Analysis

Given the nature of the data generated we mainly utilised non-parametric statistical tests. For bivariate analysis these were as follows:

(i)   Where both variables were nominal, we used the chi-square test. The p values given in the report are for Pearson chi-square statistic, except for the case of a 2×2 table where the continuity correction statistic is quoted.

(ii) Where one variable was nominal and one variable was ordinal we used the Mann–Whitney test where the nominal variable had two categories and the Kruskal–Wallis test where it had more than two categories.

(iii) Where both variables were ordinal we used a non-parametric test of correlation. The correlation coefficient quoted in the report is Kendall's tau-b.

In general for all these bivariate tests we regarded a test result as statistically significant where the p value was less than 0.05. Put another way, this is a 95% level of confidence. However, in a few instances we have included data with a p value of less than 0.1, and this is clearly indicated in the text.

For multivariate analysis we used three main techniques: partial correlation, log-linear analysis and logistic regression. Again, in most instances we adopted a significance level of $p \leq 0.05$ in using these techniques. The sample size and the level of missing data often presented problems in utilising these techniques and we therefore regard the findings based on multivariate analysis as indicative rather than conclusive.

Analysis of the Qualitative Data

Our aim in the interviews was to understand the meanings and significance that young people who go missing, social workers and residential and foster carers ascribe to their own and each other's actions. Interviews constitute narratives, or accounts, by the different players involved in a set of social processes, each making sense of those processes from their own perspective. From data of this kind we can glean some descriptive information on actions and histories, and infer the different players' understandings of these.

In respect of the factual, descriptive information which we gathered in the interviews – *what happened and when* – where accounts did not precisely coincide we made some judgements as to what had actually happened. For example, social workers could check how many placement moves had taken place from the file, while young people were sometimes unsure about how often they had moved; or a young person may have given a clear account of what happened when he or she last went missing while the carer may have known only part of the story. As for our material on the different players' understandings of events – *why it happened and what it meant* – we felt that where views did not coincide, none of the different perspectives could be prioritised as a 'truth' which rendered the others less valid. We have conceptualised each account as a narrative telling a story from a different perspective.

Taken together, these narratives give us valuable insights into complex social processes, shedding some light on the social contexts from which young people go missing, their reasons for going and social workers' and carers' responses to this behaviour. Our readings of the transcripts were therefore partly literal, insofar as they tried to discover what had actually happened in the young people's lives and how professionals had responded to this. They were also, to a large degree, interpretative, seeking to elucidate the social meanings of behaviour to each of the actors and the social processes involved in going missing and returning.

Qualitative data from the interviews and from the focus groups was analysed with the assistance of the qualitative analysis software package, Nud-ist. From an initial analysis of a small sample of interviews, some central recurring themes were developed. Some were descriptive (e.g. reasons for running away or care history) and some more conceptual (e.g. attachment or power). We wrote notes and definitions under each of the indexing categories we developed to ensure that all of the researchers were working with the same understanding of what each category constituted, so that our categories were applied as systematically and consistently as possible.

One of the problems in analysing qualitative data in applied policy research is how to grasp the complexity inherent in each individual's account while carrying out a cross-sectional analysis which can deliver useful insights across a range of subject areas. We wanted to carry out cross-sectional analysis by means of themes without losing a holistic appreciation of each case. We felt that if we employed Nud-ist to cut and paste 'slices' of dialogue from the transcripts under theme-based headings, we would lose our grasp of the context of these fragments of text. There would be a risk of our analysis becoming cut off from a holistic view of each young person's situation. We therefore addressed this problem through using Nud-ist to record our descriptions and interpretations of different aspects of each case under our descriptive and conceptual indexing categories, including lengthy quotations from the transcripts to illustrate and clarify our analysis. The analysis of each respondent's account in each case – young person, social worker, carer – was juxtaposed under each coding category, followed by any general points that we wished to make as researchers in respect of this particular case, which drew on our knowledge of the whole 'story'. The advantage of this was that each theme was analysed in the context of the whole complex set of issues for each young person, and the perspectives of each different respondent on each theme were considered side by side. Cases were second read, and the second reader would at times expand on or engage with the interpretations of the first reader, in order to deepen the analysis. Our intention in second reading the transcripts was to enhance the reliability of the research through carrying out as thorough and careful an analysis of the interview transcripts as possible.

Following this reorganisation of the data into thematic indexing categories, we then printed out our analyses and lengthy textual quotations for all 36 cases on a theme-by-theme basis. Each theme was then analysed across the 36 cases, sometimes together with other related themes, in order to build up a cross-sectional analysis of the data which was founded on an initial holistic interpretation of the interview transcripts.

THE RESEARCH CONTEXT

We selected four local authorities for the research from different parts of England, including London, the Midlands and the North.

The Authorities

City East was a thriving industrial centre for much of the nineteenth and twentieth centuries, until the onset of the recession in the 1970s. The industrial base of the city went into dramatic decline during the 1980s and it is no longer the major employer it once was. At the 1991 Census the unemployment rate was 14% for men and 6% for women. Its population was 470 000 in 1991, with a density of 13.6 per hectare, and is predominantly white. Around 5% of the population are black, of whom the largest sub-group (just over a third) are of Pakistani origin.

City West is a large conurbation which includes a number of metropolitan boroughs. It had by far the largest population in our study, with 2 600 000 inhabitants, although its population was less dense than Borough's, at 19.4 persons per hectare. Black residents comprise 6% of the population, the largest sub-group being of Pakistani origin (2%). Although, like City East, it has suffered from industrial decline since the 1970s, it has made a more successful recovery and is a thriving business area. However, areas of severe socio-economic disadvantage remain within the city. At the 1991 Census, it had an unemployment rate of 12% for men and 6% for women.

Borough, an inner London borough, is made up of urban villages and neighbourhoods which have a strong local identity, and range from very urban through suburbia to the countryside. The area has been virtually deserted by industry and is now home to limited light industry, commerce and recreational facilities, but suffers from a range of inner city problems. Nearly 1 in 5 men and 1 in 10 women in Borough were unemployed at the 1991 census and it had a substantially lower employment rate than the other areas in our study. With a population of 200 000, Borough has the highest proportion of residents from ethnic minorities, as nearly one quarter of the population is black. The largest of the ethnic minority groups is of Caribbean or African origin (18%). At the 1991 Census, the population density at 76 persons per hectare was considerably higher than in any of the other areas in our study.

County is one of the fastest growing counties in Britain, with a population of 650 000 in 1991 and a population density of 2 per hectare. Ethnic minorities comprise just over 3% of the population, mostly concentrated in urban areas. The county includes two large towns and a number of smaller market towns. The majority of the population are engaged in the service industry and construction but the high technology sector is also growing rapidly. Between 1981 and 1991 the number of jobs increased by 21% and at the 1991 Census the unemployment rate was 7% for men and 4% for women.

Children's Services and Placement Patterns in the Authorities

In City East, the smaller of the two cities in our qualitative study, fieldwork services were grouped geographically into two districts, North and South, with a total of 12 local area teams between them. Residential and fostering services were city wide resources, managed centrally, and were differentiated in terms of their purpose. There was a short term/ emergency unit, a unit for males (often offenders), one for females (often victims of sexual abuse), two units which catered for younger children (11 and under) and two long stay units. There were also three units for children with severe disabilities, which were not the subject of this research. City East made greater use of residential accommodation and less use of fostering placements than the other authorities. Nearly a quarter of its looked after children were in residential placements, more than double the national average.

City West covered a much wider geographical area and social services were divided into three large districts. Residential and fieldwork services were all organised at district level, comprising under 11 (family support) teams and 11+ (adolescent) teams. The principal managers of adolescent services also had responsibility for children's homes in their districts, aiming to deliver a coordinated local service. Within these districts there were both short term family units and long stay homes. There was a total of five emergency/short stay family units and four longer stay units providing district-based services. There was also one city wide resource, a children's home offering long term, specialist therapeutic care for young people with a history of abuse. Separate fostering managers were responsible for fostering services at district level.

Borough was divided into three districts, each with five local area teams. Each district manager also had authority wide responsibility for a particular area of service, such as child protection or looked after children. Residential and fostering services were provided on an authority wide basis. There were four community homes in Borough: a family assessment unit for children age 12 and under, a preparation for independence unit, a short stay assessment and crisis intervention unit for teenagers and a unit for 12–16 year olds who have experienced placement breakdown. Borough made considerably greater use of fostering and of residential placements in the private and voluntary sector than the other authorities.

At the time we carried out our survey County was organised into two directorates, North and South, each sub-divided into two districts. Within each of the four districts there was a purchaser/provider split. Each district had a purchasing manager and a field care manager and four or five fieldwork teams headed by practice managers. Residential and fostering services were also organised on a district basis. Apart from four homes for children with disabilities, which were not the subject of our research, there were seven mainstream children's homes providing district level services. Across the county, there was one short term reception/ emergency unit, three short–medium stay homes working towards rehabilitation or preparation for fostering, one home accommodating older young people to prepare them for fostering or independence, one to accommodate young people on remand or to prepare young people for independence and one long stay unit.

The number of children looked after on 31 March 1996, shortly after the mid-point of our surveys, varied widely between our authorities. On this date City West had a looked after population of 1183, County 1002, City East 647 and Borough 616. Borough and City West had the highest rates of children looked after in our four areas of study, with 105 children per 10 000 aged under 18 looked after in Borough on 31 March 1996 and 104 children per 10 000 in City West. Both were more than double the national average of 46 per 10 000. City East and County's rates were close to the national average, with 47 children under 18 per 10 000 looked after in both these authorities (Department of Health 1997).

The four local authorities in this study were therefore varied in terms of their populations, economic base, and the extent of socio-economic disadvantage within them. There was also substantial variation between them in the proportion of children looked after, placement patterns and the organisation of children's services. These variations provided us with the opportunity to examine patterns of going missing in very different types of authority and assess whether the incidence of going missing was related to indicators of deprivation, such as the rate of children looked after per 10 000.

3

LAW AND POLICY

NATIONAL POLICY AND GUIDANCE ON GOING MISSING

Local authorities have to fulfil a number of requirements in respect of recording and responding to going missing. Regulation 20 of the Children's Homes Regulations requires authorities to record in writing the procedure to be followed when any child accommodated in a children's home is absent without permission, and to draw this procedure to the attention of children and staff. Regulation 15 also requires residential staff to record on children's confidential records the date and circumstances of any absence of a child from a home, including whether an absence was authorised and where a child went during the period of absence (Department of Health 1991c). Local authorities are also required to issue clear guidelines to their staff on the circumstances in which the police should be notified that a juvenile is absent without permission.

Section 51 of the Children Act 1989 also makes provision for refuges for children at risk, where young people can stay for a maximum of 14 continuous days. The objectives of refuges are expected to be rehabilitation with parents or other responsible authority where this is consistent with the welfare of the child. In addition, local authorities are required to include in their children's services plans information about services for young runaways who find themselves homeless and without support. Guidance to those drawing up children's services plans suggests that local information systems which reveal the incidence and patterns of running away are important both for the planning of services and for the identification of families or institutions from which young people run away repeatedly. While there is detailed guidance to those working in residential settings, there is no advice on approaches to behaviour or control for foster carers. Equally, there is no guidance to social workers on working with young people who go missing from care placements.

Residential staff have powers which may assist them in trying to prevent young people going missing. Children who are accommodated by the local authority may be refused permission to go out, with the knowledge and preferably the agreement of those with parental responsibilities, and for children on care orders this decision can be taken by the local authority alone (Department of Health 1993). Where a child is remanded or detained within local authority accommodation under Section 3 of the Children Act, residential staff are expected to 'intervene positively if a child subject to one of these orders indicates or attempts to leave the home without authority' (Department of Health 1993).

The *Guidance on Permissible Forms of Control in Children's Residential Care* advises that when a staff member is concerned about a young person's intention to leave a unit without permission or run away, the young person should be given clear instructions and warned of the consequences of not complying with these. Staff may use their physical presence to obstruct an exit in order to create an opportunity to express concern or remonstrate with the young person and may also hold young people by the arm to secure their attention. Where it is clear that if the young person were to leave the unit there would be a strong likelihood of injury to him/herself or others, staff are permitted to use physical restraint to prevent the young person leaving the building. It is emphasised that follow-up work will be necessary to bring about longer term stability and avoid repeated use of physical restraint (Department of Health 1993).

As a last resort, when there is no appropriate alternative, a young person may be placed in secure accommodation if:

(i)   he has a history of absconding and is likely to abscond from any other description of accommodation *and*
(ii) if he absconds he is likely to suffer significant harm (Section 25, Children Act 1989).

The legislation is clear that secure accommodation must never be used simply because a child runs away from local authority accommodation but only if he or she is *also* likely to suffer significant harm in doing so, and all viable steps must first be taken to try to avoid the need for secure accommodation. In addition, the guidance to the Children Act makes it clear that a child can only be placed in secure accommodation (including any measure which prevents a child from leaving a room or building of his/her own free will) for up to 72 hours in any 28 day period before the permission of the court must be sought (Department of Health 1991b).

In certain circumstances, the police have powers to return a young person who is missing to the local authority. Paragraph 27 of Schedule 12 to the Children Act 1989 permits the arrest, without warrant, of a young person missing from a place of safety to which he or she has been taken, or from local authority accommodation in which he or she is required to live under a residence requirement attached to a supervision order, or from local authority accommodation to which he or she has been remanded. For young people on care orders or emergency protection orders, Section 50 of the Children Act allows a court to make a recovery order if a child has run away or is staying away from the responsible person or is missing. This authorises the police to enter premises to search for a missing child and allows a person authorised by the court to remove a child.

Concern that the Children Act 1989 took away from staff their power to control children and, in particular, to prevent them leaving open children's homes, led to a clarification of the implications of the Children Act in the form of a Chief Inspector letter from the Department of Health (Social Services Inspectorate 1997). This letter challenged the view that the Children Act's stress on the rights of children was at the expense of upholding the rights and responsibilities of those caring for them, arguing that it is acceptable to override the wishes and feelings of children if this is necessary to safeguard and promote their welfare. Both the Chief Inspector's letter and the earlier *Guidance on Permissible Forms of Control in Children's Residential Care* make it clear that staff in children's homes can and must intervene immediately to try to prevent young people leaving a children's home when there are grounds for believing that they are putting themselves or others at risk (Department of Health 1993).

The Chief Inspector's letter explains that it would be reasonable to assume that an 11 or 12 year old wanting to leave a children's home in the evening against the instructions of staff is likely to be at risk of harm, as would young teenagers if they are involved with vice or crime or otherwise at risk. Persuasion and the patient engagement of children are recommended, but if these fail staff have authority to prevent immediate or anticipated harm occurring. In these circumstances physical restraint may be used or staff may bolt a door temporarily to win some time to call for help (Social Services Inspectorate 1997).

However, the *Guidance on Permissible Forms of Control in Children's Residential Care* makes it clear that, for children who are not in secure accommodation, any measures to restrict children's liberty short of locking them up should be confined to circumstances where 'immediate action is necessary to prevent injury to any person or damage to property'. This action may include not only physically restraining a younger child but also holding or closely supervising him/her for a number of hours. However, attention is drawn to the fine line between the protection of children and the abuse of their civil liberties. The *Guidance* is at pains to ensure that any requirement for a child to remain in a building or part of a building does not develop into the kind of unacceptable practices revealed in the Staffordshire Pindown Inquiry. The *Guidance* is also realistic in recognising that there are practical limitations on residential staff's ability to prevent young people running away from an open children's home if they are determined to do so.

Finally, the children's services plans which local authorities are required to produce are expected to refer to provision for the assessment and follow-up of young people missing from home or care.

LOCAL POLICIES

Among our four authorities, Borough was the only one to issue comprehensive guidance to its residential staff on responding to children going missing from placements. It was also the only authority to give guidance to social workers, advising them to check the circumstances surrounding the child's disappearance, any possible reasons for going missing and details of the child's recent moods/disposition. Social workers were instructed to inform the police, parents and their line manager and to contact anyone who might know the whereabouts of the child. Once a child returned, the social worker was required to convene a placements disruption meeting. None of the authorities suggested that upon their return young people should be interviewed by their social workers, who are independent of placements, to ensure that they have not gone missing for placement related reasons which should be addressed.

There were no written procedures in any authority for foster carers or fostering social workers regarding unauthorised absence from placements. This reflects the national lack of official guidance about going missing from foster care. Foster carers were apparently told that they should inform young people's social workers if they went missing. None of the authorities gave any formal guidance to foster carers about how to respond to young people who went missing.

All authorities required residential staff to notify the police if a child went missing. The reporting time suggested was normally age related; for example in Borough staff were instructed to inform the police after two hours for under 14 year olds and by midnight for those aged 14 and over and to complete a police missing persons form. In other authorities, residential staff were given discretion as to when to inform the police, according to the age and vulnerability of the child, but in every case this had to be done by midnight. Residential staff were also required to inform parents and social workers as soon as possible. In Borough they were expected to notify the authority's principal residential manager if the child did not return within 72 hours.

Apart from requiring residential staff to notify the police, social workers and parents, three of our authorities gave little guidance to staff on responding to going missing. In City East there was no guidance referring to anything other than notification of this kind when we began our study, but during the course of our research key paragraphs from the Department of Health's *Guidance on Permissible Forms of Control in Children's Residential Care* were circulated to staff. These gave staff some guidance as to when and how they might intervene to prevent a child leaving a children's home, including clarifying issues regarding the use of physical restraint. In City West there were no written procedures on preventing or responding to going missing. However, some children's homes had included their own procedural guidance on dealing with going missing in their Statements of Purpose. County had no procedural guidance to staff other than instructions regarding the notification and recording of incidents. In Borough, however, the four community homes' Statements of Purpose contained guidance regarding the understanding of unauthorised absence, the need to intervene to prevent repeated absences and appropriate responses to young people upon their return to placements.

Residential staff in the authorities were normally expected to record absences on the child's file and incidents were also recorded on the homes' daily record sheets. However, this information was held by individual homes and not collated centrally, so none of the authorities knew how many young people were going missing from each unit or from the authority as a whole. For young people missing from foster care, the situation was even more difficult to monitor as incidents were only recorded on individual case files held by social workers, if at all. With the exception of Borough, staff were given no guidance as to whether incidents of only a few hours' duration should be recorded.

Each authority expected absences to be notified to senior managers, but the period of time after which notification was to occur varied from two to eight days and in one authority it was not specified at all. The tier of management to be informed also varied. In City East this was to be 'a senior manager' (unspecified), in City West a principal manager at district level and in County the Deputy Director was to be notified after 72 hours. In Borough social workers were required to submit a report to the Assistant Director (Children) if a child was still missing after eight days and to follow this with four weekly updates if necessary, detailing efforts made to trace the young person.

Although individual children's homes recorded absences and senior managers were expected to be notified at some stage, there was no central collation of information about absences in any authority. Two authorities explained that they relied on social workers completing placement notification forms if a young person was missing overnight, but it soon became clear that the majority of social workers did not do this. The local authorities' only central source of information on numbers going missing therefore vastly underestimated the true extent of the problem. Also, senior managers were only notified of young people who were missing for two days or more but received no authority wide information on shorter absences, which may place young people equally at risk.

The paucity of local guidance on how to prevent and respond to going missing, other than in some community homes' Statements of Purpose, also has implications for young people placed in children's homes in the private and voluntary sector. Local authorities which have not developed local procedures in response to national guidance on unauthorised absence are not in a position to communicate their expectations regarding prevention and response to those providing accommodation in the private or voluntary sector. However, in terms of national and local policy and procedures, residential staff received more guidance in this area than foster carers, who received none at all.

It appeared therefore that although one authority had procedures in place for residential staff and social workers, the guidance available in the other authorities was variable. Crucially, in terms of safeguarding children who are looked after, no authority required social workers to interview young people who went missing to ensure that there were no serious problems at their placements. Also, none of the authorities had accurate information recorded centrally to enable them to identify young people repeatedly going missing for shorter periods of time or placements with high rates of going missing.

SUMMARY

National policy and guidance on young people going missing or running away from care placements is contained in the Children Act 1989 and its associated guidance on residential care, the Children's Homes Regulations 1991, the government circular *Guidance on Permissible Forms of Control in Children's Residential Care* and a letter from the Chief Inspector of the Social Services Inspectorate. These provide guidance to residential staff but not to foster carers or field social workers.

The lack of guidance to foster carers was mirrored in the four local authorities and guidance to social workers was provided in only one authority. Local guidance to residential staff on strategies to prevent or respond to unauthorised absence from placements was variable.

All authorities required staff to notify the police when young people went missing, after a period of time which depended on age and vulnerability, but always by midnight at the latest. Parents were also to be informed and residential and foster carers were required to inform social workers.

Although children's homes individually recorded unauthorised absences, there was no effective central collation of absences from residential and foster placements. Some authorities attempted to collect information on absences by means of standard administrative child care notification forms but these vastly underestimated the actual numbers going missing. Although absences of more than two days were notified to senior managers, repeated shorter absences were not.

None of the authorities required social workers to interview young people when they returned from absences. Equally, no authority collected information on patterns of absence for individual young people or individual placements.

4

WHO GOES MISSING?

This chapter outlines the key characteristics of the young people in our main survey sample (210), our community homes sample (272) and our interview sample (36), and outlines the histories and family background of those in our interview sample. We also discuss some of the key issues that may have an impact on patterns of going missing, including ethnic origin, placement patterns, care histories and participation in education.

PROFILES

Age

Age is central to our understanding of going missing since it is significantly related to different patterns of absence, as we shall see in Chapter 6. Previous research has indicated that running away is most common among young people in their mid-teens and, consistent with this, both our surveys found that around half of the young people missing were 14 or 15 at the time of their first absence during our survey period (Abrahams and Mungall 1992). As Figure 4.1 shows, just over two thirds of the young people in both the main survey and the community homes survey were between 13 and 15 years of age. A substantial minority (17%) were under 13 and therefore particularly vulnerable in view of their age. The sharp fall in numbers for those aged 16 and over may perhaps be due to the fact that many young people leave care when only 16 or 17 years old, so there are fewer young people looked after at this age (Biehal et al 1995).

In order to explore patterns and histories of going missing at different stages in young people's lives we included a range of ages in our interview sample. Eight of these young people were under 13 years old, of whom half were age 10 or 11 years and half were 12 years old. Twenty-three were 13–15 years old and the remaining five were 16.

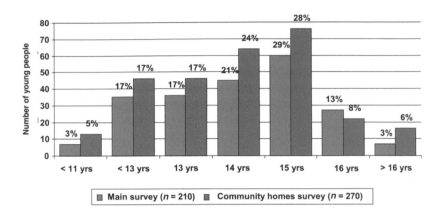

Figure 4.1 Age at time of first incident during the 12 month survey period

Sex

Although the assumption might be that boys are more likely to go missing, this is not the case. We found that females were as likely to go missing as males. Half of the young people in our main survey were male and half female, broadly reflecting the gender distribution among looked after children in the local authorities studied. However, the pattern was different for the community homes survey, where 58% of the young people going missing were male, but since a recent study of over 1000 young people in children's homes found that 58% of residents were male, it seems unlikely that males are over-represented among those missing from residential placements (Sinclair and Gibbs 1998). In our interview sample we wanted to explore any possible gender differences in histories and motivations so we included males and females in almost equal numbers.

Females in the main survey sample tended to be older. Males were more likely to have been assessed as having educational and behavioural difficulties and to have been excluded from school. They were also far more likely to have a history of offending, as only 37% of those with past convictions were female. However, gender had no bearing on the young people's histories of going missing. Our interviews revealed little in the way of gender differences in histories or reasons for going missing, other than the fact that more females had been drawn into prostitution.

Ethnic Origin

Previous studies have shown a significant over-representation of young people of African-Caribbean origin and an under-representation

of young people of Asian origin among young people running away both
from home and from substitute care (Abrahams and Mungall 1992; Rees
1993). For example, one study found that a quarter of all runaways from
substitute care in London were of African-Caribbean origin (Abrahams
and Mungall 1992).

In our study, a fifth of the sample in our main survey and a quarter of
our community homes sample were black[1]. The vast majority of the black
young people were of African-Caribbean or African-Caribbean/white
origin: 89% of the black young people in our main survey sample and
95% of those in our community homes sample. We included nine black
young people in our interview sample, of whom seven were of mixed
African-Caribbean/white origin, one of African-Caribbean origin and
one of African origin.

It is perhaps not surprising that both our study and others have found
few young people of Asian origin among runaways from substitute care,
since this group are in any case under-represented among children
looked after (Bebbington and Miles 1989). It is, however, more difficult to
explain the patterns of *over*-representation of young people of African-
Caribbean origin found in other studies. Although other research has
found a link between running away and economic disadvantage, Rees
has argued that this alone cannot satisfactorily explain high rates of running away by young people of African-Caribbean origin since young
people of Asian origin are also concentrated in economically disadvan-
taged areas (Abrahams and Mungall 1992; Rees 1993).

The majority of the black young people in both our survey samples
came from Borough, our inner London authority, which was home
to over two thirds of the black young people in the community homes
survey. We therefore decided to explore the question of possible over-
representation of black young people by looking more closely at patterns of going missing in this authority. In Borough, the majority of
young people who went missing in both survey samples were black:
57% of those in the community homes survey and 56% of those in the
main survey. In the year covered by the surveys 43% of all children
looked after were black, so at first sight it would appear that black
young people were indeed over-represented among those going missing in this authority. However, it is important to take account of the
proportion of black children aged 11 and over within the population of
children looked after, as younger children are far less likely to go

---

[1] As numbers of Asian and other black young people in both surveys were very small, and
as comparative data on ethnic origin was presented in different ways by each local authority, for the purpose of discussion we have grouped all young people of black or Asian
origin or of mixed heritage under the heading 'black' unless otherwise stated.

missing, and also of the 'flow' of young people through placements during the course of the year.

In order to look at this issue more closely we examined our survey of community homes, which had a representative sample of children going missing from residential units in Borough. Borough's children's services plan acknowledged a significant over-representation of black children among its looked after population, since 41% of all children looked after in that authority were black whereas Census data showed that only 27% of 0–15 year olds living in Borough were black (including children of African-Caribbean, African and Asian origin and children of mixed parentage). The over-representation of black children of mixed parentage among care populations has been identified in other studies (Rowe et al 1989; Barn 1993; Barn et al 1997). However, Borough's information system does not distinguish between children with two black parents and those of mixed African-Caribbean/white parentage so we could not tell whether it was specifically the latter group who were over-represented in this authority.

The over-representation of black or African-Caribbean/white young people appeared to be particularly acute in Borough's community homes. We found that during the course of the year in which we carried out our surveys, 58% of the young people aged 11 and over who were accommodated in Borough's four residential units were black/of mixed parentage, a figure that was to all intents and purposes the same as the proportion of young people going missing from these units who were of black/mixed parentage (57%). This would suggest that, once account is taken of the 'flow' of older young people through residential placements, black young people are over-represented among those looked after in children's homes but are not over-represented among those who go missing from residential placements, in this authority at least. This may help to explain why previous studies have found a high proportion of black young people among runaways from residential care (Abrahams and Mungall 1992).

Our main survey shows no difference in patterns for black and white young people relating either to the young people's history of going missing or to the particular incident recorded. There were also no differences in care careers, apart from the fact that on average white young people had been looked after for longer. For both black and white young people bullying by other residents of children's homes was sometimes a factor which encouraged them to go missing, and for two of the black young people we interviewed, racist abuse was one aspect of the general bullying they had experienced. The black young people, social workers and residential staff we interviewed felt that patterns of absence and motivations for going missing were not related to 'race' issues, although some professionals thought that black young people were more likely to return to support networks in their home areas while missing rather than head for the city centre streets, where they would be both more visible and more likely to experience racist abuse. Other than this, our findings indicate that black and white young people are not likely to go missing for different reasons, or begin their careers of going missing in different ways, or do different things while they are away.

Special Needs

Just over a quarter of the main survey sample were considered to have a disability or other special needs. The largest group were those with emotional and behavioural difficulties who had been assessed as having special educational needs under the Education Act 1981 (17% – 36 young people). These may be over-represented in our sample since a recent inspection report on children looked after in four local authorities found that 10% had emotional and behavioural difficulties (SSI/Ofsted 1995). A further 8% of the sample had learning disabilities (of whom 3% also had emotional and behavioural difficulties or a health problem). Of the remainder, less than 2% had a physical disability or sensory impairment.

The young people with emotional and behavioural difficulties were predominantly male (69%), and there were a number of other key differences in patterns for this group compared to those who had not been assessed as having emotional and behavioural difficulties, as shown in Table 4.1.

Table 4.1 Patterns for young people with/without emotional and behavioural difficulties (EBD)

	EBD	No EBD
Age first missing	First missing younger: mean age 12.6	First missing older: mean age 13.4
Times missing	Missing more often	Missing less often
Duration of absence	Away longer	Away shorter time
Nature of return	Fewer returned voluntarily	More returned voluntarily
School exclusion	39% excluded	21% excluded
Offending	71% had past convictions	44% had past convictions

The young people with emotional and behavioural difficulties were likely to have gone missing at an earlier age and to have gone missing more often in total than others in the sample. On this occasion they had stayed away longer and had been less likely than others to have returned voluntarily. They were also nearly twice as likely to be excluded from school at the time of the incident and far more likely to have been charged with at least one criminal offence prior to this incident. In these respects, patterns of going missing and of detachment for this group of young people appear more extreme. The implications of this are that young people with emotional and behavioural difficulties are a high risk group in terms of going missing from substitute care.

Histories

Our interviews offered us the opportunity to develop a more rounded understanding of the past experiences and family circumstances of a large group of young people who have gone missing from placements in substitute care, although it is important to remember that, as we explained in Chapter 2, this group was selected to give a spread of age, sex, ethnic origin and placement types and so it does not constitute a random sample. Sixteen of the young people in our interview sample had parents who were addicted to alcohol or drugs or who suffered from severe mental health problems. The most common problem was alcoholism, which accounted for around two thirds of the parents in this sub-group. Five of the young people had been severely neglected, in four cases by parents with drug or alcohol problems. Many (14) had suffered rejection by one or both parents, of whom four had entered substitute care because they had been abandoned.

Our review of the North American literature indicated that many persistent runaways from home may have run to escape severely abusing or rejecting parents (Brennan et al 1978; Johnson and Carter 1980; Farber et al 1984; Janus et al 1987; Stiffman 1989; Cohen et al 1991; Simons and Whitbeck 1991; Spatz et al 1994). These studies have shown that both physical and sexual abuse are a feature of the lives of many young runaways from home. We too found that many of the young people we interviewed had experienced abuse, although of course we may well expect to find some histories of abuse among a sample of young people in substitute care, as this is the reason why some have been separated from their parents. Seventeen of the young people were known to have experienced physical, sexual or emotional abuse and a number of these had experienced more than one type of abuse. Thirteen had been physically abused by a parent and seven had experienced sexual abuse by a family member. Another four had been sexually abused by others outside their families, including two who had been sexually abused by other young people in a foster or residential placement. Two young people were known to have sexually abused other young people. One of these was known to have been sexually abused himself, while there were strong suspicions that the other had suffered undisclosed sexual abuse. There was also concern that 16 young people had recently been or were currently being sexually exploited by adult men, of whom 10 had some past or current involvement in prostitution, a subject to which we shall return in our discussion of risk (Chapter 8).

Reason for Looking After the Young Person

In our main survey social workers were asked to record the *principal* reason for accommodating the young people at their last admission. The largest group of young people in the sample (40%) were being looked after because of the breakdown in their relationships with their families and 22% because their families were unable to provide care. Young people's behavioural problems accounted for entry in 13% of the cases and neglect was the main reason for entry for 8% of the young people. For 10% their entry to care had been precipitated by either sexual, emotional or physical abuse – in over half of these cases by sexual abuse. Our sample differed in some respects from the pattern of reasons for entry found in Sinclair and Gibbs' large study of children's homes, in that we found fewer young people were accommodated as a result of relationship breakdown or behaviour problems and more due to their families' inability to provide care (Sinclair and Gibbs 1998).

Young people often begin to be looked after for a cluster of reasons and this complexity was explored in our interviews with 36 young people. Ten of the young people in our interview sample were being looked after because their families were unable to care for them. Seven of these had parents with serious drug, alcohol or mental health problems, as did all but one of the parents of the five who had entered substitute care as a result of parental neglect. For the ten young people who had entered substitute care due to a relationship breakdown with parents there was always an additional reason, either parental abuse or the alcohol, drug or mental health problems of parents. Abuse was one of the reasons for separation from parents for 14 of these young people, and for half of this group the abuse was accompanied by rejection or neglect. For five young people, their behavioural problems had been a factor leading to their admission to substitute care, but in every case these behaviour problems were associated with histories of rejection or abuse. All of these young people had complex reasons for being looked after and even where their own behaviour was seen as being part of the problem, in every instance this was associated with histories of abuse, rejection, or parental addiction or mental illness.

PLACEMENTS

Placement Patterns

Just under two thirds of the young people in our main survey sample were in residential placements, the majority of them in community homes, and just over a third were in foster placements. Only two of the young people were in secure units but six others had had a previous admission to secure accommodation. Almost all (96%) of the young people in our main survey sample had experienced both residential and foster care since they had been looked after.

In our interview sample, 27 of the young people were in residential placements. The majority were in local community homes, but two were in private sector homes and one was in a secure unit. Eight were fostered at the time of the interview and one was placed with parents but had only just moved there from a children's home.

Time Looked After and in Placement

Most of the young people in our main survey sample had been looked after for only a short time. Four in 10 had been in substitute care for six months or less, and 6 in 10 had been looked after for one year or less. In contrast, the young people in our interview sample were likely to have been looked after for a longer period as over half had been looked after for more than a year.

For many of those in our main survey sample their time in their current placement was very short indeed, as two fifths had been in placement for a month or less. Patterns for time in placement were similar for those in residential and foster care. Our interview sample tended to have spent longer in their current placements, as only 42% had been in placement for six months or less.

Many young people were therefore still attempting to settle in to placements and form attachments to carers. In the main survey social workers considered that only 2 in 10 of the young people had formed definite attachments to their carers, and over half of these had been in their placements for seven months or more. On the other hand, well over a third were thought to have formed no attachment at all to their carers. The majority of these had been at the placement for less than six months and over half had been there for less than a month. Not surprisingly, being newly in placement, which as we have already seen is the experience of many young people in residential care, was associated with having weak attachments to carers and this is likely to make negotiation around unauthorised absence more difficult.

Placement Moves

A majority of the main survey sample had experienced a considerable number of changes of placement and over half had experienced four or more placement moves, as shown in Figure 4.2. Young people in residential placements were likely to have experienced a significantly higher number of placement moves than those in foster care, as the mean number of moves was 5.7 for those in residential care compared to 3.5 for those in foster care.

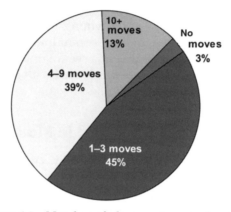

Figure 4.2 Number of placement moves ($n = 189$)

PARTICIPATION IN EDUCATION

School attendance was very poor. As Table 4.2 shows, over two fifths of the young people in our main survey were not attending mainstream school at all. Only a quarter were attending all the time, with a third attending sometimes but not on a regular basis. There was no significant difference between foster and residential placements with regard to level of school attendance at the time of the interview.

Table 4.2   School attendance

	Young people	Percentage
All the time	47	24.4
Sometimes	65	33.7
Never	78	40.4
Alternative provision	3	1.5
Total	193	100.0

The young people who 'never' attended school included both those who were reported as never attending (17%) and those who had been excluded (25%), of whom a few were receiving limited alternative provision. It was unclear from the responses to our survey how many were excluded permanently and how many temporarily. The majority of those who were non-attenders were aged 14 or 15, which tended to be older than those excluded from school. Non-attenders were also likely to have been looked after for a shorter time than those who attended, and were more likely to be unhappy in their current placement.

Although there is concern about rates of school attendance and exclusion for the general population of children who are looked after, our evidence suggests that those who go missing are at even greater risk of detachment from school. An inspection report on children looked after in four local authorities provides a useful comparison (SSI/Ofsted 1995). It found that 12% of those looked after (all ages) have poor attendance or are excluded, rising to over 25% for those in the 14–16 age group. A major study of residential care also found that 30% of those in children's homes were either excluded from school or not attending for other reasons (Sinclair and Gibbs 1998). Rates of non-attendance and exclusion therefore appear to be substantially higher for young people who go missing than for the general population of children looked after.

This disparity is even greater if we focus solely on those who were excluded from school, since the SSI/Ofsted inspection found that 5% of 11–14 year olds and 7% of 14–16 year olds looked after in four local authorities were excluded on a specific census date, whereas in our sample 25% were excluded (SSI/Ofsted 1995). The young people excluded from school were more likely to be male (75%) and young people assessed as having emotional and behavioural difficulties were almost twice as likely to be excluded. Exclusion was also significantly related to past offending, as 73% of those excluded had past convictions for offending compared to 41% of those not excluded. There was, however, no significant relationship between school exclusion and ethnic origin, which is somewhat surprising in the light of national data suggesting that black young people are over-represented among those excluded. We might speculate that perhaps, for young people who go missing from care, patterns of school exclusion are so strongly associated with emotional and behavioural difficulties or a history of offending that this overrides any association with ethnic origin (Bourne et al 1994; Brodie and Berridge 1996; Department for Education and Employment 1996).

Of the 36 young people that we interviewed, the overwhelming majority were not attending or were excluded from school, leaving only seven who attended regularly. Patterns of detachment from school often featured both non-attendance and exclusion. Twelve of the young people we interviewed had been excluded at some stage for aggressive, abusive or violent behaviour and many of these also had histories of non-attendance. Young people with special educational needs were not uncommon among those who were out of school, as 10 of the non-attenders in our interview sample were statemented as having emotional and behavioural difficulties (EBD) and many of these had also been excluded from school at some time in the past.

In common with other studies, we also found that social workers were not always clear about whether young people had been excluded or were simply non-attenders (Brodie and Berridge 1996; Sinclair and Gibbs 1998). Some young people who had been permanently excluded drifted for long periods of time with no educational provision other than short spells attending pupil referral units or EBD day schools for a day or two a week. Sometimes it was the young people themselves who subverted attempts to reintroduce them to school but in a number of cases young people who had been permanently excluded had been allowed to drift for months or, in two cases, for two years, due to long delays in arranging alternative provision.

Where young people had been out of school for a long time residential staff or social workers were sometimes unsure about whether a young person was still formally excluded or simply did not have a school to go to, and seemed unable to compel the education department to act. The long delays occasioned by lengthy referral and administrative procedures meant that the original problems at issue were unclear to those currently involved, a situation reminiscent of the protracted legal process described in *Bleak House*. For example, neither Karl's social worker nor his key-worker knew why he had been excluded two years earlier. His social worker thought he might still be 'on the books' of his old school but was unsure about this. He had spent many months going through the statementing procedure and had finally been offered a place in a specialist unit, but this would not become available for another seven months due to resource shortages. His social worker felt that no one really knew why he had been out of school for so long:

> It's just sort of disappeared into the background. No one seems to remember why he was thrown out really.

Our findings indicate that there is an urgent need for inter-agency cooperation to respond rapidly once non-attendance by looked after young people becomes a problem and to ensure that exclusion does not leave young people drifting for long periods of time detached from educational institutions. There is a clear, athough complex, link between detachment from school and motivations for going missing, and this will be explored further in Chapter 10.

SUMMARY

Most of the young people in our three samples were aged 13-15 years, but a substantial minority were aged 12 or under. Around half of those who went missing were male and half female, although there was a slightly higher proportion of males in the community homes survey.

Between a fifth and a quarter of those who went missing were black, the vast majority of whom were of African-Caribbean or African-Caribbean/white origin. Although other studies have found that young people of African-Caribbean origin are over-represented among young runaways, this was not the case in Borough, the authority from which most of the black young people in our study came. However, black young people were over-represented among children looked after in this authority and this over-representation was even more acute for those in community homes. There were no differences in patterns or histories of going missing for black and white young people.

Over a quarter of the main survey sample had a disability or other special needs, the majority of whom were statemented for emotional and behavioural difficulties. Those with emotional and behavioural difficulties were likely to have gone missing more often and to have stayed away longer. They were also much more likely to have been excluded from school and to have a history of offending.

Nearly half of the young people in our interview sample had parents who were addicted to alcohol or drugs or who had mental health problems. Almost half had experienced physical, sexual or emotional abuse and many had experienced severe rejection or neglect. Many of the young people had entered substitute care as a result of a breakdown in relationships with parents or because their families were unable to provide care. In those cases in the interview sample where behaviour problems had precipitated accommodation, in every instance this was associated with histories of abuse, rejection, or parental addiction or mental illness.

The majority of the young people in the main survey and interview samples were in residential placements, most of them in local authority community homes. Many were newly in placement; 71% of those in the main survey and 42% of those in the interview sample had been in placement for six months or less. The level of placement movement was high, with two fifths of those in the main survey having experienced four to nine moves since being looked after, even though well over half of this sample had been looked after for only one year or less.

School attendance was very poor. In the main survey, over two fifths of those of school age were not attending school, including many who were excluded from school. This appears to be a higher rate of non-attendance and school exclusion than for other looked after young people. The young people excluded from school were more likely to be male and to have past convictions for offending, and were twice as likely to have emotional and behavioural difficulties. In several cases, young people who had been excluded had been allowed to drift for long periods of time, up to two years, with no full-time educational provision from the local education authority. Resource shortages, administrative delays, lengthy and cumbersome referral procedures for specialist provision and poor liaison all contributed to the problem.

5

PATTERNS OF GOING MISSING

Concern about the disproportionate numbers of young people from residential settings amongst samples of young runaways has been growing since the late 1980s. Despite this, very little is currently known about the scale of the problem nor of what happens to young people when they do go missing from placements. How many young people go missing and for how long? Where might they go and who with? Where do they stay while away? What can we say about the nature of their return? Consideration of these questions will form the substance of this chapter.

NUMBERS GOING MISSING

Studies carried out in recent years have provided valuable information on the *proportion of young people within general runaway samples* who have gone missing from substitute care placements (Newman 1989; Abrahams and Mungall 1992). However, our study approaches this phenomenon from a different angle, by attempting to estimate the *proportion of looked after young people* who go missing.

As the vast majority of young runaways are in the 11–16 age group, it would be misleading to compare them to the total numbers of looked after young people in order to establish the proportion going missing, since nationally 39% of looked after children are under 10 years of age (Department of Health 1997). We have therefore attempted to establish the proportion of 11–16 year olds looked after in our authorities who went missing at least once during the survey period.

Numbers Missing from Residential Placements

The children's home survey provided the basis for an estimate of the numbers and proportion of 11–16 year olds in the four authorities who went missing from mainstream children's homes during the 12 month survey period. Table 5.1 shows that, across the four authorities, just over two fifths (43%) of the total population went missing at least once during the year.

Table 5.1 Proportion of young people in residential care going missing from community homes (community homes survey)

	Young people aged 11–16 in residential placements	Young people in homes survey	Young people aged 11–16 in homes survey	% 11–16s missing from children's homes
County	159	44	39	25
City West	141	96	92	65
City East	164	51	43	26
Borough	94	81	67	71
Total	558	272	241	43

This high level of absence, together with the findings of earlier studies on young runaways, suggests that going missing is indeed a widespread phenomenon in children's homes. There was considerable variation between authorities, with around two thirds of all young people in community homes in City West and nearly three quarters of residents in Borough's homes going missing. For the other two authorities the proportion was around a quarter[1]. The variation between authorities that we have identified points to the need for some caution in generalising these findings to the national population of young people looked after in children's homes, since rates of absence are likely to vary from one authority to another.

Earlier studies have found wide variations between similar types of establishment in the numbers that run away (Clarke and Martin 1971; Sinclair 1971; Abrahams and Mungall 1992; Sinclair and Gibbs 1998) and that these variations could not be satisfactorily explained by differences in intake or length of time in the home (Sinclair and Gibbs 1998). We also found that there were considerable differences between children's homes in the numbers going missing. Of the 32 community homes surveyed, just four homes accommodated 42% of those who went missing. The difference is even more marked if we consider the number of incidents in different units, as two thirds of the incidents of absence occurred in just seven homes. The problem was particularly severe in Borough, where just

---

[1] The young people missing from children's homes in Borough tended to be older than those in the other authorities, with 61% aged 15 or 16. In this respect there was a significant difference in the age distribution between Borough and the other authorities.

two of this authority's four community homes accommodated 28% of all the young people in the sample and these young people were responsible for nearly a third of all incidents in the survey.

However, it was equally the case that in most units with high rates of absence a small number of young people accounted for a high proportion of incidents in that unit. In City East, although one unit accounted for 46% of all absences in the authority, one young person was responsible for nearly half the incidents in that unit during the year (105 out of 226). In County, although one unit accounted for 52% of all incidents, just three young people were responsible for more than half of these. Finally, in one of the previously mentioned units in Borough, 47% of the absences involved only five young people.

While our survey data cannot help us to understand the *processes* associated with these patterns, it does suggest a need to focus both on the cultures and regimes of units and on young people's careers of going missing and the life experiences they bring with them to a placement. Drawing on our qualitative data, these are issues to which we shall return in subsequent chapters.

Numbers Missing from Foster Care

An accurate estimate of the proportion of young people who went missing from foster placements was impossible to obtain. While the community homes in each of the four authorities kept records of unauthorised absences which made our supplementary survey possible, no data was available on unauthorised absences from foster placements in any authority. We can therefore only estimate the *minimum* proportion of young people missing from foster placements based on our main survey sample. Across the four authorities, *at least* 5% of all 11–16 year olds placed in foster care during the course of one year went missing from their placements at least once. Although it seems probable that going missing from foster placements is a less common occurrence than is the case in the residential sector, this figure is likely to be an underestimate.

The absence of central information on unauthorised absences from foster and residential placements represents an area of weakness for these authorities. As we shall see in Chapter 13, the failure to accurately record, collate and monitor absences meant that these authorities had little idea of the scale of the problem nor where pockets of high absence existed, which had implications for planning strategic service responses. In addition, at an individual level, inadequate recording could impair information sharing between social workers and caregivers and, in consequence, the future protection and support of young people.

WHAT HAPPENS WHEN YOUNG PEOPLE GO MISSING?

The main survey enabled us to gather information from social workers and carers about the contours of a single instance of unauthorised absence. This will be supplemented here by illustrative material drawn from the interview sample that takes account of young people's perceptions of what they do when missing.

How Long Were They Missing?

The vast majority (85%) of the young people were missing overnight on this occasion. Figure 5.1 shows that just over two fifths were missing for less than 24 hours and three fifths for one day or less. At the other extreme, more than 1 in 10 were missing for a week or more. In the duration of their absences, young people in substitute care do not appear to differ from runaways in the general population, for whom the pattern is similar (Abrahams and Mungall 1992; Rees 1993).

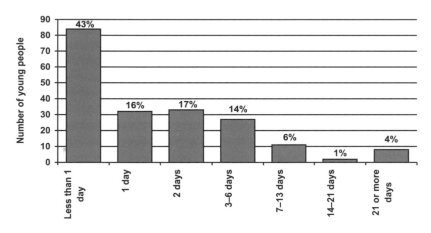

Figure 5.1   Length of time missing: main survey sample ($n = 197$)

Turning to the children's homes survey sample, Figure 5.2 shows that viewed over a 12 month period a higher proportion of the absences from these children's homes were for one day or less.

The difference between the two surveys can be explained by the fact that the young people in foster care in the main survey sample were more likely to be missing for more than a day, while the absences of those in residential placements tended to be of shorter duration.

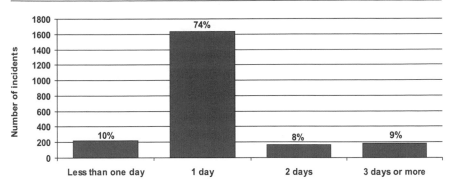

Figure 5.2   Length of time missing: children's homes survey sample by number of incidents (n = 2211)

Age also influenced the length of absences. Those under 13 years of age were more likely to be missing for less than one day, with the likelihood of being missing for one day or more steadily increasing with age up to 15 years. At 16 and over, this age effect lessened considerably. So in overall terms, the younger children stayed away for shorter periods while those at the peak ages for going missing, the 14 and 15 year olds, tended to stay away longer.

Information gathered from our interviews with young people, social workers and carers tended to suggest that the patterns an absence might take were quite closely related to the motivations for going missing, although there were exceptions. Where young people were unhappy being looked after, either because they wanted reunification with their families or were experiencing problems in their placement, and where they had a definite destination with family or friends, absences tended to be of longer duration – several days rather than overnight. For example, one young male who had been placed in an out-of-authority unit 100 miles from his family regularly ran back to his family/home area because he felt 'homesick'. He would stay away until picked up by the police and returned. Another male (aged 14) regularly went missing for two to three days at a time to be with his father. According to his keyworker his pattern was to return voluntarily when he needed a change of clothes, a bath and extra food, stay a few days and then return to his father. In some instances, even where absences lacked a problem focus, if young people knew friends who had their own accommodation (sometimes themselves care leavers) they were likely to be away longer. One extreme example was of a young female (aged 15) who had spent the past three months virtually living at her boyfriend's flat. She liked her residential placement, had a close and confiding relationship with her keyworker, and would return voluntarily on a regular basis whenever she wanted security, advice or simply a chat.

Where young people lacked a destination and absences centred on spending time on city centre streets, absences tended to be of shorter duration, although there were extreme examples of young people living on the streets for three to five weeks. Young people were more likely to return in the early hours or the next morning when tired, cold and hungry. One typical pattern, especially though not exclusively for young males going missing from units as part of a peer group, was to leave in the late evening, spend the night out and return in the early hours. These absences were closely associated with offending (taking cars, thefts, criminal damage), alcohol and drugs. These young people would then sleep during the day and, for those heavily involved, repeat the pattern nightly. The rationale given by young people for this type of absence was the buzz and excitement of being free of adult authority although, as we will see, some felt coerced. A similar pattern was apparent for those, more often females, who 'stayed out' on the town at clubs or parties. Again these absences were linked to having fun, getting drunk and often sexual encounters. These young people would usually return voluntarily the next day. Although of relatively short duration, it should be apparent that these kinds of absence involved quite high risks of involvement in criminal activities, substance misuse, victimisation and sexual exploitation. Although rationalised as fun they were often underpinned by deeper unhappiness and carried real dangers.

However, patterns were rarely fixed. The duration of an absence was sometimes simply related to what happened when young people were on the streets, who they met and what was suggested. Patterns also shifted over time according to age or maturity or to changes in contexts or circumstances. These are issues to which we shall return later.

Who Did They Go Missing With?

The majority (55%) went alone and two fifths (42%) went with friends, either from the placement or outside it. Those who went missing alone tended to be older and nearly two thirds of those who went missing to be with friends/family had gone alone. In contrast, those who went missing with others were likely to be younger and were more likely to have run away. Nearly one in five of those who went missing with others slept rough on this occasion and were twice as likely to have done this as those who went missing alone.

From our interview sample there is evidence to suggest that a number of factors are associated with going missing with others, as part of a group experience. First, as we have seen, a key rationale for peer group inspired absences from residential settings was the fun and excitement of being 'free'. Hanging about in city centres alone was not fun, it was too isolating. As one male (aged 12) said:

> You've got no one to hang about with. When you've got your gang you know what to do, you know where to go.

Second, and linked to this, a number of young people felt that being with others afforded greater protection when on the streets or at clubs. For them, being out at night was understandably scary. However, being with others could also lead to an escalation in risk activities. For example, there were a number of instances of younger boys and girls being inducted into criminal activities or finding themselves in dangerous circumstances with strangers through their involvement in peer-based absences.

Third, although many were enticed into going with peers for these reasons, some were coerced or were reluctantly attempting to seek acceptance within the peer group. For example, David, a 12 year old black male who had learning difficulties, had been inappropriately placed in a residential unit (due to a lack of alternatives) that had a very strong negative peer culture centred around a group of older males. He was the youngest and was subjected to sustained racist bullying. Initially he went missing alone to escape the pressure but eventually, in order to gain acceptance, he started stealing and distributing the fruits to the others and joining in their peer-based absences. Not only was the bullying never effectively tackled within the unit but his 'career' of going missing and offending was at risk of escalation.

While a majority of incidents involving others tended broadly to fit these patterns, there were also instances of young people going with one or more friends to visit family or friends and one or two examples of a young person going with a sibling. In contrast, young people tended to go alone when they had a definite destination in mind, usually with family or friends, or when they were experiencing personal difficulties – for example trying to relieve mental pressure, escape conflict with carers or young people or, as with David, escape bullying. Going alone was also a feature for some young people adjusting to the trauma of entering care or settling into a new placement. One young female recounted going missing nearly every day, mostly to friends' houses, as she struggled to adjust to a new residential placement:

> I would not stay in here, I didn't like it . . . 'cos it were just a completely different environment to what I'd been used to.

As she found her feet in the unit the scale of her absences gradually diminished.

Where Did They Stay While Away?

Returning to the main survey, over a quarter (28%) of the young people's social workers or carers did not know where the young people had stayed while away on this occasion, a matter of some concern in itself. As shown in Figure 5.3, where the young people's destinations were known, three quarters had stayed with friends or relatives, the vast majority with friends, and a further 15% had slept rough.

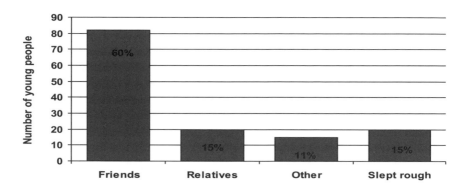

Figure 5.3   Where the young people stayed while absent ($n = 137$)

Those who slept rough tended to be in the younger age range and were clearly at considerable risk, as nearly two thirds of them were aged between 11 and 13 years, and over a third of those described as having run away had slept rough on this occasion.

Most of the young people did not travel far when they went missing. Over a third remained within the local area and over four fifths remained within the boundary of their local authority.

Rees (1993) found that, for his sample of runaways, those running from residential care were less likely to have slept rough than those running from the family home and speculated that those from care may have a wider network of places to stay while away. Findings from our interview sample suggest that, while a consistent pattern of where young people were likely to stay was hard to discern in many cases and while many of the young people had slept rough on occasion, a repeat pattern of going missing tended to lead to a wider network of places that could be used.

Some young people appeared to repeat a pattern of returning in the early hours of the morning to sleep and others of going to the same family members or friends. While some of these young people were not considered by carers and social workers to be at risk, staying with relatives or friends did not always lessen professional concern about young people's safety.

As young people's careers progressed their networks could become ever wider, incorporating older siblings, care leavers, friends, new acquaintances or strangers or contacts in the 'street' scene. One young female (now aged 16) whose boyfriend was a homeless care leaver was introduced through him to the homeless hostel and street culture in City West. Eventually, according to her social worker, her network of contacts and supports, including those of voluntary agencies providing services for those on the streets, enabled her to stay away weeks at a time. Some, less 'street-wise' than this young woman, who allowed themselves to go off with strangers were considered especially vulnerable. As one key-worker said of a 12 year old male:

> The beginning of this week . . . he met up with some 16 year old boy on the first day, don't know where he stayed. Then the second day he was at someone's house who was 22; both lads. I mean, why would they want to knock around with a 12 year old? I haven't got a clue, but the next day he's found on the streets full of drugs. That's how vulnerable this boy is.

The keyworker felt that this boy had been abused sexually, had no sense of danger and would meet up and go off with people immediately. For those with more extreme careers of going missing, not knowing where young people were likely to stay seemed to be a permanent state of affairs for practitioners. It is hard not to have some sympathy with this exasperated keyworker who already had a list of 15–20 addresses where this boy had stayed in the past, all of which had to be passed to the police each time he went missing. A number of carers and social workers spoke of the problems associated with trying to track young people, identify whether these addresses contained adults known to have past convictions for sexual offences against children, and then liaise with the police. We shall return to these issues in subsequent chapters.

Return to the Placement

Just over half the sample (52%) returned of their own accord, while just over two fifths were brought back and these proportions are similar to a recent survey of runaways in general (Rees 1993). A small group (5%) of young people refused to return to a substitute care placement and placed themselves in alternative accommodation with friends or family. This *fait accompli* was then 'negotiated' with social workers who, perhaps reluctantly, allowed the young people to remain in the accommodation of their own choosing. Of the young people who were brought back to their placements by others, nearly two thirds were returned by the police and nearly a quarter were collected by a carer.

The vast majority (85%) of the young people were able to return to the same placement. Where they did move to new accommodation, a third placed themselves with family or friends and a tenth went to a new foster or residential placement. In two thirds of cases social workers felt that the decision to return to the same placement or to move to a new one was in keeping with the aims of the care plan. However, for a fifth of the young people the decision was forced through lack of alternative resources or through the carer refusing to have the young person back. Whether returning to the same or a new placement, not all the young people were happy with the arrangements made. Over a quarter of the young people were unhappy with the choice that was available to them.

SUMMARY

In this chapter we have reviewed descriptive findings from the main survey and our supplementary children's homes survey and, where appropriate, introduced some illustrative findings from the interview sample which included the perceptions of young people themselves. We have used these data sources to identify the numbers of young people who went missing from these authorities over a 12 month period and to explore the patterns associated with a single absence in some detail.

From the children's home survey we estimated that 43% of all those aged 11–16 accommodated in mainstream children's homes in the four authorities went missing at least once in a 12 month period. Considerable variations in the rate of absence were observed between the authorities and between individual children's homes, although most units with high rates of absence contained a small number of young people who accounted for a disproportionate number of incidents. This suggests the need to situate going missing in terms of both the culture and regimes of units and the life course of young people, the kinds of experiences they bring to a placement.

No data in any authority was available on absences from foster care and we can only estimate, from the main survey alone, that *at least* 5% of 11–16 year olds went missing at least once from foster settings, a likely underestimate. Evidence suggests that greater attention to record keeping and the collation of monitoring data about absences would help authorities to have a clearer understanding of the scale of absences, identify pockets of high absence and plan strategic responses.

In relation to patterns associated with the single incident, we found that these young people did not stay away longer than has been the case for previous samples of runaways from home and care, although length of absence tended to increase with age. Just over half had gone missing alone and they tended to be older and to have gone missing to be with 'friends/family'; those going with others were more likely to have 'run away or stayed out'. Going with others was often thought to enhance enjoyment on the streets and offer greater protection, although it could escalate risks. Going alone tended to be linked to having a definite destination, usually friends or family, or to absences related to relieving pressure or escaping conflict. Where destinations were known, nearly two thirds stayed with friends, 15% with family and 15% slept rough. Over one third of those thought to have 'run away' slept rough and two thirds of rough sleepers were aged 11–13. Most did not travel far and just over half returned voluntarily, usually to the same placement.

6

COMPARING TYPES OF ABSENCE

In the last chapter we described in some detail the patterns associated with a single unauthorised absence for the main survey sample. We were also interested to know from social workers and caregivers what meaning they ascribed to that absence. Did they think the young people were running away? If not, in what other way would they categorise their behaviour? Through this we hoped to gain a better understanding of the varied types of unauthorised absence that might exist. Analysis of this data has enabled us to identify two broad groupings of young people within the sample – those who went missing to be with friends or family and those who ran away or stayed out. The young people in these groups tended to have different characteristics, for each group the pattern of the incident was significantly different and, as we shall see, young people who closely fit the profile of one or other of these groups may require different professional responses.

One of the limitations of this type of survey analysis is that it cannot capture the depth and complexity of young people's lives. We shall therefore end the chapter with some case profiles designed to illustrate these types of absence, but also to show how patterns of going missing for young people can be complex, involving different types of absence, and shift over time in response to growing maturity or changes in circumstances.

DIFFERING TYPES OF ABSENCE

Figure 6.1 shows that over half of the young people were described as going missing to be with friends or family on this occasion. Over two fifths went missing to be with friends, while one in ten either went missing to be with a member of their family or failed to return from a visit home. Nearly a third were described as having 'run away', while a further 15% were reported to have stayed out.

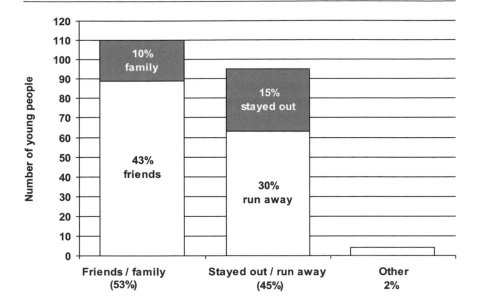

Figure 6.1   Nature of the absence ($n = 209$)

The sample therefore broadly divides into two groupings, with 53% missing to be with 'family or friends', the vast majority with friends, and 45% thought to have 'run away or stayed out'. There were no significant differences between those in the 'friends' and those in the 'family' groups in terms of personal characteristics, care careers, the features of their absence or histories of going missing. So for the purpose of further analysis we have grouped them together as the *friends* group.

As regards those who 'ran away' or 'stayed out', there were also few significant differences. Those described as 'running away' were more likely to be male and, on this occasion, to have stayed away longer and to have slept rough than was the case for those who 'stayed out'. Despite these small differences, we have categorised these young people as the *runaways* group in order to compare them to the *friends* group.

COMPARING THE *FRIENDS/FAMILY* AND *RUNAWAYS* GROUPS

A number of significantly different tendencies can be seen in both the personal characteristics and the pattern of the incident for these two groups of young people.

Differences in Age, Sex and Current Placement

Table 6.1 shows differences for these groupings in relation to age, sex and current placement.

Table 6.1   Nature of absence by age, sex and placement type

	Friends group	Runaways group
Age (p = 0.001; n = 205)	Older	Younger
Sex (p = 0.004; n = 205)	More females – 59% were female	More males – 38% were female
Placement type (p = 0.008; n = 199)	More foster – 66% of those fostered	More residential – 54% of those in residential placements

There was a greater concentration within the *friends* group of females, of those who were in foster placements at the time of the incident and of older young people. The mean age for the *friends* group was 14.3 years compared to 13.6 years for the *runaways* group. The *runaways* group, as well as being younger, tended to have more males within it and a slightly higher proportion of young people from residential settings. Looked at from another angle, three quarters (73%) of those who 'ran away or stayed out' were from residential settings.

Differences in the Pattern of the Absence

Distinctive differences were also apparent for these groups in relation to key features of the absence as Table 6.2 indicates.

A greater proportion of the young people in the *friends* group tended to be away longer, to have gone alone, to have stayed with friends or family and to have returned voluntarily. They were also less likely to have committed an offence while away. Where immediate reasons for the absence had been identified by social workers and carers, more of this group were considered to have gone missing to spend time with friends or for family-centred rather than placement-centred reasons. As we have seen, they also tended to be older, female and to have been in foster placements at this time.

In contrast, the *runaways* group tended to be younger, male and to have been in residential settings. They tended to be away less time, were more likely to have gone with others and less likely to have returned voluntarily. The immediate reasons for the absence were more likely to have been ascribed to a placement (which included peer group dynamics) or personal problem focus. While away they were less likely to have stayed with friends or family and more likely to have slept rough. They were also more likely to have been involved in offending.

Table 6.2 Nature of absence by characteristics of the absence

	Friends group	Runaways group
Length of time away ($p = 0.02$; $n = 194$)	Away longer	Away less time
Immediate reasons ($p = 0.001$; $n = 128$)	Time with friends/family-centred reasons (51% of 'friends group') Placement-centred reasons/personal difficulties (36%)	Time with friends/family-centred reasons (17% of 'runaways') Placement-centred reasons/personal difficulties (75%)
Alone or with others ($p = 0.06$; $n = 202$)	More likely alone (62% of 'friends group')	More likely with others (53% of 'runaways')
Where stayed ($p < 0.001$; $n = 135$)	92% with friends/family	49% with friends/family; 30% slept rough
Offending while away ($p = 0.001$; $n = 75$)	27% committed an offence	68% committed an offence
Nature of return (p 0.07; $n = 188$)	62% returned voluntarily	48% returned voluntarily

The distinctions according to age for these two groups would seem to be influential in providing one logical explanation for these different patterns. The *friends* group, comprising more older teenagers, contained within it more young people who, without negotiation, left their placements to visit friends, stayed away for as long as they wanted and then returned voluntarily. Their absence was less problem focused and they were less likely to be in trouble with the police while away. The younger *runaways* group were more likely to be experiencing problems and their absence tended to be more problem related. Although they tended to be away a shorter time, they would appear to have been at greater risk while away, as evidenced by the patterns for sleeping rough and offending, and were more reluctant to return.

Predictive Influences on the Nature of the Absence

Given the range of variables that had a significant relationship to the nature of the absence, we used a variety of statistical techniques to identify those which were most influential in explaining the different patterns for these two groups of young people. As a consequence of this analysis we were able to eliminate certain variables, their effects on the nature of the absence weakening once controlled for other factors. For example, although the relationship between sex and type of absence was significant at a two-way level, once we controlled for age its significance disappeared. This relationship therefore needs to be understood as an effect of there being more older females within the sample. The three variables that remained as predictive influences upon the nature of the absence are presented in Table 6.3.

Table 6.3   Factors influencing the nature of the absence

	Friends group	Runaways group
Age	Older	Younger
Placement type	More foster	More residential
Total absences in the past year	Recent low rate of absences	Recent high rate of absences

As we have indicated, age is central to understanding the distinctions between these groupings. In addition, the type of placement young people are in and the number of times they have gone missing in the past year are also predictive of the form that a given incident is likely to take. Where young people are older, in a foster placement and where they have not gone missing many times in the recent past, it is more likely that any given absence will follow a pattern associated with the *friends* group. Equally, where they are younger, in a residential placement and have had a high rate of absences, the nature of their absences is more likely to fit the *runaways* group profile.

The Practice Dimension

Looked at from a practice viewpoint, these findings suggest that it would be helpful for social workers and carers to think carefully about how they might structure their support to these different groupings of young people. Taking the *friends* group first, the key words might be flexibility and negotiation. Recent research has pointed to the complex negotiations that take place between older teenagers and parents within the family home around money (Jamieson and Corr 1990), domestic tasks (Jones and Wallace 1992) and the freedom to visit friends and stay out late. These informal negotiations about boundaries require greater flexibility and power sharing from parents (Coleman 1997) and attempt to balance risks with the need for exploration. Studies have also pointed to the restrictions in these areas that are often experienced by looked after young people (Fisher et al 1986; Stein and Carey 1986; Who Cares? Trust 1993; Sinclair and Gibbs 1998). Clearly this is a difficult area for practitioners charged with the care and control of young people. Many young people may exhibit challenging behaviour, may engage in practices that carry undue risk and the consequences of staff mistakes may be more public and formal. However, wherever possible, a negotiated solution for young people who fit this profile would be preferable to the risk of their developing a persistent pattern of going missing. As we shall see, going missing often is associated with a growing detachment from adult authority that may make later negotiation much more difficult.

The *runaways* group brings the issue of protection into sharper focus. They tend to be younger, more often in residential settings and are likely to have had more extensive careers of going missing. Their absences are more likely to have a problem focus and to place them at greater risk. For a greater proportion of this group running away may have become an established response to difficulties in their lives and changing this behaviour is likely to prove difficult. The support offered to these young people is therefore unlikely to be successful unless it is highly structured and manages to balance their need for protection and consistent boundaries with a concerted attempt to unravel the problems that underpin their behaviour. However, as we shall see in subsequent chapters, the level of urgency required to make such an approach effective was often not evident in this study. Even for young people placing themselves at high risk of sexual exploitation, child protection procedures that might have provided a framework for a coordinated multi-professional response were rarely invoked and case conferences were often not held. The development of an agreed practice framework, similar to that developed in child protection work, is therefore likely to be necessary to provide a structured and consistent response to young people, especially for those whose absences more closely approximate a *runaways* profile.

ILLUSTRATIONS OF DIFFERING TYPES OF ABSENCE

The survey analysis has therefore enabled us to identify broad groupings within the survey sample, the *friends* and *runaways* groups, and has suggested that where young people closely fit the profiles of one of these groups the pattern of any given incident is more likely to take a particular course. Furthermore, taken in the round, the risks for those 'running away' or 'staying out' appeared to be higher, an issue to which we shall return in subsequent chapters.

The case illustrations that we provide below are designed to put flesh on the bones of these findings. Survey analysis based on patterns associated with a single absence, while both valid and meaningful, cannot offer a dynamic picture of process and change. As practitioners are undoubtedly aware, young people's lives when viewed over time are considerably more complex and volatile. Data from our interview sample suggests that, while some young people tended to repeat similar patterns each time they went missing, for example visiting the same friends or family members, others simultaneously engaged in different types of absence. For most, however, the nature and intensity of their absences and the patterns associated with them shifted over time in response to changes in their circumstances. For some young people, a move to a foster placement or closer attachment to unit staff led to a diminution in the scale and intensity of their absences. For others, involvement in a children's home peer culture or with new acquaintances and friends outside led to an escalation in their careers and the risks associated with going missing. For a few older young people, growing maturity led to a change in the type of absence (for example, from 'running away' to staying with 'friends') or even to negotiated stays away.

The picture that emerges from the interview sample, therefore, is one of careers in flux; some remaining constant, some improving and others deteriorating over time in response to changes in young people's lives and the support being made available to them. Hopefully the illustrations will highlight this dynamic view in a more holistic way and also suggest that, while those with a *runaways* profile may be at greater risk, those going missing to be with *friends/family* are often by no means in risk-free situations.

The first two illustrations relate to young people who, at least to this point in their careers, have tended to do similar things each time they have gone missing, one going to her family and the other out with friends.

Family

Lisa, aged 13, had had a number of previous short stays in care linked to her mother's problem with alcohol and drugs. During this stay of six months she had run back to her grandmother or mother twice from two previous foster placements. One was too far from her family and the other she had not liked. Her social worker had been aware of her problems but had no other placements available. On the second occasion she stayed with her gran while a new placement was found. At the time of her interview, she had been at her new foster placement eight weeks, had settled well as it was close to her family and she liked her carers. By the social worker interview, she had been missing again with her mother for two days. Although at minimal risk with her family, the social worker had some concerns about her mother's associates and her ability to care. Her main fear was that if the pattern continued what seemed a very appropriate placement would be put at risk.

Friends

Mary, aged 14, had been settled in her foster placement for seven months and had a close relationship with her carer. Her pattern, linked to her school exclusion and the non-

attendance of her friends, was to spend time with them in the local area or at their homes. Although she had been missing overnight in the past, she usually returned of her own accord in the early hours and sometimes phoned her carer to reassure her she was all right. While clearly at risk outside at night, her absences were not associated with offending but were connected to a lack of structure in her daily life.

The next illustration, of a young lad with a pre-care itinerant lifestyle and an unstable care career spanning 10 episodes and littered with failed foster and residential placements, points to the way in which a quite serious *runaway* career can, at least to some extent, be lessened by a change in circumstance, in his case by finding a settled foster placement for 18 months.

Runaway

Paul (aged 12) started running off from home for a few hours at a time and a number of his foster breakdowns were linked to his behaviour problems and to running off to hang out with friends on the streets. His career escalated with two stays in residential units. He described his involvement in a continuous pattern of group escapes. Young people from a number of different units would gather in the city centre and often stay away as long as possible until picked up by the police and returned. 'When we were caught and got taken back, we'd get something to eat, . . . get some money and go back out again and find the rest.' He linked this to the inability of these units to apply sufficient controls. Although these absences were associated with opportunist crime and Paul has a charge for street robbery, he was too young to get convictions. He felt the risks of being on the streets were mitigated by the protection afforded by the older members of his 'gang'.

According to his social worker, the last 18 months at his present foster placement had been the most settled of his life. Although Paul desperately wanted to be with his mother, he liked his placement and was less inclined to break the rules. Described by his carer as a 'free spirit' who refused controls and boundaries, while he still went missing regularly, the pattern was less intense. Some of the links with his past peer group had been broken and, although he would still hang out with friends and go to the city centre, this happened less often and he usually returned in the early hours of his own accord.

However, at the time we interviewed young people, some careers were clearly intensifying.

Runaway

Gary (aged 13) was considered a very disturbed lad with a family background of physical abuse and abusing behaviour. He had never gone missing pre-care and only once or twice from a past foster placement to be with his grandmother or mother. His move to a short stay unit (where he had been for six months) had led to an escalation in his career as he sought acceptance with an older peer group that regularly went out at night stealing cars, drinking and taking drugs and would return in the early hours, if not picked up by the police. Although too young for convictions, he had been assaulted and sexually abused by an older man while away. Both his keyworker and social worker were aware of his progress but were at a loss to find a more appropriate placement. Both felt a move to a long stay unit, the only offer on the table, would hasten his decline.

The next profile shows how, for some young people, career patterns can change over time in relation to growing age and maturity, even though they may still be under-written by certain risks.

Runaway to family/friends

Neil (aged 16) had been in and out of care on six occasions linked to behaviour difficulties and a long history of offending. His career of going missing passed through three phases. When younger in residential units, he said his pattern was to go out with peers for the 'buzz' and that this was linked to drinks, drugs and offending. As with others we have described, they would usually return in the early hours. During a subsequent episode, he was placed in a unit in Wales and, although he liked it, would run back to his mum and home area. He would stay 'hidden' until taken back. However, more recently, his absences had become associated with a need for greater independence and less unit restriction. He stopped hanging out on the streets and would visit his mother, aunt or sisters and go clubbing or to parties with his friends. As he put it: 'I come in when I'm ready to and I phone up when I'm going to be late.' Sometimes he returned in the early hours and sometimes was away two or three days. He liked the unit and appreciated the room for manoeuvre they allowed him. His keyworker and social worker felt that there were few risks attached to his absences except for his underlying offending behaviour. He was possibly one offence away from a custodial sentence.

However, sometimes the shift in pattern could be achieved by foster carers or residential staff managing to tackle the problems which underlay young people's absences.

Geri (aged 16) had had a pattern of going missing from past foster placements (some with relatives and family friends) and at a past short stay unit. She had been away weeks at a time and slept rough, begged and stayed with strangers. On entering her present unit nine months previously she experienced bullying. Her response was to run away and she stayed with a new acquaintance for three weeks. Once tracked down by her keyworker, he agreed to negotiate her return and tackle the bullying. A formal complaint was made out and, once the bullying stopped, she settled and no longer felt the need to 'run away'. She still went missing occasionally, but saw this as 'staying out' until the early hours and, more often than not, her late nights were negotiated with staff.

Although the case profiles we have presented still tend to flatten the sharp contours of young people's lives and, inevitably, underplay the level of distress many felt at their rejection by or separation from their families, it has hopefully helped to flesh out the drier bones of our survey findings. It cannot fully capture the complexity of all types and patterns of absence for two reasons. First, for some young people, there was very little consistency in the nature and patterns of their incidents at all. Second, at the level of individual biographies, young people's personal histories, experiences and careers of going missing were almost inevitably unique. No one follows the same path precisely. However, the profiles have highlighted in greater depth the main types of absence identified from our survey analysis and the kinds of patterns associated with them, and have shown how these patterns may change over time, some for better and some for worse, in response to shifts in young people's circumstances and maturity.

SUMMARY

In this chapter we have presented findings based on further analysis of the main survey data concerning a single incident of unauthorised absence. From the meaning ascribed to this incident by carers and social workers, we were able to identify two broad sub-groupings within the sample – those who had gone missing to be with 'friends/family' and those who had 'run away or stayed out'. Distinctive differences were identified in the personal characteristics and in the contours of the incident for these two groupings. Those in the *friends* group tended to be older, female and more were from fostering backgrounds. Their absences tended to be longer, less problem focused, less associated with offending and they were more likely to return voluntarily, when they were ready. Those in the *runaways* group had a profile that was more often male, younger and from residential placements. They were more likely to go with others and for a shorter time and their absences were more likely to be associated with sleeping rough and offending. The key predictive influences on the nature of the absence were age, placement type and the number of recent absences. These findings point to the need for different responses to young people who closely fit the profile of these sub-groups. Those in the *friends* group, more often older teenagers going to stay with friends or family may benefit from a more flexible, negotiated approach. Those who fit the *runaways* profile bring child protection issues into sharper focus. However, none of this is to say that those going to friends or family are necessarily risk free, as data from our interview sample has shown.

Finally, a number of case studies drawn from the interview sample were presented to illustrate these different types of absence. By presenting a dynamic picture, rooted in the lives of young people, we were able to show how these differing types of absence, and the patterns that tended to be associated with them, shifted over time – some for better and others for worse – according to changes in young people's circumstances or growing levels of maturity.

7

ASSESSING RISKS

The assessment and management of risk is an integral feature of social work practice. Gauging the likely risks to which young people might be exposed when they go missing and therefore appropriate levels of response is a difficult task which practitioners grapple with on a daily basis. In this chapter we will present evidence that highlights the degree of uncertainty that surrounds these processes and the need for caution in this area.

First, for those young people in the survey sample who had gone missing more often in the past, we will explore whether the contours of each incident necessarily became more protracted, deeper or riskier as their careers progressed. If such a pattern existed, if absences necessarily got worse, then practitioners would have a more certain basis for their assessment. Second, we will look at the problem from a different angle. How much did social workers and caregivers who participated in the survey actually know about the risks to which their young people were exposed while missing and what are some of the difficulties associated with knowing? Finally, we will look briefly at differing perceptions of risk amongst young people, social workers and caregivers.

IS GOING MISSING OFTEN ASSOCIATED WITH MORE PROTRACTED, RISKIER ABSENCES?

The information gathered about a single recent absence in the main survey enabled us to test out the following hypothesis: did the patterns associated with young people's absences necessarily get worse the further their careers progressed? When comparing those who had gone missing often in the past with those who had not, would the former have been more likely to have 'run away' and stayed away longer on this occasion? Were they more likely to have travelled further and placed themselves at greater risk? Were they less likely to have returned voluntarily? In short, was there evidence to support the idea of a progressive pattern in which each episode deepens and becomes more protracted the more often young people go missing?

The short answer is no. One of the more surprising findings was the limited degree to which past careers of going missing were reflected in the contours of the specific incident. Those who had gone missing more often in the past were not significantly more likely to have gone missing on this occasion for different reasons, nor to have stayed away longer than those who had gone missing less often. They were no more likely to have gone with others, travelled further, stayed in certain places rather than others, nor to have been at greater risk while away. Equally, they were not significantly more likely to have received a different police response, nor were they less likely to have returned voluntarily. The only significant finding was that those who had gone missing more often in the past year and in total were more likely to have 'run away or stayed out' on this occasion.

Surprised by these findings we made two further checks. First, we calculated the length of time that young people had been going missing: a tentative career length variable. This was done by subtracting the age they first went missing from their current age. The career length variable was then tested against key features of the absence and, as before, the only significant relationship was with the type of absence; those who 'ran away or stayed out' tended to have had longer careers. Second, as we only had data on the number of absences whilst looked after, we carried out the same tests just for those young people who had first gone missing while being looked after. In relation to those first missing from home our concern was that, since we had no data on their number of absences prior to being looked after, the data in relation to their absences whilst looked after may be less reliable. They could be at different stages in their careers of going missing. However, even for those first missing from substitute care, there was still no evidence of a developing pattern apart from a weak positive correlation with length of absence ($p = 0.06$; $\tau + 0.16$).

As a result of this analysis we can be very confident that going missing more or less often is not associated with a progressive pattern that can be discerned in the contours of any given incident. The number of times young people go missing from substitute care is not significantly associated with each successive episode becoming deeper, riskier or more protracted.

How might this finding be explained? As we saw in our last chapter, viewing young people's careers over time pointed to quite a complex picture. While some young people tended to repeat a similar pattern each time they went missing, whether visiting or staying with the same family members or friends, for most young people, patterns shifted over time according to changes in their age or circumstances. Moving to a new placement, forming closer attachments to carers or falling in with a negative peer group could influence the course of their careers for good or ill. It is this picture of continuity and change with some careers escalating, others constant and some diminishing, that helps to explain our survey finding that there is no necessary connection between going missing often and a progressive pattern of riskier absences. It is what young people do on any particular occasion and their particular circumstances at the time that are the key factors here, rather than simply the number of times they have gone missing in the past.

Returning to our main argument, what might these survey findings mean for assumptions about young people's safety when missing? If going missing more or less often is not necessarily reflected in discrete incident patterns, then young people are equally likely to be safe or at risk *on any occasion they go missing* and similar levels of caution and concern should be shown about all absences. It cannot simply be assumed that because a person has gone missing frequently or infrequently in the past they are likely to be at greater or lesser risk now. The assessment of the likely risk to a young person on any particular occasion needs to be based upon a detailed knowledge of an individual's history, their skill levels and self-awareness, their motivations for going missing and the places they are likely to go.

However, we should make it clear that going missing often is definitely not good for long term health. As we shall see in our next chapter, when viewing young people's careers over time we found, consistent with other studies of runaways, that persistent exposure to risk situations while missing did tend to increase the likelihood of young people becoming criminalised, victimised or sexually exploited (Newman 1989; Simons and Whitbeck 1991; Stein et al 1994). In addition, as we shall see in Chapter 9, going missing often is significantly associated with a growing detachment from placement and school and with involvement in subcultures of offending and substance misuse. The long term prognosis for these young people was often bleak.

KNOWLEDGE OF RISKS

In relation to the single unauthorised absence in the main survey, we were interested to know, for this sample, what risks were associated with the particular absence. To limit speculation about potential risks, we asked social workers and carers if they *knew* whether young people *had been involved* in a range of specified risk activities while away. In respect of *half* (51%) the young people, respondents had no idea if they had been at risk while missing, even after the event. Over a quarter of the sample (28%) were known to have been at risk. The main risks involved committing offences, substance misuse and being the victim of crime, including physical and sexual abuse.

However, data gathered on a single incident is likely to under-report risk for two reasons. First, although young people may or may not have been at risk on that occasion, viewing their careers over time may lead to a somewhat different picture. Second, a large proportion of carers and social workers were unaware of significant aspects of the absence, even after the event. Over a quarter did not know where they stayed on that occasion and, as we have just seen, one half did not know whether or not they were at risk.

We also found that the contours of this absence were significantly different for those who were thought to have gone missing to be with 'friends or family' and those thought to have 'run away or stayed out'. Those in the latter group, more often younger, male and from residential placements, were more likely to go with others, for a shorter time and their absences were more likely to be associated with sleeping rough and offending. For these reasons, they appeared to be at greater risk when away.

One reading of these findings might be that, given the different patterns of absence associated with these groupings, where young people closely fit the profile of the *friends* group and are thought to have gone missing to be with friends or family, concern about their welfare may lessen. They are likely to be at less risk and therefore be a lower priority for action. Whilst there is some truth in this, our findings suggest that the ability of practitioners to assess the level of risk *in advance* was cloaked in a fair degree of uncertainty.

To look more closely at risk, as can be seen in Figure 7.1, we took the different categories of absence and superimposed upon them what social workers and carers knew of the risks to which young people were exposed while away.

We adopted a conservative definition of risk, excluding offending and substance misuse. Young people were only placed in the 'risk' category where they were known to have been a victim of crime, including physical and sexual abuse, were involved in prostitution or where they were known to have slept rough or stayed with a stranger. Young people were placed in the 'don't know' category where their social worker and carer either did not know where they had stayed or whether they were at risk where they were staying. The 'no risk' category applies where there was reasonable certainty that no risk was attached to the absence. Those responsible knew where the young person had stayed and that they were not at risk there.

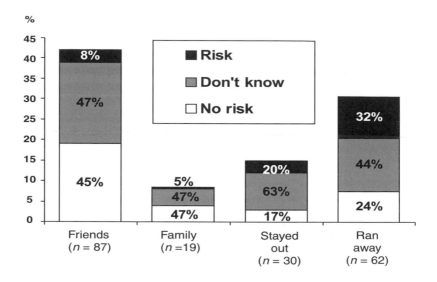

Figure 7.1 Absence by risk (*n* = 202; remaining 4 cases in 'other' category)

The figure illustrates that nearly half of those who went missing to be with friends or family were not considered to have been at risk while away and that a far smaller proportion of young people in these group-ings were known to have been at risk than was the case for those who had run away or stayed out. However, it also points to the degree of uncer-tainty that existed for social workers and carers. Not knowing one way or the other represented the largest category for each type of absence. We also need to be aware that this assessment was based on knowledge available *after the event*, at the time the questionnaires were completed. Predicting vulnerability in advance would therefore probably pose fur-ther difficulties for practitioners and points to the complexities involved in undertaking risk assessment for young people who go missing. We will pick up these issues again in Chapter 13 when we focus on reporting procedures and risk assessment for young people going missing.

Findings from the interview sample can shed some further light on the problems of knowing about the risks to which young people are exposed. Young people, especially those who went missing frequently, often re-fused to tell where they had been, what they had been doing and who with. Even though most caregivers and some social workers did try to follow up absences to find out where young people had been and whether they were safe, their questions could be met with a stony silence. This was less likely to be the case where young people had stayed with family or with friends who were known to their carers as reasonably safe;

in these cases there was usually little to hide. Even where young people had been involved in riskier absences where they may have offended, taken drugs or exposed themselves to danger, the information could sometimes be prised from them with careful questioning if they had a longer standing relationship and greater attachment to carers or social workers. Knowing what had happened opened up the possibility of exploring the risks associated with these absences and offering advice about harm reduction, even where prevention may have been unrealistic. It also reinforced to young people the level of care, concern and value that was placed on their well-being, even if they were reluctant to listen to the advice at the time. In a few cases, where young people were more open about themselves and trusted the advice that would be offered, they volunteered the information and actually sought advice.

Where young people lacked this attachment or where absences did involve risk, especially offending, they were generally much less likely to tell. This was often the case for those who went missing from children's homes as part of a peer group and whose absences were closely associated with offending and substance misuse. Their concern was clearly to avoid admitting their own part in the proceedings but also to avoid 'grassing up' others. For those seeking acceptance within the peer group or coerced into going, the implications could be particularly severe since it carried the threat of further bullying by older peers. However, it also has to be said that in a few units where the formation of a negative peer culture had taken a firm grip and where these kinds of absence had become a nightly pattern, the staff group appeared to have lost control. It had become so much a feature of everyday routine that, effectively, questions no longer seemed to be asked.

However, some young people going off to stay with friends simply wanted to keep their contacts and addresses secret, especially where they thought these contacts would not meet with approval, often for good reasons. They were aware that, if divulged, some carers and social workers would feel obliged to try and follow up to check out the credentials of these contacts. More seriously for the young person, these known addresses were likely to be passed to the police when they next went missing and they were more likely to be picked up, and their absence curtailed. Indeed, these considerations could apply to friends or contacts coming to meet young people at children's homes since, in order to assess vulnerability, similar questions would need to be asked. Some residential staff were aware that this may push young people to meet up outside and plan activities from there, but felt they had little choice. At times it appeared that attempts to identify who young people were with and where they were staying took on the qualities of a game of 'cat and mouse' as caregivers attempted to trace addresses and identify risks. This represented an important arm's length protection role. A number of carers mentioned attempts to identify names of contacts, car registration numbers, addresses where young people had stayed and whether these contained known paedophiles. Information gathered would then be passed to the police for further inquiry. As one social worker said, even if they could not prevent young people going missing nor control where they stayed, building a profile of likely places was important:

> We have more knowledge. We can now say, we have lists of addresses where these young people go now . . . Those addresses are building up and the characters we're coming across . . . we do notify the police.

In one authority, concerns about young people's vulnerability to sexual exploitation had led to the child protection unit attempting to collate and monitor this information and undertake police liaison at a broader level.

The consequences of uncertainty could be serious and, in a number of cases, prevented early and appropriate intervention. To give just one example, Victoria (aged 14) had been going missing overnight with an older female from her children's home known to be involved in prostitution. Although her keyworker and social worker were aware of the relationship and that her regular absences were drawing her into the twilight world of pimps and drugs, they were completely unaware that she had been directly involved in prostitution. They underestimated the dangers to her, thought her absences were essentially about 'staying out for the buzz of being out and about', which perhaps for the most part they were, and missed the seriousness of the dangers to which she was exposed. Uncertain knowledge, combined with some complacency, inhibited prompt action. Given the vulnerability of looked after young people to exploitation, the kinds of patient investigative work described above and close police liaison with regard to this information are an important feature of a child protection approach.

PERCEPTIONS OF RISK

There was a considerable degree of congruence between social workers, caregivers and young people about the risks attached to going missing, although there were some subtle differences. It is not surprising, given their role as substitute parents, that carers and social workers tended to view these with serious concern and, given the evidence we will present below, rightly so. Charged with these protective responsibilities, they were more likely to view young people as wilfully disregarding or being unable or too young to see the risks associated with their behaviour. Attempts to discuss risks were often met with a shrug of the shoulders, a laugh or the abrupt statement, 'I'm not bothered'. While in many cases the failure to recognise risks may have been true, it also smacks of many encounters between concerned parents and recalcitrant teenagers reluctant to express their feelings. Another perception, sometimes shared by young people, was that the tendency to disregard risks and emphasise the fun aspects of going missing could be reinforced if they had gone a few times, usually with others, and nothing frightening had happened. Finally, excessive risk taking was linked to the lack of expressive controls and moral authority associated with substitute parenting itself. One residential staff group, recollecting their own experiences of teenage risk taking, spoke of the parental 'voice' present in their minds that drew them back, partly through fear, from excessively dangerous encounters, whereas young people in children's homes knew that staff could neither prevent nor punish them; a view firmly shared by young people themselves.

Given their professional role, practitioners were also more likely to take a longer view. Exposure to risks was often linked, quite correctly, to young people's past experiences of abuse, emotional distress and to the implications this had had for their sense of self, their self-esteem:

> There's a carelessness of their person and there's a pursuit of immediate gratification . . . but there's no idea of the risk they're putting themselves in. (social workers' focus group)

Some even wondered, in the light of many young people's past experiences, whether it was possible to transfer accepted notions of risk onto them:

> When they have been abused and . . . go missing . . . we'll say to them, 'Well, you shouldn't be in town at 2 o'clock in the morning, it's dangerous'. And then when you think what's happened to them, that isn't dangerous to them. We can't imagine what is dangerous to 'em given what they've experienced. (residential social workers' focus group)

In contrast, young people's appreciation of risk tended to be rooted in the here and now. Many young people, though by no means all, did see going missing as primarily being about going out with friends, having fun and escaping the boredom and controls of 'home'. In this sense there was a tendency to downgrade risks, to see their absences as less serious even where, to outside observers such as ourselves, they appeared to carry great risks. However, our individual and group discussions with young people also showed that there was considerable appreciation of the risks attached to going missing, especially in relation to being out at night, as the following comments suggest:

It's risky for anybody that goes out because . . . there's a lot (that) happens, but I'm not really bothered.

You could get kidnapped, get killed, get raped or beaten up.

The problem was not so much a failure to see the dangers, indeed many had direct experience, but rather that either they were reluctant to draw out the implications for them as *individuals* or the pull of what was outside was simply too great. Some persisted in the belief that they would be safe, even when they had already experienced quite serious abuse. Others felt, rightly or wrongly, they could defend themselves. Some, fearful of the streets at night, ensured they returned to sleep or made sure they stayed awake. Some others, reluctantly drawn to sleeping rough, tried to ensure they were part of a group.

Going missing as part of a group was seen as one of the main ways of mitigating risk. For one young male (aged 11) who regularly went out with older peers from his children's home, going with them made him feel safer:

Wherever they'd go they'd take you with them. Like, they didn't have to really, but in a way they made me think it'll be all right.

A few young people who had spent longer periods sleeping rough in city centres also claimed to have found a sense of camaraderie amongst the young homeless:

There's quite a few people . . . where I was sleeping on the streets, they stick up for each other. If anything happens to one of them it happens to all of 'em . . . 'cos we're all in the same situation.

However, as we turn to look at discrete areas of risk we shall see that, whatever the protective effects of being with others, going as part of a group often led to a reinforcement of young people's careers of going missing and to an escalation in the levels of risk.

SUMMARY

In this chapter we have viewed, from a number of angles, the problems associated with assessing the risks to which young people may be exposed while missing. We explored the hypothesis that, for those in the main survey sample who had gone missing more often in the past, there would be a progressive pattern in which successive episodes would necessarily become more protracted and riskier; that young people would stay away longer, travel further, engage in higher risk activities and would be less likely to return voluntarily. No evidence was found to support such a contention. This finding has implications for assumptions that may be made about young people's safety while away. it suggests that young people may be as likely to be at risk *on any occasion* they go missing, whether the first or the twenty-first, and that all absences should give cause for concern. What is important for the assessment of risk, therefore, is not how many times young people have gone missing but having a detailed knowledge of an individual's history and the circumstances of a given absence, including their motivations for going, who they are going with and the places they are likely to go.

With regard to this type of knowledge, uncertainty was a common problem for social workers and caregivers. For each type of absence in our main survey – whether young people were thought to have gone missing to be with friends, with family, to have run away or stayed out – uncertainty about the risks attached to that absence was the most common response of practitioners, even after the event. Assessing levels of risk *at the time young people go missing* is therefore likely to present serious difficulties to practitioners. Young people often refused to tell where they had been, what they had been doing and who with. This was particularly likely where they lacked attachment to carers or had been involved in risk activities, especially offending, and was often motivated by a desire to avoid telling on others, sometimes through fear. Others simply wanted to keep addresses secret as they were aware their carers would be obliged to follow up and, if passed to the police, future absences might be curtailed. In a few children's homes, with strong negative peer cultures, staff appeared to have lost control and fewer questions were asked. Attempts to trace where young people were and the risks attached to their absences represented an important arm's length child protection role and involved extensive police liaison.

Although there was considerable congruence in the perceptions of social workers, caregivers and young people about the risks associated with going missing, there were some differences. Perhaps not surprisingly, given the parental role of practitioners, this was nearly always the subject of serious concern. They were more likely to see young people as wilfully disregarding or lacking awareness of risk and were more likely to take a longer view, often linking risk taking to past experiences of abuse and neglect. In contrast, young people's perceptions were more rooted in the here and now. Although many saw going missing as about having fun, most did appreciate the risks attached. The main strategy for mitigating risk was to go as part of a group. While this could offer protection on the streets, as we shall see in our next chapter, it could also lead to a reinforcement of young people's careers of going missing and to an escalation in the levels of risk.

8

THE RISKS FOR YOUNG PEOPLE

In this chapter we shall draw together information from our main survey and interview samples to examine more closely the kinds of risks to which young people were exposed when away from their placements without permission. Our discussion will include the relationship of offending to going missing, the risks of sexual exploitation, including prostitution, more general risks to young people's personal health and safety and the responses to these risk behaviours by social workers and caregivers.

OFFENDING

Offending was one of the main risks associated with going missing and, for many young people, going with others could initiate or escalate criminal careers. Data from the main survey and interview samples enabled us to examine young people's patterns of past offending, the links between offending and going missing and the kinds of scenarios that induced young people to commit offences while they were absent from placements.

Previous Offences

The level of previous involvement in committing offences was high for our main survey sample. Nearly half (49%) had been charged with a criminal offence prior to the incident of going missing reported in the survey. Where past disposals were known, 23% of the total sample had been cautioned, but 20% had received a non-custodial sentence and 1% a custodial sentence.

If we compare our data to Sinclair and Gibbs' (1998) sample of nearly 1100 young people in residential care, we see that young people who go missing are more likely to have a prior conviction or caution than the general population in children's homes[1]. In their study just under half of the males (49%) and nearly a quarter of the females (23%) had a prior conviction or caution and this compares to nearly two thirds (63%) of the males and over a third (37%) of the females in our sample. This is broadly consistent with Sinclair and Gibbs' finding of a strong association between conviction while in a children's home and running away. Those with past convictions were far more likely to run away and those who ran away were more likely to be convicted while living in the home. Roughly half of those who ran away but only 1 in 10 of those who did not were convicted or cautioned while living in the home, and this association was particularly strong where young people had no convictions prior to admission (Sinclair and Gibbs 1998). Taken together, both studies suggest that many young people, both males and females, who go missing from substitute care are likely to have committed offences. Similar patterns have also been found for those running away from home, as a major Home Office study found that, among young runaways from home, 71% of males and 46% of females had offended (Graham and Bowling 1995).

In our main survey, those who had been charged with offences prior to this incident were likely to be older – 83% of past offenders were aged 13–16. They were more likely to have first gone missing from their family and to have gone missing more often in the past. While absent on this particular occasion, they were likely to have stayed away longer and, perhaps not surprisingly, were more likely to be reported as having committed an offence while absent. In addition, as we have already seen, there was also a strong relationship between past offending and school exclusion.

Turning to our interview sample, many of those who had started offending before entering substitute care had already committed numerous offences, but for some this pattern was reinforced when they were placed in a residential unit together with other young offenders. Others only began offending once they were accommodated. Anxious to gain acceptance by their peers, in some cases in order to avoid bullying, they were initiated into criminal activities by other residents in children's homes. The concentration of young offenders in some children's homes led to a situation where groups of males in certain units, often as young as 11 or 12, went out together in order to commit offences.

The stories of David and Richard illustrate different ways in which a pattern of offending was initiated or escalated by accommodation in a

---

[1] Ideally, we would like to compare our sample to offenders in both residential and foster care but we have not been able to obtain data on offending rates for all young people looked after in all types of placements. However, as 70% of those who had previously offended were in residential placements, compared to 56% of those who had not, this comparison may be able to indicate some broad differences in patterns.

children's home. David, 12, was first introduced to crime by young people in his children's home. Bullied and suffering serious physical and racial abuse by older males at the unit, he reluctantly became involved in the 'gang' culture of crime and was used by them to steal. He began going missing with them at night to steal and engage in car crime and also shoplifted in order to buy acceptance from his peers. As his keyworker explained: 'They started leaving him alone when he started giving them things.'

Richard, 13, began running away from home to escape abuse and started truanting during the same period. While on the streets he became involved with older teenagers and joined with them in committing criminal damage. In the 18 months since he entered a children's home his offending had escalated through his involvement in the criminal peer culture prevalent in the unit. He joined group escapades to engage in car theft and burglary for the shared excitement it generated.

Around half of the females in the interview sample also had past offences and, in many instances, these were no less serious than the males'. Most had been involved in car crime, burglary or assault and often more than one of these. Most had started offending because their friends were doing it, either while living at home or in substitute care, and some had joined in groups from children's homes who went out offending overnight, usually to engage in car crime. The high proportion of females with past offences in our survey points to the strength of the relationship between going missing and offending.

Offending While Missing from Placements

During their recent absence from placement over a fifth (22%) of the young people in our main survey were known to have committed a criminal offence. This is likely to be an underestimate, given the limited knowledge about risks amongst social workers and carers. Our interviews with young people indicate that there are a number of scenarios in which offending is likely to be linked with going missing. First, as described above, there are young people who go missing together from children's homes in order to offend, for the 'buzz'. Usually linked to the existence of a criminal peer culture in particular units, newer residents may be drawn in by the more established and powerful young people within the unit, sometimes willingly and sometimes under pressure. A second scenario is one where young people commit opportunist crimes while away in order to have the money or food they need to survive on the streets. Gary, 13, described how he would steal food when he was hungry and steal cars to shelter in when he was cold. Alternatively, young people would commit offences in a spontaneous search for excitement. As a young person in one of our focus groups explained:

> When you get out there and it's night time and all the shops are shut and that and it's boring, you think of what else you can do and it's mainly nicking cars and car radios and stuff like that.

Opportunist crime was also linked to the attraction of inner city street cultures. Young people could be drawn into high risk situations in city centres through their association with older people involved in crime, with procurers and prostitutes. Several of the young people spoke of the excitement of life on the margins, the buzz of city centre street sub-cultures, the attractions of feeling part of a 'community' of outsiders. One young person managed to live in the city centre for several weeks and even managed to get a job selling *The Big Issue*, preferring the attractions of this lifestyle to being accommodated in a children's home. Crime is a feature of the inner city street cultures to which some young people were drawn. For example Jason, 14, would go missing regularly from his children's home in order to join the 'community' on the city centre streets and would steal to order for homeless people he knew there.

For a number of young people crime became a routine feature of their lives while they were missing. Several residential workers and social workers mentioned how some young people had lost any sense of right and wrong, making it very difficult to do any effective work with them around their offending. In a few cases this was quite extreme, as the social worker of Curtis, a deeply rejected 13 year old with serious behaviour problems and a long history of running away, explained:

> I think he's got no conscience, he's got nothing going for him. He just wanders around aimlessly, robbing and smoking dope or whatever drugs he can get hold of.

Many of those involved in offending were very young – six were only 11 or 12 years old and five were aged 13. For some young people under 14, the awareness that they were unlikely to be prosecuted could reinforce their incipient criminal careers, making it even harder for professionals to work with them effectively on their offending behaviour. As one young person explained:

> The more you do it, it don't matter. Until I was 14 I'd never been charged with nothing, because they couldn't touch me. I was untouchable. And that's the way a lot of kids look at it now, especially in care. (care leavers' focus group)

Other workers said they were hampered by the fact that some young people were missing so often that they were rarely around long enough for work on offending, or indeed on any other issues, to be done effectively.

Our evidence, taken together with evidence from other studies, suggests that there is a strong relationship between going missing and offending. Those with a history of offending are also likely to go missing from placements, and those with no past offences are at risk of being drawn into criminal activities if they go missing. Placement in certain residential units where criminal peer cultures have developed can increase the risk that young people will offend. For those under 14 who went missing, work on offending was hampered by the fact that there were few clear legal sanctions. These findings also suggest that effective interventions need to take place at an early point in young people's careers of going missing and offending. Once these patterns become set, as we have seen, opportunities for constructive support on either problem are likely to recede. We will pick up these issues again in our next chapter where, in viewing young people's histories or careers of going missing, the strength of the relationship between going missing and offending will be further clarified.

SEXUAL EXPLOITATION

Studies of young people who run away have identified their vulnerability to the risks of sexual exploitation, including prostitution (Newman 1989; Van der Ploeg 1989; Simons and Whitbeck 1991; Stein et al 1994). The risk of victimisation is closely associated with frequency of running and therefore the length of time young people are exposed to risks on the streets. Although our interview sample may not be representative of all young people who go missing from substitute care, these risks were very apparent for them. Eight out of the 36 young people had been subjected to rape or other serious sexual assaults while missing from placements and 10 young people had been or were currently exploited as prostitutes.

Of those who suffered sexual assault, five were female and three were male. One young female was raped by a group of men while sleeping rough and two others, whose frequent absences were associated with heavy drug use, were raped and sexually abused by men they were staying with. A young male with learning difficulties, who regularly truanted with a school friend, was led by him to an older man's house where he was sexually assaulted. There was clear awareness on the part of carers and social workers that looked after young people, especially those who went missing frequently, were targeted by child abusers, sometimes as part of organised networks, and one described the city centre, where many young people congregated, as 'a glue pot for paedophiles'. However, as with going missing generally, preventing or limiting the risks to which these young people exposed themselves seemed an intractable problem to many practitioners.

To give one example, Robbie (aged 11) had frequently gone missing from home with his older brother prior to being looked after. His move to residential care had, if anything, worsened the situation, according to his social worker. He went missing regularly, had more young people to go with and a wider range of contacts. He would simply go off with strangers to their homes, some of whom were known to have past convictions for sexual offences against children. Despite being fairly certain he had been sexually abused, the home was unable to contain him and, apart from passing these addresses to the police, warning him of the dangers and counselling him to stay, all appeared to be at a loss as to how to prevent him undertaking these dangerous excursions. As with many young people, no child protection procedures had been initiated.

Prostitution

Equally disturbing was the evidence concerning those drawn into prostitution. Of these 10 young people, 7 were female and 3 were male. Some studies have highlighted the links between past sexual and physical abuse, running away and involvement in prostitution (Finkelhor 1986; Spatz et al 1994; Lee and O'Brien 1995). Within this group of young people, 8 had been victims of sexual abuse prior to being looked after and 9 had suffered past physical abuse, neglect or rejection by their families. In addition, for 9 out of the 10, these experiences had left them with serious behaviour difficulties, including tendencies for aggression and/or self-destructiveness, difficulties in forming relationships and a low sense of self-worth. Despite their vulnerability to exploitation all were placed in ordinary children's homes at the time of the study.

Kelly et al (1995), concerned with identifying routes into the sex industry, point to a range of factors that can increase young people's vulnerability to exploitation, including those described above, combined with the presence of adults or other young people who act as procurers or organisers. Those in our sample, with the exception of one female, appeared to have been drawn into prostitution while being looked after and, in all cases, while it may not have been the main rationale for their absences, it was closely associated with going missing.

The exception was Gemma (aged 15). Both her parents had serious alcohol and drug dependencies, her home background had been violent and she had been sexually abused by a friend of her father. At the age of 11 she ran away for two months and mostly lived rough or stayed with contacts she made. She was raped and then placed under the 'protection' of a pimp, who she saw as her boyfriend. Her mother was aware of her prostitution and took money from her for drugs. On entering care (aged 12) her pattern of going missing and involvement in prostitution continued. She sank deeper into a world of sexual abuse, violence and drugs and eventually began to draw other young people into prostitution, including her younger sisters and a younger resident at her children's home.

As we have suggested, all the other young people first became involved while being looked after. Farmer and Pollock (1997), in their study of looked after sexually abused and abusing children, found that, for their sample, where young people were led by their peers towards prostitution this only occurred in residential settings and while, for some, this was linked to going missing together, for others, it appeared to be a compulsive activity that involved rehearsing their own initiation – as the example of Gemma might suggest. Some of our young people were clearly influenced by the involvement of peers in their children's homes while others were led to prostitution through contacts made outside.

Involvement through peers could involve enticement or threats, it could be accidental or by design. One young male (aged 13), for example, who went missing with an older lad from the unit was procured by him and, in consequence, he was sexually abused by an older man. Although the police were involved, the man placed on remand and the older lad was moved out, no child protection procedures were implemented and the boy was not currently receiving therapy, despite his deeply disturbed background. In contrast, a young female (aged 14) who regularly went missing with two friends from her unit, both of whom had involvement in prostitution, viewed her absences as primarily about fun and freedom. Her brief involvement in prostitution was, in her view, about accessing the means to that enjoyment. She stopped when one of her friends was made subject to a secure order. Living in homes with others involved in prostitution could be frightening, as one young woman who had successfully resisted attempts to coerce her stressed:

> If you're in care with a prostitute they'll try and get you to go out with them. If not, then you get bullied from them.

These findings suggest that greater attention needs to be placed on the 'mix' of young people in residential and foster settings. Placement decisions, driven in part by financial considerations and a shortage of placement options, can only heighten risks where vulnerable young people are placed alongside others engaging in dangerous behaviour. Appropriate matching is inevitably sacrificed (Triseliotis et al 1995a) and the ability of heads of homes or foster carers to resist pressures to accept inappropriate referrals is compromised (Farmer and Pollock 1997). Returning to the lad who procured a younger boy for sex, at the time of our interviews and after he had gone on to involve his siblings, the head of home was attempting to resist management pressure to accept him back at the unit!

However, some young people's involvement emerged through contacts made outside their homes. Shireen (aged 15), for example, who had been involved in prostitution prior to her current placement, regularly went missing to stay with an older woman. The woman was known to be involved in prostitution and, through her, Shireen became ensnared in a cycle of abusive sex for money with older men. The residential staff were deeply worried but felt unable to protect her in the context of an ordinary children's home. In contrast, her social worker, whose involvement was quite distant, felt that being there was 'safer than the streets', that many of the 'stories' were fabricated and was not sufficiently concerned to press for therapy or an alternative placement, even though aware that Shireen might have benefited from either of these.

Recent research has pointed to the ways in which child abusers target children's homes, either directly or through the use of young people recruiting others (Wild 1989; Shaw et al 1996). The protection of children's homes was a major worry for residential staff, especially where some residents were already involved in prostitution. If problems were intense, the units could temporarily appear to be under siege. In some instances pimps would hang around the units and enter if not seen. In others, men would arrive at or ring the unit to seek out specific young people. As one keyworker said in relation to one female, at times they were being used 'like an escort service'. Concerns rested not just on the individuals involved but on the risk to other residents. Most practitioners were clearly aware of the strategies abusers might use:

> (Some adults) . . . tap into vulnerable young children in the units and get them involved in what's going on in the city centre . . . People involved in the red light scene in town, drug scene . . . they know where the units are.

> It seems to me that what they do is . . . encourage the older kids to truant, let them into their flat, let them play music, give them money, maybe drink alcohol and encourage them to take the younger kids back.

Where units were experiencing serious problems, considerable energy was invested in trying to identify contacts, in police liaison to deter these adults and, often unsuccessfully, in trying to prevent young people leaving with them.

Kelly et al (1995) point to the potent combination of factors that can hold young people once they become involved in prostitution and to the difficulties that are likely in helping them extricate themselves. These can include the lure of money, the possibility of greater independence and freedom, coercion by abusers often coinciding with confused loyalties to them, drug dependency and debts that may be associated with this and, in some instances, a sense of belonging to a community bonded by societal disapproval. A number of these factors were apparent for young people in our sample.

For young people abused in the past, initial involvement may link to a search for physical closeness or the illusion of affection (Shaw et al 1996). For some, it may represent the first time they have felt some control over their own bodies (Jesson 1993). Gemma, whom we have mentioned before, was introduced to prostitution through a pimp she perceived as her boyfriend. Initially he persuaded her by saying:

> If I loved him I'd do it, and all that. So I just carried on doing it more. Then he started taking cocaine and then he let me have some . . . and I started taking it from then on, to block everything out me head.

As her involvement increased, the mechanism of control shifted to coercion and violence, she was pressured to involve others and, although outwardly she maintained an illusion of control to other people, her only respite came through a stay in a secure unit. Not only was she out of control but she represented a serious threat to other young people in the unit. In the case of another young female, her need for physical attention, to be valued, was so great that she would often burn the money she received from men.

However, the lure of money and excitement could be seductive. It offered opportunities for greater freedom, independence and to fund the more enjoyable activities associated with going missing. For example, one female who went missing with her friends and for whom going missing was primarily about fun, viewed her involvement in prostitution as a necessary evil:

> 'Cos it was fun and they (her friends) have no rules and you could just be free. All my life there's always been rules and things that I've had to do. With them I could just do what I wanted. I didn't want to prostitute. If I could have got money some way else then I would have done it, but . . . I would have money and then I could do what I wanted and not what people told me to do.

Returning with money, whether through offending or prostitution, could make young people feel that they were reclaiming some control over their lives, when often their past experiences had been of powerlessness; it could also enhance their power and status within the children's home. However, as a number of residential workers pointed out, it could also make attempts to divert young people from such activities much more difficult. It could make the usual strategies of counselling them about the dangers and of involving them in organised activities within and outside the unit, designed to access an alternative positive sense of self-esteem, appear meaningless to them. While these strategies may have had some success with younger children on the fringes of involvement, once their behaviour had taken a grip, they rarely brought much success. As one keyworker said of a young male involved in offending and prostitution:

> He's used to the bright lights of the big city and all that's happening around there . . . Nothing (that we do) is going to be fun for him because he's sort of beyond that now.

Responses to Prostitution

The sense of powerlessness contained in that comment was quite pervasive amongst practitioners. Where young people were missing frequently and engaging in very risky sexual behaviour, many carers and social workers clearly felt out of their depth. They often felt they lacked the skills and knowledge required to intervene effectively. This is not surprising given that work aimed at diverting young prostitutes is a relatively recent development. Social work lacks an agreed practice framework in this area, consistent with a child protection perspective, and there is no guidance available to practitioners to aid their work with young people (Jesson 1993; Farmer and Pollock 1997).

Our evidence, and that of others, highlights the need for a rapid preventive response whenever a young person is suspected of becoming involved in prostitution. Not merely are they themselves at risk but they may well endanger others. Although, as we have seen, many practitioners were aware of these dangers, there was no great evidence of such a response being put into practice. Child protection procedures were rarely invoked and, in many instances, case conferences were not held. One female was enabled to stop by a change of placement, which separated her from her peers, and two others when the friends they were going with were made subject to secure orders. However, in one case, the difficulties involved in obtaining an order led to an eight month delay and extended the period at risk.

Farmer and Pollock (1997) found that, for those more deeply involved, separation from their peers was important and that geographical distance from their networks was an ingredient in more successful placements, preferably in specialist foster homes. While our findings would endorse this, it is not without problems. A number of young people with more persistent careers of going missing had already run back to their home areas from out-of-authority placements, even when they quite liked them. In addition, while professional and specialist foster placements would represent a way forward, neither City East nor City West had many placements of that type. Young people not attending school, often the most troubled and troublesome, were therefore very rarely offered a foster placement and resource constraints meant that residential placements in therapeutic environments or special schools were very difficult to achieve. Meeting the particular needs of sexually exploited young people must therefore be situated in a context of wider reforms to the child care system.

The measure of last resort was a secure placement. While these offered a period of respite and recovery, there was little evidence of them achieving longer term change. Gemma, for example, spent a short period in a secure unit. While there her health and appearance improved. She was offered therapy by a rape specialist, although she found the process too painful to continue. She was determined not to resume her old life. However, within a very short period back at the same children's home she had again become immersed in her old networks. A similar pattern occurred for two others who had experienced brief spells in secure units.

In the main, unable adequately to contain or protect, the support strategies of residential and social workers focused on harm reduction. One residential worker, responsible for a female heavily involved in prostitution, felt these dilemmas keenly:

> It's not really the right place for them 'cos there's very little we can do. We can advise her about using safe sex, we can certainly make appointments at the clinic and the hospital for her, we can certainly advise her about all the dangers she's running by going with these men, but at the end of the day . . . she disappears and we can't do anything. I feel we ought to protect her more.

Although a number of young people had been additionally offered therapeutic help, aimed at unravelling the problems associated with their past abuse, some rejected this as too painful and others only attended erratically due to their lifestyles and patterns of going missing. In addition such help was hard to come by. One deeply disturbed young male had been placed on a six month waiting list at the local children's hospital and another was unable to commence as he was in a short stay placement, despite having been there for six months.

In addition to a practice framework capable of supporting more effective interventions, there is a need for a more coordinated joint approach between social services and the police. As we have seen, concerned practitioners were attempting to trace contacts and pass these names and addresses to the police and child protection teams were attempting to collate information and monitor developments at a broader level. However, a more formal and coordinated joint approach aimed at containing and protecting young people is likely to be necessary. Kelly et al (1995) point to some systemic weaknesses that would need to be addressed to make such an approach more effective. First, the individual casework approach of social work may be ill-suited to the kinds of investigation, evidence gathering and support needed for young prostitutes, especially where such abuse is organised in networks or 'rings' and numbers of young people are involved. Second, those under 16 are still liable to be dealt with by the police under soliciting legislation rather than the Children Act. The risks associated with punishing and further labelling those sexually exploited are therefore likely to be exacerbated. An effective joint approach between police and social services would need to be firmly grounded in a child protection perspective.

There is a depressing symmetry between our findings and those of Farmer and Pollock's (1997) more specialist study of sexually abused and abusing children in care. They found that, out of all the groups in their sample, those involved in prostitution had the worst outcomes and that there were few, if any, examples of effective practice in relation to them. Together, these findings point to this as an area that requires quite urgent action if some of the most damaged and vulnerable young people within the care system are to be offered more effective protection.

PERSONAL HEALTH AND SAFETY

Going missing, especially if it was a repeated pattern, involved both immediate and longer term risks to the personal health and safety of young people. In the short term, in addition to the risks of offending and sexual exploitation that we have described, young people were at risk of violence and victimisation. One young male had been stabbed, several had been the victims of street robberies and a few mentioned being stalked at night. Some young people, during more extended stays away, had resorted to begging for money, cigarettes or food. One young female summed up her fears about being on the streets at night:

> I've stayed out on the streets all night. Sometimes it was horrible. Like once we'd seen this man driving past, trying to get us in his car and everything, so we wouldn't get in. But sleeping on benches and everything was pretty horrible. You'd come back and it was cold and you felt dirty.

Other young people found themselves in dangerous situations over which they had lost control. For example, one female, who had gone missing with a friend from her unit, found herself in the back of a taxi with two men they had just met, one of whom had a gun. The men robbed the taxi driver and coerced the girls into spending the night at their flat. Another found herself locked for two days in the flat of a man who was a heroin user.

Longer Term Health Risks

In addition to these immediate risks, going missing often also carried longer term risks to young people's health. As the comments above suggest, young people would often return in a poor mental and physical condition, especially when they had stayed away for a while. Where going missing was part of an habitual pattern there were obvious concerns about its implications for the diet, weight, appearance and self-image of young people. The lack of structure to their daily lives meant they were often not around for appointments with social workers and carers and their basic health care needs could therefore not be met. The social worker of one 11 year old boy felt that he looked worse than he did before entering care. He was out all day and most nights, his diet was poor and he was never around for medical checks or visits to the dentist.

Sexual Health

The problems associated with providing personal and social education to looked after young people have been quite well documented (Audit Commission 1994; Biehal et al 1995) and, according to one recent study, the provision of such education remains 'extremely variable' (Farmer and Pollock 1997). Patterns of movement in care, the absence of one consistent carer throughout their period in care and problems of truancy, mean young people may miss out on what is on offer, which even in schools can often be patchy (Hudson and Ineichen 1991). For those going missing often from placements, the problems can be even more acute.

Concerns about the sexual behaviour of looked after females is not new. Lawrenson (1997) notes that 10 years ago, during screening of 210 teenage girls from residential care at a genito-urinary clinic, 22% were found to have engaged in prostitution and 31% had had two or more sexual partners in the preceding month. In our study, many social workers and carers were extremely concerned about the risky sexual behaviour of females in their care, often involving unprotected sex, although much less appeared to be known about the sexual activities of males. The latter, unless prone to going off with strangers or involved in prostitution, tended to be considered at greater risk of offending or substance misuse. The gendered assumptions that may underpin this reasoning have been quite well documented (Cawson 1987; Farmer and Pollock 1997).

Most practitioners had serious concerns about the sexual health of young females going missing, especially where they were known to be involved with multiple partners. None were optimistic about the possibility of restricting this behaviour, even for girls as young as 13, and the realistic alternative was to focus on a harm reduction approach. To give just one example, Catherine (now aged 15) had a history of going missing regularly with friends. They would spend the night on the town getting drunk and meeting boys, sometimes two or three times a week, and usually return the next day. Unable to prevent this pattern, her key-worker had spent time counselling her about the importance of safe sex and the risks of sexual diseases, including HIV/AIDS. She had tried to get her to take the pill, although Catherine was reluctant, and had given her condoms as she was leaving. Their relationship was quite close, Catherine would tell her if she had unprotected sex and her keyworker would provide a morning after pill. In addition, she focused on trying to get Catherine to tell her where she was going and when she would return, which she sometimes did, and was concerned to 'keep the channels open' so that Catherine could ring at night if in difficulty. This example, which could have been replicated for any number of the young females, is both sad and quite realistic. Sad in that Catherine felt the need to place herself in situations that involved immediate risks and that she could not be better protected, realistic in that the support offered may help to protect her longer term health.

Substance Misuse

Prior to the absence reported in our main survey sample, over a third of the young people had been involved in substance misuse while being looked after, as shown in Table 8.1.

Table 8.1 Previous involvement in substance misuse

	Young people	Percentage
Yes	71	35.0
No	81	39.9
Don't know	51	25.1
Total	203	100.0

There was a clear indication of a relationship between substance mis-use and offending, as nearly 7 in 10 of those involved in substance misuse had offended in the past and nearly two thirds were reported as having committed a crime while missing on this occasion. Like those with a history of offending, these young people were more likely to have first gone missing from home and to have gone missing more often in the past. However, unlike the offending group, there was no relationship with either sex or age, so involvement in substance misuse was not concen-trated among the older young people in the sample. There was also a clear relationship between school non-attendance and substance misuse, as half of those not attending school (including both truants and those excluded) were known to be involved in substance misuse.

Twenty of the young people in our interview sample admitted to regu-lar drug use, heavy drinking or both. Eighteen admitted to using drugs and nearly half of them were only 11–13 years old. Most were only using cannabis but two had used heroin regularly and five others had used cocaine, speed, LSD and anti-depressants. A few also spoke of using ecstasy or sniffing gas or glue. Some put themselves very much at risk from adults involved in the drug scene. For example, a group of residents in one children's home had discovered a cannabis plantation concealed in a local churchyard and were regularly raiding it, while a 13 year old who was fostered sold some heroin he had found, undercutting local dealers. Heavy drinking was also a problem for a number of the young people. Foster carers in one of our focus groups commented that alcohol use by young people in their early to mid-teens was a serious problem they had often encountered and they suggested that young people in foster care often go missing in order to get drunk.

A few of the young people said they had started drinking or using drugs once they entered residential care, including one 15 year old who was introduced to heroin by her boyfriend at her children's home. Some of the young people linked their drug or alcohol misuse to their emotional prob-lems and some felt they had been influenced by peers in residential units:

> I only done it 'cos my mates was doing it and I was depressed. (male 14)

> They were doing it, the other kids, and I thought it were good to do it. So I started doing it. (male 12)

For some, using drugs or drinking heavily was one of the things they did when they went missing, part of the excitement:

> We go out and have a laugh, get drunk and get stoned all the time. (female 15)

Very few of the young people saw their drug or alcohol use as prob-lematic and most refused to listen when social workers or carers tried to talk to them about the risks involved. They tended to view the use of drugs and alcohol as part of the excitement of being free from the constraints of adult authority while missing, whether hanging out on the streets or visiting clubs or parties, and appeared to have little concern about the potential longer term impact on their health, as can be the case with many teenagers. However, as we turn to look at young people's histories of going missing, we will find that, for those with careers that involve going missing often, involvement in sub-cultures that include offending, school non-attendance and substance misuse forms part of a package that significantly increases the risks of gradual detachment from the main centres of adult authority and makes effective intervention much harder to achieve.

SUMMARY

For young people in our survey sample, levels of offending were higher, for both males and females, than is the case for young people in children's homes more generally. Going missing is therefore closely associated with offending. Those with past offences were more likely to be male, older, in residential settings, to be excluded from school, to have first gone missing from home and to have gone missing more often in the past. While those with past offences were more likely to have gone missing often from placements than those who had none, it was also the case that those with no past history of offending were more likely to begin offending if they went missing. Placement in certain units where criminal peer cultures had developed increased the risk that young people would offend.

While some young people had quite extensive offending careers prior to being looked after, others were either initiated or their careers escalated once looked after. For some young people going missing had become inextricably linked with offending, especially for those going with peers from children's homes, but for others offending was more opportunistic, part of a spontaneous search for excitement while away. For some, particularly those away longer, offences were sometimes linked to survival strategies on the streets, while a minority, drawn to the fringes of 'street culture', were influenced by older people associated with that scene. Where patterns of going missing and offending had become entrenched, most practitioners found effective intervention very difficult to achieve and, given that nearly half the offenders in the interview sample were under 14 years of age, their nascent careers were less likely to be inhibited by convictions or a sense of responsibility for their actions.

Although the interview sample was not representative of all young people who go missing, the risks associated with sexual exploitation were apparent for many of them – 8 had suffered serious sexual assault while missing and 10 had some past or current involvement in prostitution while absent from their placements: 7 female and 3 male. Virtually all of the latter group had been sexually abused in the past; had experienced physical abuse, neglect or family rejection; had often quite serious behaviour difficulties associated with these experiences and were therefore vulnerable to sexual exploitation. For all but one, their involvement in prostitution had started whilst looked after and all were placed in ordinary children's homes. Some had been enticed or coerced by others within their units and some became involved in prostitution through links they had made outside. A search for physical closeness and affection, in lives often bereft of these qualities, marked the initiation for some. For those deeply involved, their involvement with procurers, drugs and violence meant that they were sometimes held through fear. For others, more often with fringe involvement, the money enabled them to access other enjoyable activities associated with going missing; it represented a distasteful means to an end. Returning with money could give young people added power and status within their homes and make the task of assisting them more difficult.

Despite the obvious concern of practitioners, there were few examples of positive practice directed at protecting them from such high risk behaviours consistent with a child protection perspective. Where young people were more deeply involved, workers often felt out of their depth, lacking the skills and knowledge to intervene effectively. Practice tended to centre on dissuasion and harm reduction strategies which, while useful in themselves, were usually unsuccessful in preventing repeat exposure to risk. Recent research in this area has pointed to the need for a rapid response and, due to the risks such behaviour presents to others, the need for young people to be separated from their peers and, where possible, placed at some distance from their networks, preferably in specialist foster homes. There was little evidence of such an approach in this study. Child protection procedures were rarely invoked and case conferences were often not held. Although one young person stopped when moved to a new placement and two others when their friends were placed in secure accommodation, this pattern was not common. Placement in a secure unit was a last resort and, while it provided respite, their was little evidence of longer term benefits when young people were returned.

Effective practice was not helped by the wider organisational and resource context in which practitioners found themselves. There was neither a clear practice framework nor guidance in this area. There were very few specialist foster placements in either City East or City West and access to specialist out-of-authority residential placements were closely circumscribed by financial considerations. Practitioners were only too aware of the limits of trying to work with these young people in ordinary children's homes and of the need for greater protection.

Protecting units from child abusers and procurers and tracing young people's contacts was an important area of work for practitioners. Child protection teams were trying to collate information and liaise with police at a broader level. However, a more formal and concerted joint approach between social services and the police, aimed at containing young people and based on the child protection principles within the Children Act, is likely to be necessary if this very vulnerable group of young people is to be afforded better protection.

Going missing also involved other immediate and longer term risks to young people's personal health and safety. A number of young people were the victims of sometimes violent criminal acts while missing and a number found themselves in dangerous situations over which they had lost control. The longer term health of those missing often would also suffer and the monitoring of basic health needs often proved impossible. Carers often had real concerns about the risks associated with the un-protected sexual encounters of young females in their care, although less concern was apparent for males in this regard. Finally, a large number of young people in both the survey and interview samples had involvement in alcohol and drug misuse. In the interview sample nearly half of those who admitted drug use were aged 11–13. While few of the young people thought of their substance misuse as problematic, seeing it as part of the excitement of being free of adult supervision, it was closely associated with going missing often, school non-attendance and offending.

9

HISTORIES OF GOING MISSING

In previous chapters we have focused on the patterns associated with a single incident of unauthorised absence, on the risks associated with going missing and the uncertainties surrounding attempts to assess risks. This chapter will explore the careers or histories of going missing for young people in the main survey and interview samples. The main survey enabled us to examine a number of issues for those who had gone missing more or less often in the past. First, we were interested in exploring the implications of going missing often for young people's lives. Was it associated with greater instability in young people's care careers and with patterns of school non-attendance, offending and substance misuse? In short, was going missing often linked to a progressive detachment from the centres of adult authority for young people? Second, if so, were these risks of detachment the same for all young people in this sample? For example, might there be differences in these longer term risks for those who, on this single occasion, were thought to have gone missing to be with 'friends or family' as compared to those who 'ran away or stayed out'? Finally, might these factors associated with progressive detachment be influential to differing degrees and in differing ways for those who first went missing from home when compared to those who first went missing from substitute care? The answers to these questions will form the main substance of this chapter.

CAREERS OF GOING MISSING

In addition to the detailed information about a single absence, the main survey enabled us to gather some information about these young people's histories of going missing. However, the level of knowledge social workers had of young people's past careers was variable, suggesting that data about past events were not always clearly recorded on case files. For example, 12% were unable to estimate how many times young people had gone missing from placements in the past and one quarter did not know at what age their young person had first gone missing.

For those who did know the age first missing, the distribution is presented in Figure 9.1.

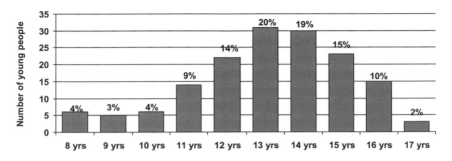

Figure 9.1   Age at which young people first went missing ($n = 155$)

Although the majority first went missing between the ages of 12 and 16 years, one in ten were under 11 years of age. While the proportion first going missing at 17 years of age tails off dramatically, and this may reasonably be expected given what we know about the relationship between going missing and the mid-teen years, it may also be a feature of our sample profile. We had very few 17 year olds in the sample and therefore very few who could have first gone missing at that age. The mean age at which young people first went missing was 13 years and this is consistent with the findings of other recent studies (Rees 1993; Graham and Bowling 1995).

For just a quarter (23%) of the young people the reported absence was their first experience of going missing. As Figure 9.2 demonstrates, of those who had gone missing previously, just over half had only been absent without permission from substitute care placements one to four times in the past. However, at the other end of the spectrum, nearly one fifth had gone missing 20 or more times.

Looking solely at young people in residential placements, our survey of children's homes found that nearly one third (30%) of the young people went missing only once during the 12 month period and more than half (54%) went missing four times or less. This means that a minority of the young people were responsible for the majority of the incidents. Just over a quarter (28%) of the young people in the community homes sample went missing 10 or more times during the course of the year and these young people were responsible for nearly three quarters of all incidents.

We now compare those in the main survey who had gone missing often in the past with those who had not.

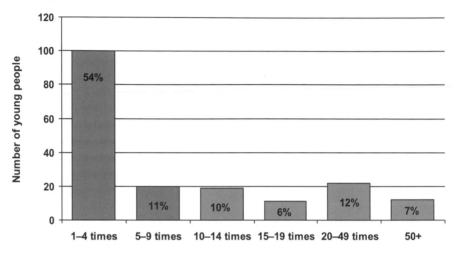

Figure 9.2   Total number of times missing prior to this absence (n = 184)

GOING MISSING OFTEN: THE RISK OF DETACHMENT

Other studies of runaways in general have suggested an association between going missing often, or for longer periods, and a tendency for young people to become progressively more detached from family, school or care system (Kurtz 1991; Stein et al 1994; Brennan et al 1978). Analysis of this association for our large survey sample of looked after young people confirms this tendency.

Going missing more or less often was not significantly associated with young people's personal characteristics. Age, sex and ethnic origin did not have a significant influence upon careers of going missing. However, there was some evidence that those who had been statemented for emotional and behavioural difficulties (p = 0.05) and those with learning difficulties (p = 0.08) were over-represented amongst those who had gone missing more often. This also proved to be the case for those who had first gone missing from home rather than from substitute care, but we will be looking at the differences between these sub-groups in greater detail later. Finally, there was a clear, if not surprising, association between the age young people first went missing and the number of times they had gone missing in the past year. Those who started going missing at a younger age had gone missing more often (τ – 0.268), a finding consistent with earlier research on absconding (Clarke and Martin 1971).

More Unstable Care Careers

Those who had gone missing more often were likely to have experienced greater instability in their care careers, as reflected in the key measure of placement movement. A positive correlation was found between the extent of placement movement and the number of absences in both the past year ($\tau + 0.22$) and throughout their care careers ($\tau + 0.3$). In addition, this relationship held true even when we controlled for other factors such as the length of time looked after, the age they first went missing and whether they had first gone missing from home or care. Differences in the scale of absences in the past year were quite striking. For example, just taking those young people who had been continuously looked after for more than 12 months, the mean number of absences for those who had made no or one move during their care careers was 4 compared to 21 for those who had moved 10 or more times.

Placement-centred Problems

Going missing often was also connected with young people's current circumstances. Those in residential settings had gone missing more often in the past. Of those young people in a residential placement, 46% had gone missing 10 or more times during their care careers compared to only 18% of those in foster placements. There was also some evidence that those young people who had gone missing more often were less likely to have a positive attachment to their current carers ($p = 0.08$), were likely to be less happy in their current placement and more likely to be experiencing problems there. Although there was a tendency for a greater proportion of these young people to be concentrated in residential settings, these findings were not statistically significant. This suggests that although placement difficulties were associated with going missing often, they were not confined to residential placements per se. However, the central point for us here is that going missing often was associated with both unstable care careers and current placement-centred difficulties.

School Non-attendance, Offending and Substance Misuse

However, the story in relation to the risks of growing detachment did not end there. Those young people who had gone missing more often in the past were significantly less likely to be attending school. Social workers were more likely to report that they were either excluded at the time of the incident or 'never' attended school than was the case for the sample as a whole. Taking only those who had been looked after continuously for more than one year, the mean number of absences in the past year was 1.9 for those attending 'all the time', 8.6 for those attending 'sometimes' and 17.9 for those who 'never' attended.

Finally, going missing often was also linked to past offending and substance misuse. Those who had been convicted of a past offence and those who had been involved in substance misuse had gone missing significantly more often during their care careers. Indeed, as we shall see below, offending has a stronger link with going missing often than does school non-attendance.

Although we are unable clearly to distinguish cause and effect in this network of relationships, our findings suggest that where young people establish a repeat pattern of going missing, this process is associated with a gradual weakening of their links with some of the key centres of adult authority for teenagers. Their care careers are likely to be more unstable. Their relationships with carers and the ability of carers to influence their behaviour are likely to weaken. They are unlikely to have a positive relationship with their school and its teachers, if they attend at all. They are also likely to be in difficulty with the youth justice system and, finally, to be at risk of involvement in sub-cultures associated with substance misuse.

The Relationship Between School Attendance, Offending and Going Missing Often

Graham and Bowling's (1995) research into the influences that may lead young people into offending behaviour found a close association between offending and school non-attendance. For both males and females, the odds of offending were more than three times as great for those who had truanted as for those who had not. Alongside poor parental supervision, truancy correlated most strongly with starting to offend. Connections have also been made between running away and both involvement in criminal activities (Kufeldt and Nimmo 1987) and greater detachment from school (Brennan et al 1978; Kurtz 1991).

We too identified a close link between school non-attendance and offending for our sample of young people who have gone missing from placements and we have suggested that both are separately associated with going missing often. Is it possible to go a step further, to say something more about the relative strengths of these relationships? We have attempted to do this by looking at the median rate of absence in the past year for those who were attending/not attending school and for those with/without past offences.

Table 9.1 suggests that the link between offending and going missing often is stronger and clearer than is the connection with school non-attendance. In terms of overall rates, the table points to a greater disparity in the median rate of absence for offenders (6) and non-offenders (1) than was the case for school non-attenders (4.5) and attenders (2). It also shows that offenders had a higher median rate of absence irrespective of whether they were attending school or not. The closeness of the relationship between offending and running away in residential institutions has been a consistent theme in the literature from the 1970s (Clarke and Martin 1971; Porteous and McLoughlin 1974; Millham et al 1977a; Sinclair and Gibbs 1998) and suggests that any strategy aimed at reducing the number of times young people go missing should pay very close attention to signs of offending behaviour.

Table 9.1 Median* rate of absence in the past year by offending and school attendance

	Offenders	Non-offenders	Overall rate
Attenders	5.0	1.0	2.0
Non-attenders	6.0	2.0	4.5
Overall rate	6.0	1.0	

* The median was chosen as a measure because the mean rate of absence for these groups was affected by outlying cases and therefore proved less reliable.

Similar patterns of increasing detachment were apparent for many young people in the interview sample who had gone missing often, although there were variations in the degree to which they had become disaffected. Thirty out of the 36 young people in this sample had gone missing often whilst looked after, ranging from 10 to more than 70 absences.

The vast majority of these young people (26) were placed in residential settings, often as a result of previous foster placement breakdowns. Eleven of those who had previous placements in foster care had experienced breakdowns in which going missing, often allied to other behaviour difficulties, had been an ingredient. The relative fragility of foster placements for teenagers has been well documented (Berridge and Cleaver 1987; Rowe et al 1989) and this would particularly appear to be the case where going missing is one of the problems they present to carers.

Patterns of school attendance, offending and substance misuse were poor for those missing often: 24 were not attending school, either through refusal or exclusion; 23 had past offences, although a few had not yet received a conviction due to their tender years; and 20 had some past or present involvement in substance misuse. As we have suggested, it is when all these elements are articulated, as they were for many of these young people, in a manner which serves to remove structure from or destabilise young people's lives that the risks of longer term detachment are at their most acute.

Runaway profile: *To give just one example at this extreme end of the spectrum. Curtis, aged 13, although looked after for four years, had first gone missing from home when eight years old. His mother was unable to control his behaviour or set appropriate boundaries, he had truanted from six years of age, and he would go off with friends for two days at a time. His absences both pre- and in-care were associated with offending (criminal damage, theft, stealing cars and arson) and substance misuse (mostly glue and gas).*

During his stay in care no placement had been able to cope with his behaviour nor contain him. He had moved 10 times between foster placements, residential units, a residential special school and a secure unit. In the two months he had been at his current children's home, the only one that would have him and which he liked, he had been missing nine times. Apart from his stay at a residential school he had not attended school for two years. He had stayed away weeks at a time begging and sleeping rough or staying with 'dubious' characters. His social worker felt he had lost all sense of 'conscience', spending his days aimlessly stealing and taking drugs and, perhaps still more poignantly, she felt he had 'lost his childhood'.

Are the Risks of Detachment the Same for All?

Our findings have pointed to a fairly clear association between going missing often and the likelihood of increasing detachment. Whilst this was true for the survey sample as a whole, it was more true for some than for others. If we recall the *friends* and *runaways* groupings identified earlier, we shall see that going missing often had different implications for these groups. Table 9.2 demonstrates this by showing the degree of relationship of the key variables identified above to a high absence rate in the past year for each of these sub-groups.

Table 9.2 Relationship of key variables to high absence rate for 'friends' and 'runaways' groups

	Friends group	Runaways group
Placement moves	Some relationship ($p = 0.09\,\tau + 0.092$)	Strong relationship ($p = 0.01\,\tau + 0.298$)
School non-attendance	No relationship ($p = 0.93$)	Strong relationship ($p = 0.01$)
Past offences	Strong relationship ($p = 0.01$)	Strong relationship ($p = 0.01$)
Past substance misuse	No relationship ($p = 0.3$)	Strong relationship ($p < 0.001$)

Taking the *runaways* group first, it is clear that the association between going missing often and the risks of a growing detachment was stronger for this group. Where young people 'run away' and where they do this repeatedly, our findings suggest that this pattern of behaviour is likely to be associated with placement instability, truancy or exclusion, offending and substance misuse. For those who, on the single occasion for which data were collected, went missing to be with friends or family (the *friends* group), the picture is more complex. Going missing more or less often for them was not associated with school attendance or substance misuse. There was some link with placement instability and a strong one with offending.

While instability and offending may still lead to these young people having poorer outcomes at the end of their period of being looked after, they appeared, in a general sense at least, to be at less risk of detachment.

Although we have established that going missing often is risky for all looked after young people, these findings tend to reinforce the need to approach these two groups in subtly different ways. Where young people more closely approximate the characteristics of the *friends* group – usually older teenagers going to be with friends or family, often from foster placements – a more flexible negotiated approach may be beneficial. Where they more closely fit the *runaways* group – younger, often from residential placements and where absences have a sharper problem focus – a greater priority needs to be given to structured intensive support, as they appear to be at greater long term risk.

Curtis's level of detachment was obviously extreme. However, as we have noted, not all those who had gone missing often appeared to be as disaffected. This seemed to be the case, as suggested by the survey, for those few young people whose repeat pattern of going missing more closely approximated a 'friends' group profile. For example, one female who had a stable residential placement and a close relationship with the staff would go out regularly with her friends and return in the early hours or, occasionally, the next day. The longer term risks for her seemed low. She regularly attended school, was not involved in offending and, apart from getting drunk with her friends, had no serious involvement in substance misuse.

The Practice Dimension

Although the range of professional responses to young people who go missing will be dealt with in greater depth in Chapter 12, a few comments would seem appropriate here. Despite, as we have just seen, some differentiation in the likely impact of going missing often for longer term detachment, nonetheless, from a practice viewpoint, the prognosis for young people who do go missing often would appear to be quite a bleak one. Research on leaving care has found that where young people's care careers are marked by movement and instability, offending, and a failure to obtain educational qualifications, their chances for a successful transition from care to community as young adults are seriously reduced (Garnett 1992; Broad 1994; Cook 1994; Biehal et al 1995).

Our survey findings therefore point to the need for an early response. Once a pattern of going missing becomes set, the possibilities for engagement with a young person and opportunities to explore any underlying issues or difficulties they are experiencing are likely to become more remote. Evidence from our interview sample suggests that, for those who had gone missing often, there were only limited examples of successful interventions bringing about a positive change. In a few cases a change of placement or a shift in the nature of a unit peer group helped to arrest careers that were heading towards detachment. For some others, as we have seen, increasing age and maturity led to a reappraisal of their priorities. For those adjusting to care or a new placement, a growing attachment to their homes and carers could help to moderate their behaviour.

The range of factors associated with 'going missing often' also points to the need for an inter-agency approach to supporting young people. The links we have established suggest that young people's behaviour may initially come to the attention of social workers, teachers, youth workers or youth justice workers. Early intervention is therefore likely to require a strategy for joint working that enables the needs of young people who do go missing to be viewed in a holistic way: an even-handed approach that pays close attention to signs of offending behaviour, school non-attendance and involvement in substance misuse.

COMPARING THOSE WHO FIRST WENT MISSING FROM HOME WITH THOSE WHO FIRST WENT MISSING WHILE BEING LOOKED AFTER

Previous research on runaways has suggested that a majority of those young people who run away from substitute care/accommodation first started running from the family home (Rees 1993; Stein et al 1994). In our main survey sample of young people who had gone missing from placements we found that nearly half (46%) were known to have first gone missing from home. The sample therefore divides into two broad groupings, one having a history of going missing before they entered substitute care and the other going missing for the first time after entering substitute care. We were interested in seeing the extent to which these groupings of young people (the *home* group and the *care* group) had different characteristics and what implications these might have for their patterns of going missing. This has proved a productive line of inquiry. However, some caution needs to be exercised when extrapolating from these findings. Once broken down into these groupings the numbers of young people in them were quite low for some of the tests conducted and the findings in this section therefore need to be seen as indicative rather than conclusive.

The personal characteristics of these young people had little bearing on their distribution into these groups. Gender, ethnic origin and disability had no influence. However, there was some evidence that those who had first gone missing from home had a higher current age; their mean age was 14.2 years compared to 13.8 for those in the *care* group ($p = 0.08$).

Differences in Care Careers

Table 9.3 points to a number of significant differences in the pattern of care careers for these two sub-groups.

Table 9.3   Care history by 'home' and 'care' groups

	Home	Care
Reason for entry ($p < 0.001$; $n = 197$)	Relationship breakdown (56% of home group) Family unable to provide care, or abuse (19% of home group)	Relationship breakdown (28% of care group) Family unable to provide care or abuse (40% of care group)
Time in care ($p < 0.001$; $n = 193$)	Shorter time – (76% 12 months or less)	Longer time – (44% 12 months or less)
Status ($p = 0.01$; $n = 192$)	More likely accommodated (70% accommodated)	Less likely accommodated (48% on care orders)
Placement movement ($p = 0.03$; $n = 178$)	Less movement (mean number 4.5)	More movement (mean number 5.3)

A greater proportion of those in the *home* group were older at the time of the incident and had been looked after for a shorter length of time, which suggests that they were older when they first entered the care system. In fact teenage entrants were twice as likely to be in the *home* group ($p < 0.01$). Consistent with teenage entry they were more likely to have entered for reasons of relationship breakdown rather than for reasons associated with 'protection'[1] – the family's inability to provide care or physical/sexual abuse. They were also more likely to be accommodated rather on care orders and to have experienced slightly less placement movement. On the other hand, more of the *care* group entered at a younger age for reasons associated with 'protection', had been looked after longer, were more likely to be on care orders and had experienced more movement.

Differences in Degree of Disaffection

When we look at patterns of school attendance, offending and substance misuse some further interesting divergences can be noted.

---

[1] The distinction drawn here between the 'protected' and the 'disaffected' derives from Farmer and Parker (1991) and is useful in thinking about the differences between those first missing from home and substitute care.

As can be seen from Table 9.4, those who had first gone missing from home were less likely to be attending school and more likely to have had past offences and involvement in substance misuse. These findings tend to confirm the picture that proportionately more disaffected young people were concentrated in the *home* group. Even when we controlled for current age, the differences between these groups remained significant, suggesting that this greater degree of disaffection was not simply an effect of those in the *home* group being older at the time of the survey. A number of questions spring to mind. What is influencing these patterns for those who first went missing from home and who tended to enter care later? Do these indices of greater detachment derive from difficulties they were experiencing in the family home prior to being looked after? We will return to these issues in a moment.

Table 9.4   School attendance, offending and substance misuse by 'home' and 'care' groups

	Home	Care
Current school attendance ($p = 0.001; n = 179$)	12% attending 'all the time' 51% 'never' attending	36% attending 'all the time' 33% 'never' attending
Past offences ($p = 0.02; n = 185$)	More likely (58% had a past conviction)	Less likely (40% had a past conviction)
Past substance misuse ($p = 0.003; n = 191$)	More likely (47% had been involved in substance misuse)	Less likely (27% had been involved in substance misuse)

Differences in the Pattern of Going Missing

Moving on to the issue of going missing for these groups, first going missing from home or substitute care/accommodation was not significantly linked to the features of the particular incident, except for some evidence that more of those in the *home* group tended to stay away longer on this occasion ($p = 0.05$). This suggests that the young people in these sub-groups were not tending to do different things while away nor, indeed, that they were going for significantly different reasons.

However, those in the *home* group had gone missing significantly more often in the past year ($p = 0.001$) and throughout their care careers ($p = 0.002$). When we looked only at those young people within the sample who had been continuously looked after for more than one year, the significance of this relationship was reduced ($p = 0.09, n = 70$) – the mean number of absences in the past year for the *home* group being 10.6 compared to 8.4 for the *care* group.

The closeness of these findings presented us with some problems. Given what we already knew, it would have been reasonable to expect that those young people exhibiting symptoms of disaffection and detachment, as the *home* group tended to do, would have gone missing more often. While this picture was confirmed, it was not as striking as we might have expected. Absences in the past year can only accurately reflect what is happening for those young people who have been looked after *for more than a year*, since only they have had the opportunity to go missing throughout the 12 months. As we have seen, the findings here showed less difference between the *home* and *care* groups. Our suspicions were that both of these groups contained young people who had gone missing often and we therefore undertook further multivariate analysis to try and unravel the factors at play.

This analysis suggested that, although in overall terms those in the *home* group had tended to go missing more often, both groups contained young people who had gone missing often. It further suggested, as we shall see below, that the influences upon going missing often for those who first went missing from home or substitute care were subtly different, although these findings are tentative given the low numbers involved.

Care Careers, Going Missing Often and Disaffection/Detachment

We knew that, in relation to care careers, those in the *home* group tended to have been looked after for a shorter time and to have experienced less placement movement. We also knew, in overall terms, that they had tended to go missing more often and were likely to be more disaffected. What we did not know at this stage was whether the relationship between care careers and going missing/disaffection was similar or divergent for the *home* and *care* groups. In other words, was the relationship between care careers (length of time looked after, placement movement) and going missing often likely to be stronger for those who had first gone missing from substitute care than for those in the *home* group?

Our findings suggest that this is likely to be the case. For both groups the length of time they had been looked after was not significantly related to the number of times they had gone missing in the past year, nor to the likelihood of their attending school, offending or being involved in substance misuse. With regard to placement movement, our key measure of a less stable care career, some interesting differences were observed. For the *home* group there was no significant relationship between higher placement movement and higher levels of absence or greater disaffection/ detachment. However, there was evidence for the *care* group of a close association between more unstable care careers and going missing often (p = 0.03, τ +0.237) and involvement in offending (p = 0.01). It is therefore likely that the experience of being looked after, especially where that experience is unstable, is more closely associated with going missing often and offending for those who first go missing from substitute care/accommodation than is the case for those who first went missing from the family home.

The Practice Dimension

In relation to those first missing from home, our findings suggest that this group had within it a greater preponderance of teenage entrants and those more disaffected. They were older at the time of the incident, had been looked after for a shorter time, were more likely to be accommodated and to have been accommodated through relationship breakdown rather than for traditional 'protection' reasons. They were likely to have gone missing more often in the past and were also more likely to be detached from school and involved in offending and substance misuse. In addition, their experience of being looked after was less closely associated with their pattern of going missing. It therefore seems reasonable to assume that, for a greater proportion of the young people in this grouping, going missing was rooted in difficulties experienced in the family home and that the patterns of detachment associated with going missing often were already taking shape *prior to being looked after*. Once accommodated these patterns were more likely to continue irrespective of placement stability.

Evidence from the interview sample can shed further light on the tendencies identified here. Just over half this sample (19) had first gone missing from the family home. While, for some, patterns established at this stage were continuing to be played out in a care setting, for others, their experience of being looked after had influenced these patterns for better or worse. Where some positive change had been achieved, this had been brought about through a change of placement, through closer attachment to and support from carers and/or social workers or through increasing age and maturity. Where careers of going missing were escalating this was usually linked to involvement in negative peer cultures.

For half of those first missing from home (nine), their experience of being looked after had made little or no difference to patterns of going missing and detachment that were being shaped prior to entry. All had extensive careers of going missing, involving days or weeks away from home. Most had slept rough at times, begged on the streets and, for seven, their absences had involved offending. None were attending school regularly and seven had involvement in substance misuse, usually linked to their absences. The following illustration, by no means the most extreme, should help to make these connections clear and point to the difficulties inherent in trying to influence change once these patterns become set.

Victoria (aged 14) had been accommodated at her mother's request a year previously due to her behaviour difficulties. After a stay of a few months at a short term unit, she had been at her present children's home for four months. Her running away from home was originally rooted in conflicts with her mother, who had alcohol problems and could be violent, and with her step-father. She would regularly go off to stay with friends and gradually her absences lengthened. On one occasion she was away five weeks and lived on the streets, using drugs and stealing to survive. She rarely attended school and this was one source of conflict at home. Upon entering care she went 'wild'. She was missing all the time and, through her involvement with another young woman at the unit, was introduced to prostitution. Her offences, mostly burglary and criminal damage, increased and she often breached a curfew imposed by the court. Despite the best efforts of staff to get her to return to school, and she was being taken two days a week by a support tutor, the signs were not optimistic, as only one other young person in the unit was attending. Although no longer involved in prostitution, she would still go missing regularly, now mostly overnight, partly to escape the pressures of institutional life and partly in search of excitement. Her social worker felt during her period in care she had gone from 'bad to worse'.

In contrast to those first missing from home, the young people in the *care* group tended to be younger, were more likely to have entered for 'protection' reasons and to have been looked after longer. They were more likely to be on care orders, to have had more placement moves and, in overall terms, to have gone missing less often. They were also more likely to be attending school and less likely to have offended or been involved in substance misuse. In this sense, they seemed to have a greater degree of attachment. However, there was a core of young people within this group who had gone missing often and, for them, their absences were more closely associated with instability in their care careers and offending.

Seventeen of the young people in the interview sample had first gone missing from substitute care. Four were engaged in infrequent or low key absences and were not showing signs of serious disaffection. Seven young people whose careers appeared to be escalating were clearly at risk of longer term detachment. For a further four young people, careers that appeared at risk of degenerating were helped, in one instance by a move to a foster placement, in another by an appropriate response to bullying and, for the other two, through closer attachments to and continuing support from staff. The following illustration, of a female who quite closely fits a care *group profile, points to the importance of these factors in protecting young people from further risk.*

Carron (aged 13) came into care aged three at the request of her mother, who was unable to cope. Although she had moved seven times during this period and had a number of foster breakdowns, none had been associated with running away. After a period at an out-of-authority placement, she returned to a short stay unit and went missing for the first time as she was 'depressed with living there'. Her absences increased at her present children's home where, at the time of the interview, she had lived for two years. She went missing regularly with another female resident and, through her, became involved in prostitution and other high risk activities which she felt, at the time, were exciting. After this period she calmed down again, partly because this female was sent to a secure unit and partly due to her keyworker, with whom she had developed a close relationship, encouraging her involvement in constructive activities which helped her build contacts outside. She had never been very disaffected. She had no involvement in offending or persistent substance misuse. Her main problem was school. She was excluded on entry to the unit and it took a year to find a school place. Although still truanting quite regularly, she was managing to attend two days per week and her keyworker felt they were 'getting there slowly'.

From a practice viewpoint, the tendencies associated with those first missing from home point to the need for a rapid preventive response, preferably while young people are still within the family home. Where young people establish a pattern of going missing from home, associated as it may be with truancy, offending and substance misuse, the problem once they are looked after is likely to prove more intractable. Indeed, these problems are not only likely to contribute to the *need* to look after them but, once accommodated, this group is likely to be a high risk one for repeat bouts of going missing. Although these patterns are clearly not irreversible, they are likely to pose a deeper challenge to those practitioners charged with their support than ought to be the case for those who first go missing whilst looked after. While potentially beneficial for all young people, for those in this latter group, offering and working to maintain the structure of a stable placement, regular school attendance and dissuading them from involvement in crime and substance misuse, may well prove especially protective.

SUMMARY

Evidence from past studies of runaways has suggested an association between going missing often and a progressive risk of detachment from family, substitute carers and school. Findings from the main survey confirm this association but also suggest that the factors associated with detachment – placement disruption, school non-attendance, offending and substance misuse – are influential to differing degrees and in differing ways for sub-groups of young people identified in this study.

For the survey sample as a whole, going missing often was not associated with young people's personal characteristics (age, sex, ethnic origin). However, those with statements for emotional and behavioural difficulties were over-represented amongst those with more protracted careers of going missing. Those young people who had gone missing more often in the past were likely to have had less stable care careers. They were more likely to be in a residential placement, to have experienced more placement movement in the past and to be experiencing difficulties in their current placement. They were less likely to be attending school and more likely to have had past involvement in offending and substance misuse than was the case for those who had not gone missing often. These findings suggest that where young people establish a repeat pattern of going missing, this process is associated with a gradual weakening of their links with some of the key centres of adult authority for teenagers. It is where these elements articulate in a manner that acts to destabilise young people's lives that the risks of detachment are most acute.

While both school non-attendance and offending are separately related to going missing often, the relationship with offending is both clearer and stronger. Strategies for reducing unauthorised absences therefore need to pay close attention to signs of offending behaviour. An early response to unauthorised absences is also likely to be necessary. Once a pattern of going missing becomes established, opportunities for caregivers, social workers, teachers or youth justice workers to engage young people and explore any underlying difficulties they might be experiencing are likely to become more remote. The range of factors associated with going missing often also suggests the need for inter-agency collaboration that can address the needs of young people in an integrated way.

The risk of detachment, while true for the sample as a whole, seemed more true for some than for others. Those young people whose absences closely approximated a *runaway* group profile appeared to be at greater long term risk of detachment than those whose absences fitted a *friends/ family* group profile.

Significant differences were also identified between those who had first gone missing from the family home and those who had first gone missing from substitute care. The *home* group contained more teenage entrants; they were older at the time of the incident and more of them tended to be disaffected. They had been looked after a shorter time and experienced less movement during their time looked after. However, overall, they had gone missing more often, were less likely to be attending school and more likely to have offences and involvement in substance misuse. For this group, patterns of going missing and detachment were rooted in the family home and were already taking shape prior to being looked after. Their subsequent care careers appeared to have less impact upon these patterns.

In contrast, more of those in the *care* group were younger, had entered for protection reasons and had been looked after longer. Overall, they showed more signs of attachment to school and less involvement in offending and substance misuse. However, for those in this group who had gone missing often, instability in their care careers was more closely associated with their tendency to go missing.

From a practice viewpoint, the patterns associated with the *home* group point to the need for a rapid preventive response while young people are still within the family home. Where young people establish a pattern of going missing from home, and where that career is associated with growing signs of detachment, the problem once they are looked after is likely to prove more intractable. While these patterns are clearly not irreversible, as evidence from the interview sample showed, they pose a much deeper challenge to practitioners than ought to be the case for those first missing from substitute care.

10

WHY YOUNG PEOPLE GO MISSING

Motivations for going missing are often complex and multi-layered. For some young people, issues deriving from their personal histories may dispose them towards going missing, while others may be prompted by the placement contexts in which they find themselves. Often, issues arising both from personal biographies and from placements are inter-woven to prompt young people to go missing. Even for those whose absences are spontaneous rather than planned, the reasons underlying their behaviour may be complex, arising from pressures within a place-ment or from past experiences of life in families and in substitute care. This chapter attempts to unravel the meanings that young people and professionals give to the experience of going missing and for the most part is based on our interviews with young people, residential workers, foster carers and social workers.

Young people's reasons for going missing, including absences which they described as running away, could be placement centred, family cen-tred or derived from their own histories, anxieties and aspirations, a cluster of reasons we have called 'young person centred'. In most cases, young people's absences were prompted by a combination of reasons, often a mix of placement-centred and young-person- or family-centred reasons. Another important underlying reason was that they had already established a pattern of going missing while living at home.

RUNAWAYS FROM HOME

As we saw in the previous chapter, nearly half of the young people in our main survey had previously gone missing from home. In our interview sample, 19 of the young people had run away from home. Once this pattern had been established, these young people continued to go missing from residential and foster care placements. Many of the young people we interviewed had started going missing from home at a very early age, at least ten of them at age 11 or under and four at only 7 or 8 years old. Some had stayed with their friends' families while away, but at least five had stayed out on the streets and slept rough at only 8–12 years of age. These very young children wandering the streets were very much at risk of detachment from school and involvement in crime, as we saw in the previous chapter, quite apart from the risk to their personal safety.

There were four main reasons why young people had originally gone missing from home, and for most of these young people it was a combination of these reasons that had prompted them to go missing. The most common reason was a background of neglect and a lack of parental boundaries, so that children had been able to wander off from the family home, sometimes for days or weeks at a time. More than half of the children who had gone missing from home for this reason had parents suffering from drug or alcohol addiction and the remainder had been rejected or abused by parents. This is consistent with a number of North American studies that found that many runaways had suffered parental rejection or had parents with drug or alcohol problems (Brennan et al 1978; Johnson and Carter 1980; Stiffman 1989; Simons and Whitbeck 1991). Most of those who had gone missing from home at a very early age had done so as a result of neglect.

A second reason for running away from home was to escape abuse, a finding consistent with many of the American studies cited in Chapter 1 (Johnson and Carter 1980; Farber et al 1984; Janus et al 1987; Stiffman 1989; Cohen et al 1991; Simons and Whitbeck 1991; Spatz, Widom and Ames 1994). Tara, 14, graphically described how she had first started running away following abuse by her step-father: 'I jumped out of me bedroom window in just me socks and I got cold. It all started off like that.' The remaining reasons given were family conflict, often combined with abuse or neglect, and teenage rebellion against parents and other authority. Two of these young people had run away from parents on some occasions and had been thrown out by them on others.

At least two of the young people who had first run away from home had followed a pathway which closely approximated to one identified by North American researchers (Simons and Whitbeck 1991). In their study of 84 runaways they found that, for males in particular, parental abuse increased the likelihood that young people would run away persistently, and that frequency of running away increased the probability of involvement with deviant peers. This, in turn, increased the likelihood of substance abuse and criminal activity.

For those who had first run away from home, the experience of substitute care was clearly not responsible for initiating their careers of going missing. The question remains, however, how far substitute care reinforces these careers and how far it is able to deter young people from continuing this established pattern.

PLACEMENT-CENTRED REASONS

Some of the placement-centred reasons for going missing from foster placements differed from reasons for absences from residential care. The intensity of family life could be difficult for some young people to adjust to and if they fell out with their foster carers, or did not like them, they did not have the option of turning to other adults as they might in a residential unit. In this context going missing is one way in which young people can demonstrate their unhappiness, either to draw attention to placement problems or, alternatively, to avoid dealing with them. Faced with having to resolve a difficulty or argument, some young people simply walked out of the situation. As one foster carer explained:

> A lot think well, running away's better than sitting down and talking to you about problems.

The intensity of relationships with foster carers could also operate in other ways to prompt young people to go missing. One young person who had experienced rejection in the past feared abandonment by his carer too so that, feeling anxious and unsettled, he went missing to pre-empt anticipated rejection. Others, anxious about the forthcoming disruption of their relationships with foster carers, went missing when a move away from a foster placement was planned.

Young people usually explained their reasons for going missing from foster placements in terms of being unhappy there, not liking their foster carers or resenting the restrictions placed on them by carers. Several foster carers, however, located the problem in the difficulties that young people had in settling into a family environment, where certain boundaries were imposed on them and assumptions made about behaviour that would be considered acceptable. Some young people's experiences in past residential placements or in their own families, where they had been allowed to come and go as they pleased with little adult intervention, made it hard for them to accept any restrictions on their activities, leading to arguments and unauthorised absences. In these situations, clarifying the expectations that young people and foster carers have prior to placement might allow some of these issues to be addressed.

Some placement-centred reasons for going missing were similar for those in both foster and residential placements. As we saw in Chapter 1, the trend in recent years is for young people to stay in placements a shorter time than in the past and this is particularly the case in residential care, where a high proportion of the residents are likely to have arrived in the past few weeks or months. As a result, at any one time a proportion of those living in children's homes are likely to be unsettled. We found that one of the reasons that a number of the young people had gone missing was that they felt unsettled in new placements and had not yet established strong relationships with foster carers or staff. Several spoke of how frightened they felt about entering a residential unit, fearing bullying by other young people or feeling anxious, unsettled and alienated by the institutional nature of the environment: 'It don't look like a home, it don't feel like a home', as one young woman put it. In a residential context, some young people who had not yet had the opportunity to form attachments to any staff were particularly vulnerable to the influence of other unsettled or disruptive young people. Others rapidly went missing with no encouragement from others, in one case within 10 minutes of admission, prompted by their own anxiety and distress at the new placement.

Feeling generally unhappy in a placement was also given as a reason for going missing by those in both foster and residential placements, as was a desire to escape restrictions at the placement. In substitute care, one young person explained: 'You feel like you're locked up and people tell you what to do and everything.' For others, carers' attempts to talk about painful issues were sometimes distressing and could spark sudden flight from placements. Finally, sometimes young people went missing from both foster and residential placements because they felt no one was listening to them or helping them deal with problems such as bullying.

Some reasons for going missing were specific to residential placements, arising from the way in which the institutions were run by staff, from the powerful peer cultures that existed in some units or from the interaction of both of these. Young people quickly realised that there was little staff could do to control their behaviour. As 10 year old Adam, who was deeply unhappy at separation from his family and sometimes ran away in the hope that he could stay with them, explained:

> Staff can't really do anything bad, like, so then I thought oh I'm getting out of here, I don't like it.

In a few units there was little structure and little evidence of any staff authority, which made it easy for young people to feel that there would be few consequences if they simply walked out. As one social worker complained: 'I think a lot of the time the kids run because they can . . . because no one cares about what they do.' A residential worker commented: 'I think there's a sort of atmosphere around that people can come and go, that nobody's bothered really.' In this way, it was easy for going missing to become an established pattern, reinforced by the placement contexts in which young people found themselves, as one residential worker described:

> Once you've gone out a few times and nothing's happened and you've had a good time, it's easy to carry on doing it, isn't it?

The composition of the particular staff team on duty could also influence young people's behaviour, as other studies have found (Sinclair 1971; Martin 1977). One young person talked of 'group escapes' that were planned to coincide with certain staff being on duty, while another explained that he never went missing when his keyworker was on duty, as his relationship with this worker was extremely important to him. This indicates the crucial impact that relationships with carers can make on going missing. A few went missing partly to provoke a reaction from staff, to make them take notice of their distress or to test out whether staff cared about them – a phenomenon identified in studies of absconding in the 1970s (Millham et al 1977a). They would go missing partly to escape from problems and partly to generate concern, so that caregivers would understand how they were feeling:

> Like, I'd be gone for such a long time and they'd think, what happened to her? And then I'd come back and then they'd try to sort it out with me. (16 year old in residential care)

A few young people commented on their need to escape at times from the pressures of institutional life, talking of how stressful group living could be. Children's homes were not portrayed as peaceful places, as young people had to deal not only with their own problems, but with the day-to-day distress, arguments and fights of others. As Chloe and her residential worker explained:

> It's like some days when people do things and I get upset and I run away . . . people showing off and shouting and I want some peace and quiet.

> If you're living in a children's home with people that are feeling pain, it can be quite an oppressive thing . . . she's not only dealing with her own problems, she's dealing with five other people's problems as well. And that's something I think makes a difference when people are wanting to run away.

The weakness of adult authority and the permissive atmosphere in certain units not only made young people feel that going missing would lead to few repercussions but also made these units frightening places for younger or less well-established residents. Young people's cultures could be primarily positive or negative (and will be discussed in the following chapter), but in units where adult authority was weak, negative peer cultures were able to flourish, so that bullying was widespread and younger or newer residents were encouraged or pressurised into going missing. Bullying was a serious problem mentioned by a number of young people as a reason for going missing:

I'd spoke to staff but the staff weren't really doing much, so I run away. Like, I'm not staying here while I'm being bullied and everything, so I'm going.

Other research has also identified bullying as a major reason why young people run away from residential care (Rees 1993; Barter 1996).

Where negative peer cultures were powerful within units, some young people felt they had little choice but to succumb to group pressure to go missing when others did, simply in order to survive. If most others were going missing, those reluctant to do so were nevertheless drawn in for fear of being excluded by the group. Unsettled young people who felt in a vulnerable position in relation to a powerful group of other residents were led into going missing in order to gain acceptance by the group, and some later went on to put pressure on younger or newer residents in the same way. Peer pressure could therefore operate in two ways: some young people ran away alone to escape bullying, while others were pressurised into going missing with others in order to gain acceptance by the group and escape further bullying. These issues regarding the way in which residential units were run and the impact of peer cultures among young people will be examined more closely in the following chapter.

Other research has pointed to the difficulty of managing the mix of young people passing through residential units and encouraging supportive rather than destructive relationships in the group (Whitaker et al 1998). Some staff felt that peer-led absences were most common when there was a particularly unsettled or disruptive group in a unit. In these circumstances, a new young person with a history of running away could rapidly influence others to do the same, even in a unit that was previously settled. In a number of ways, then, placement-centred reasons for going missing could act as 'push' factors, prompting unauthorised absences from placements.

FAMILY-CENTRED REASONS

In most instances, family-centred reasons acted as 'pull' factors. In one extreme case, the parents of a young boy who was accommodated as a result of severe parental neglect actively tried to undermine his placement, encouraging him to run away. In common with several other younger children, this child ran away because: 'I wanted to see them and be at home.' Another feared that failure to demonstrate his loyalty to his father by running away would jeopardise his relationship with him. His keyworker explained:

His father would say to him 'if you don't run away you're no son of mine'
. . . and he would come off the phone and say 'my dad wants me to run
away' and he'd have to go.

In most cases the 'pull' of the family was more subtle. Young people
simply did not want to be separated and although they may have liked
their placements, they did not want to be in substitute care. It was not
uncommon for young people who had been rejected by their families to
go missing in order to be with them and to find it hard to settle in
placements because of their desire to be with their parents. As Paul, a 12
year old who had been abandoned by his family, poignantly explained:

I like it here and there's nothing wrong with living here, but I prefer me
own, you know, to live with me own flesh and blood, to live with me family.

A few young people who longed to be reunited with their families
clung to the hope that if they ran away repeatedly residential or foster
carers would wash their hands of them. Most of the young people going
missing for family-centred reasons had been rejected by their parents or
even abandoned by them and the remainder had been abused. A few of
them dealt with their distress about parental rejection by blaming Social
Services for keeping them apart from their families, understandably finding it hard to accept that their families were unwilling to care for them.
One of the underlying reasons for their absences was therefore an attempt
to engineer placement breakdown in order to put pressure on social
workers and parents to allow them home.

Other young people who went missing partly for family-centred reasons did not do so in the hope of returning home permanently. Some
went missing from placements in order to spend some time with their
families while others went missing when they were feeling particularly
upset about their parents, but did not actually go to see them while away.
There were also two young women who had been abused who ran away
from settled placements because they feared that plans were afoot to
return them to their parents. However, it was unusual for family-centred
reasons alone to prompt young people to run away. They often interacted
with placement-centred and/or young-person-centred reasons to generate different types of absences at different times.

YOUNG-PERSON-CENTRED REASONS

Some of the young-person-centred reasons for going missing derived
from their pre-care histories and some from their current experiences. As
we have seen, for some of the young people, going missing was an

established pattern which had begun before their entry to substitute care or in previous placements. Another underlying reason for going missing was the lack of controls or boundaries that many of the young people in our interview sample had experienced while living with their families. Many had no experience of adult concern over their day-to-day behaviour and no experience of restrictions on their comings and goings. As one residential worker explained:

> Adam resents anyone putting any kind of rules and regulations on him. His lifestyle has always been to go where he wants and do what he wants, and he finds it very difficult to accept that people may be doing that for his safety, and just sees it as one more rule or regulation to break.

Several of the young people whose parents had failed to provide boundaries had also been abused. Their experience of inconsistent parenting that was both weak and sometimes abusive had left them with little respect for adult authority, making it hard for carers to set limits to their behaviour in order to protect them. The keyworker of Kate, 13, who was involved in prostitution while missing overnight, described her history of ineffectual parenting from her mother combined with physical violence from her father and explained that:

> She hasn't had a great deal of appropriate boundaries put on her life, she doesn't have any respect for adults. And it's very much about, well, I'm taking control of my life here.

Several of the young people with this type of history had become so used to an adult lifestyle that, on entry to substitute care, they found it hard to exchange this autonomy for an acceptance of the protective boundaries that carers sought to impose.

A number of the young people explained that one of the reasons they went missing was to escape from emotional problems when they were feeling particularly unhappy. Some used going missing as a safety valve, a means of escape from pressure when they were feeling upset or angry, as one young person explained:

> It's free. There's no one there telling you what to do, you do whatever you want. Plus you get some time to straighten out your head.

For others, going missing was a cry for help when painful feelings were too much for them, a means of demonstrating their need for attention from carers. Mark, a 12 year old living with foster carers, described the way his pain and confusion over his past experiences of rejection and abuse had led him to run away:

My dad says he loves me, and even though he hits me he still loves me. But it's hard for me to understand that because how can he love me when he beats me up and he doesn't want me at home? It's like no one's understanding what I'm feeling and what's going on with my behaviour and it's not really fair. Sometimes it's when it's going round in your head and you can't control it and you just lash out at everything . . . Running away is going overnight to get it out of your mind, or something like that. I've run away really bad and I won't come back for the night. And make them worried and make them understand what I'm feeling.

In a number of cases an underlying reason was young people's weak attachments to foster or residential carers. Although this may not directly have prompted young people to go missing, a lack of strong attachment to carers may have made it easier for young people to go missing, feeling that no one would care. Many of the young people in both the interview sample and the main sample had been in placement for less than six months, as we saw in Chapter 4, so it was unlikely that this group would have had the opportunity to have formed strong attachments to carers.

In every case where problems with attachment were mentioned, the young people had experienced parental rejection or abuse. A number of the young people were wary of forming attachments to carers and some became anxious if they started to form stronger relationships with them, fearing that they would yet again experience rejection or abandonment. For those in residential placements, this was likely to happen sooner or later as staff left establishments or young people moved to new placements. As one social worker commented: 'They anticipate failure and they won't give of themselves, or they can't'. Claire, a 16 year old in a children's home who had been abandoned by her mother and had spent much of her life with a cold, rejecting private foster carer, explained:

I just didn't want to get too close to anybody 'cos of the things that happened in the past.

Where young people had strong attachments to carers this sometimes deterred them from going missing, but where attachments were weak this could create the conditions in which going missing was more likely to happen.

Other young-person-centred reasons for going missing derived from the young people's current lifestyles and networks of friends. Many talked of going missing simply for fun, for the excitement of staying out on the streets, spending time with friends or going clubbing, 'having a laugh', free of adult controls. For some, this was an opportunity for heavy drinking or for using drugs. A number of the young people talked of the 'pull' of city centre streets, the irresistible excitements of the street lifestyle. The city centre of City West, in particular, exercised a strong 'pull' on young people, particularly those in residential units. Some described the sense of having an alternative 'family' on the streets to which they felt they belonged. Many talked of the sense of adventure that spending nights in the city centre could bring, and of the pleasures of being free from adult rules and restrictions, which could become compulsive:

> It's like smoking. Once you've got the habit of going into town and doing all the things that you used to do . . . you can't stop it. (12 year old boy)

> The longer they're round the city centre the longer they'll stay round it. It becomes their family, it becomes their community. (social worker)

However, the city centre streets were also portrayed as dangerous and sometimes violent places to be at night, peopled by pimps and drug dealers as well as pleasure seekers, particularly in City West. Some young people drawn into prostitution or going missing to the city centre to commit offences saw this as an exciting, adventurous lifestyle. Their networks on the streets had a far stronger influence on their attitudes and behaviour than the interventions of carers, who found it hard to deter those young people who were enmeshed in prostitution or a culture of offending and regularly went missing to carry out these activities.

DETACHMENT FROM SCHOOL

As we have seen, over two fifths of those in our main survey sample were not attending school or had been excluded. For these young people, going missing could lead to detachment from school. Alternatively, detachment from the school system and the ensuing lack of structure in their lives could indirectly draw them into going missing. A number of those we interviewed had been allowed to drift without receiving any education for several months and had become entrenched in a pattern of non-attendance, which made them susceptible to encouragement from their peers to stay out on the streets at night.

Some had been non-attenders before they began to be looked after. A large scale Home Office study has shown that truancy is two to three times more likely among young people where parental attachment and supervision are weak, and that this tendency is compounded where young people have delinquent peers (Graham and Bowling 1995). It is clear that this was the background of many of the young people we interviewed. Their school attendance been poor while they were living with their families and one reason for their continuing non-attendance was that they were locked into an established pattern which substitute care had failed to counter. The question is whether this established pattern of non-attendance is compounded by the nature of substitute parenting and by the social context of the placement once young people enter substitute care. Several young people spoke of how hard it was to return to school once a pattern of non-attendance had been established:

> I was scared that if I went back I wouldn't know what to do . . . I was scared really.

The other non-attenders had begun to truant from school only after they had entered substitute care. In some cases the reasons they stopped attending were similar to those of any other young people: fears of bullying, difficulty in managing group relationships, feeling that they did not fit in and anxiety about their inability to cope with schoolwork. However, other reasons which related to their being looked after were also mentioned. For example, a 10 year old boy who could not concentrate in school because he was so distressed by separation from his family explained that he was upset by teachers shouting at him for daydreaming. The disturbance and stress relating to young people's pre-care experiences and their separation from parents can clearly have a major impact on young people's school careers (Heath et al 1994; Stein et al 1994; Biehal et al 1995). Circumstances of this kind led one social worker to abandon attempts to ensure school attendance and prioritise work on emotional issues, a practice that has been identified in other studies (Jackson 1988/9; Aldgate et al 1993).

For others, non-attendance was linked to the culture of residential units. Despite efforts by residential staff to encourage residents to go to school and, in many cases, good liaison with local schools, there was a culture of non-attendance in some units which made it difficult for even the well motivated to attend. For some, the realisation that staff could do little to enforce attendance was key:

> You're only in care, it doesn't matter what I do. Like, they're not going to get into trouble because they're not exactly with their real parents, are they?

Staff simply could not force determined non-attenders to get out of bed and go to school in the mornings and were sometimes too busy to make non-attenders stick to the programmes they were supposed to follow during school hours. Also, living in a unit where no one else was going to school made it hard for new residents to attend and some felt compelled to stop going in order to gain acceptance within their peer group, often after having been bullied by the older residents. As one demoralised residential worker put it:

> School goes, everything else has gone, like it usually does when you come into care. I mean you can't cope with school within a residential unit . . . No

matter how much you try they just sort of start following each other and one stops going and it just escalates.

As one young person explained, when all, or most, other residents in a unit are up late into the night and sleeping until midday, and no one else is doing any homework in the evenings, a great deal of determination is needed to be the only one who gets up early and goes to school.

Detachment from school and going missing were closely interrelated. Young people whose attendance at school was interrupted when they were missing often found reintegration into school life difficult once they returned:

> I used to like school, but when I went missing for those three weeks I went back and I didn't feel like I could belong to school no more . . . so I just walked out of school.

Equally, for those who did not attend school or were excluded for lengthy periods of time, the lack of structure in their lives made them vulnerable to the 'pull' of alternative pursuits out on the streets at night. Those who regularly went missing became used to a lack of structure and restrictions and to the excitements of life on the streets, so that school became incongruous with their lifestyle. A number of the young people were in the habit of staying out all night and sleeping for much of the day, which was obviously not conducive to school attendance. Spending time on the streets with other non-attenders also reinforced this pattern. Going missing regularly simply made it impossible for these young people to maintain school attendance:

> I like school. I just kept running off.

> I just suddenly stopped 'cos I were running away . . . and I didn't give a shit about school.

Once patterns of persistent running away and detachment from school had been established, they were mutually reinforcing.

UNDERLYING AND IMMEDIATE REASONS

For the young people in our interview sample, it was common for different types of reasons for going missing to coexist and reinforce one another. In many cases it was possible to see the interplay between underlying reasons and more immediate reasons. Distressed by past abuse or parental rejection and upset about family separation, some young people were very clear that they simply did not want to be looked after, however congenial the placement. Others may have grown to accept family separation, but were unable to settle in placements and form attachments to carers.

These difficulties might be generated or reinforced by the particular care contexts in which they found themselves. Those who had established a pattern of going missing while living at home, or who had little pre-care experience of consistent parenting and adult-imposed boundaries, were also likely to be predisposed to go missing from placements. Underlying issues such as these could in themselves lead young people to go missing, or could make it easier for more immediate experiences to trigger un-authorised absences – for example, 'push' factors such as bullying, peer pressure and poor substitute parenting or 'pull' factors such as the desire to see parents, the excitement of staying out all night with friends or the lure of street networks, offending and prostitution.

REASONS FOR GOING MISSING AND PATTERNS OF ABSENCE

For those who had gone missing from foster placements, underlying reasons relating to distress at family separation, conflicting loyalties to family and foster carers, a lack of past boundaries or a fear of further rejection appeared to be particularly strong. The most common immedi-ate reasons mentioned for this group were conflict with carers, often over carers' attempts to impose boundaries to young people's behaviour. Our survey found that those going missing to be with friends or family were more likely to be in foster placements. This pattern appears to be broadly consistent with both these underlying and immediate reasons, as these young people either felt drawn to their families or tried to escape the restrictions of foster family life by staying with friends.

As for those in residential care, we saw in Chapter 6 that nearly three quarters of those in our main survey whose absences fitted the contours of the *runaways* pattern were in residential placements. Our survey showed that *runaways* were more likely to go missing for placement-centred rea-sons, or due to personal difficulties, than those whose absences fitted the pattern of the *friends* group. *Runaways* were likely to be missing for a shorter time (often only overnight), and were more likely to sleep rough than those in the *friends* group. In our interview sample, there were several accounts of young people persistently going missing from residential placements who used their children's homes as a 'watering hole' or 'hotel', a place to return to briefly for a bath, a meal, a change of clothes and a rest before venturing out on the streets again. This group included those young people repeatedly drawn to the city centre streets, including those going missing to offend or because they had been drawn into prostitution.

However, just as for those in foster care, these immediate reasons were in almost every case entwined with underlying reasons. Established patterns of running away, past instability in life at home or in care, and histories of rejection, neglect or abuse, all unsettled and distressed young people. Of course, those who were placed in residential units which had a strong peer culture of going missing would find it hard to swim against the tide, especially if this was reinforced by bullying. However, where these underlying reasons are at play, even those in happier and more settled placement contexts might go missing in certain circumstances.

We are not arguing here that all young people who go missing from residential placements will do so for one cluster of reasons and that their absences will follow the *runaways* pattern, nor that all young people who go missing from foster care will do so for another set of reasons and that their absences will follow the *friends* pattern. What we have identified here are two common patterns of going missing which are often associated with certain clusters of reasons for absences – each of which are more likely (though not exclusively) to be found among young people in certain types of placement.

It is important to remember that, in discussing the *friends* and *runaways* patterns of going missing, we are referring to types of incidents, not young people. These patterns refer predominantly to *what the young people do* while missing, which of course is closely linked to the reasons *why* they go missing. Although it was common for young people's absences to follow predominantly one or the other pattern, the same young person might go missing for one reason on one occasion and a different reason on another occasion. As a result the nature of each incident might approximate more closely to the *runaways* or the *friends* pattern.

> Robbie's mother had died when he was five and while living with his alcoholic father he had been neglected and had had a very unsettled lifestyle. He had been allowed to roam the streets, sometimes going missing for days at a time. Although there was a strong bond between Robbie and his father, his father made little effort to maintain contact and his social worker did nothing to encourage this. Robbie, now 11, liked his children's home but desperately longed to return to his father and sometimes ran away in the hope of engineering this return. However, his transient lifestyle pre-care also made it hard for him to accept any boundaries imposed by residential staff or by his former foster carers, so he also went missing at times to spend the night on the streets. He was sometimes absent for two or three days at a time, staying with male strangers or other young people. His social worker felt that, despite efforts to contain him, residential care had actually allowed his predilection for street life to flourish.

In the failure of substitute care to impose any effective controls on Robbie's behaviour, his desire to be reunited with his family and his pre-care history of going missing, we can see how placement-centred reasons, family-centred reasons and young-person-centred reasons can interact.

His absences for different reasons on different occasions included some incidents that followed the friends pattern, when he attempted to return home, and others that followed the runaways pattern.

For some of the young people, reasons for going missing changed over time. The most common pattern of change was for young people to start by going missing from placements because they were unsettled, unhappy or being bullied, or because they wanted to see their families. As they grew older, they continued in this established pattern but their absences became less problem focused as they went missing in order to spend time with friends or to spend nights on the streets. Elliott, an 11 year old placed in a children's home, summed up this shift succinctly: 'Well at the beginning I ran away to see me mum all the time and then I started running away to see me mates.' The pathway followed by Catherine, a 15 year old in a residential unit, was not uncommon.

Catherine had first run away from home to escape her father's abuse. She had had little experience of any parental controls other than through physical abuse and when she entered the authority's short stay unit she was rapidly drawn into its negative peer culture and became out of control, going missing at night in order to drink, take drugs and steal cars. When interviewed, she was happier in a more settled placement where she had good relationships with staff, but she continued to go missing – now in order to spend time with friends overnight rather than because she was unhappy. She saw herself as going missing to have fun with friends, as the unit could not give her permission to stay out all night: 'We go out and have a laugh, get drunk and stoned all the time.'

LINKING BIOGRAPHIES AND CONTEXTS

As we saw in Chapter 1, British studies of the 1970s argued that it is institutions, rather than the individual characteristics of their residents, which produce running away. These earlier studies charted the variation in rates of running away between residential institutions and established that differences in intake could not explain these variations, a finding that has been replicated in a recent study of children's homes (Clarke and Martin 1971; Sinclair 1971; Sinclair and Clarke 1973; Millham et al 1977a, 1977b, 1978; Sinclair and Gibbs 1998). Our exploration of young-person- and family-centred reasons for going missing alongside placement-centred reasons may at first sight appear at odds with the findings of these earlier studies, but this is due to the fact that this study was conducted differently.

The earlier studies took institutions as their focus and so were able to identify the environmental effects of different residential units. However, the accounts of individual residents of their reasons for running away were not the primary focus of these studies. Our study differs in taking individuals, rather than institutions, as its focus. It attempts a holistic analysis of histories and relationships, examining the impact of past family and placement experiences on young people's current behaviour and motivations through the accounts of the young people themselves and of those working with them. Individual accounts of why some young people go missing from placements may raise placement-related issues, but will also include reasons deriving from individual biographies.

Young people's behaviour is not entirely determined by what happens in residential or foster care, as they bring with them their own past experiences, attitudes, expectations and aspirations to the placements they enter, which interact with placement influences. Placement-centred reasons are interwoven with motivations arising from young people's personal biographies as well as the contemporary influence of their families and of their friends and associates, both within and outside placements. Perhaps because children's homes and foster homes today bear little resemblance to the closed, controlling residential institutions studied 30 years ago, our understanding of going missing from these open institutions and substitute families must be located within wider social networks than those of the placements alone.

Drawing on findings from North American research on the backgrounds and motivations of runaways and the findings from British research on the importance of placement contexts, our life course approach has led us to examine both the personal biographies of young people and the social contexts in which they find themselves. In the chapters that follow, we will look more closely at the placement contexts from which young people go missing and also consider the wider context, including field social work, the resource context and the inter-agency context.

SUMMARY

Reasons for going missing may be multifaceted and for some young people these reasons may change over time. Young people often went missing for a combination of reasons, including placement-centred, family-centred and young-person-centred reasons. A large proportion of young people in both our main survey and our interview sample had already established a pattern of going missing from home prior to their entry to care. The initial reasons for these absences included a background of neglect, abuse and a lack of parental boundaries. Once this pattern had been established it often continued when the young people were accommodated.

Placement-centred reasons for absences included escaping from bullying and other pressures of institutional life, feeling unsettled in placements, peer pressure to go missing and young people's feeling in certain children's homes that there would be few consequences if they absented themselves.

Family-centred reasons came into play mainly as underlying reasons contributing to absences. Some young people wanted to be with their families even when these families had previously been rejecting or even abusive. Some of them would go missing in the hope of engineering a permanent return home, while others went because they felt upset about family issues.

Some young-person-centred reasons derived from pre-care histories and some from current experiences. Young people who had experienced few boundaries to their behaviour while living at home or in previous placements found it hard to accept any restrictions placed on their behaviour. Others went because they were feeling unhappy or hoped to generate concern on the part of those caring for them. Poor attachment to carers and a feeling that no one would care if they went was sometimes an underlying reason. For others, motivations derived in part from young people's lifestyles and networks of friends, the 'pull' of the city centre streets and excitement of the street lifestyle.

Motivations for going missing were also intertwined with exclusion from school and non-attendance. In some residential units there appeared to be an entrenched culture of non-attendance which made it difficult for even the well motivated to attend. Although staff in some units tried hard to encourage residents to go to school, many residential staff were demoralised by their inability to enforce attendance. Once patterns of non-attendance and going missing had been established they were mutually reinforcing.

Young people from foster placements were more likely to have gone missing to spend time with family or friends and this group tended to stay away for longer. Those from residential placements were more likely to have run away or stayed out, and stayed away for a shorter time. For 'runaways', absences were more often linked to placement-centred or personal difficulties and young people following this pattern of absences were at risk of sleeping rough, offending and prostitution. Placement-centred reasons were interwoven with motivations arising from young people's personal biographies as well as the contemporary influence of their families and of their friends and associates, both within and outside placements.

11

THE PLACEMENT
DIMENSION

We have seen that young people's motivations for going missing often included reasons that were placement centred. This chapter looks more closely at the ways in which the organisation and practice of residential and foster care, and the staff and resident cultures within children's homes, may be related to going missing.

CHILDREN'S HOMES

The community homes in both City East and City West tended to be larger than is usual today. In both authorities several units had 8 to 10 beds, whereas nationally homes with 6 or fewer places are the most common (Department of Health 1996b). Recent research on residential care has come to the conclusion that children's homes should be small, as homes with 6 or fewer residents were found to be likely, in combination with other factors, to provide better quality of care (Sinclair and Gibbs 1998).

One residential worker in City East argued that occupancy levels were rising due to pressure on resources. This is reminiscent of findings in other recent studies that changes in homes were not usually driven by young people's needs but tended to derive from acute agency problems or were essentially finance led (Berridge and Brodie 1998; Brown et al 1998).

A number of residential staff complained about the problems of caring for a large group of difficult teenagers in one unit. Both staff and young people agreed that sheer numbers made adolescent units very stressful places in which to work or live:

> You can't manage ten adolescents together, they all feed off each other and wind each other up and they don't feel like it's a home, it's an institution . . . these places are too big, they look like prisons so nobody wants to be in them. (residential worker, City West)

With everyone shoved in one big house together you end up fighting and arguing and then the place gets smashed up, your bedroom completely wrecked. (young person, City East)

Residential staff sometimes argued that young people were inappropriately placed in their units and that this led to difficulties. Unplanned admissions could disrupt a relatively stable group of young people, but pressure on resources meant that homes were sometimes directed to take young people at short notice. If units had no control over admissions the mix of young people in particular homes was often felt to be inappropriate, driven by pressure on bed spaces rather than the needs of young people. Residential staff working with young people who had been abused complained of being directed to accept others who were themselves abusers, or who had a history of sexually exploiting younger children. The turnover of young people even in long stay units, together with high staff turnover in certain units, could also have a very unsettling effect. Berridge and Brodie's study of 12 children's homes found that homes pressurised by managers to take in any young person in order to solve short term accommodation needs were less effective in providing good quality of care, as some residents' needs and the tasks required to be undertaken appeared to be mutually exclusive. They argued that it was important for homes to have some say in admissions, partly in order to keep to their aims and objectives as a unit (Berridge and Brodie 1998).

However, while both the mix of young people and emergency admissions could cause problems, the characteristics of the young people as individuals may not in themselves have been the primary cause of the difficulties staff experienced. Two recent studies found that a home's intake was not related to the quality of care it provided (Berridge and Brodie 1998; Sinclair and Gibbs 1998). A study of 48 children's homes found that young people with more serious behaviour problems tended to be placed in the larger homes, and grouping a large number of difficult young people together in this way made it hard for homes to provide good quality care. They argue that homes with difficult intakes do badly because of their size (Sinclair and Gibbs 1998).

Sinclair and Gibbs found that there were major variations between homes in the incidence of running away and getting into trouble with the police after allowance had been made for intake and length of time in the home. They also found that the proportion of residents running away rose with length of time spent in the home, as the longer young people stayed the more likely it became that they would have run away at some point. They argued that the readiness with which young people became involved in running away varied greatly between different homes and suggested that behaviour is very much a creation of the immediate environment, reiterating the findings of earlier studies on absconding from approved schools and probation hostels (Clarke and Martin 1971; Sinclair 1971).

We found major environmental effects between our four authorities, as the incidence of going missing was much higher in Borough and City West than in County and City East. This may have been a reflection of differences in levels of social deprivation between the authorities (as outlined in Chapter 2), in the relative attractions and development of local 'street' networks, in child care policy and practice in the authorities or a combination of all three. As reported in Chapter 5, we also found variations in the incidence of running away between the 32 homes in our sample. In City West one long stay home accounted for 28% of all un-authorised absences from community homes during the previous year, and in City East a long stay unit accounted for 46% of incidents. In both authorities the next highest number of absences occurred in short stay units. In City West 19% of absences were from a short stay family unit (Pearl) and in City East 19% of absences were from the short term/emergency unit (Opal). Social workers clearly thought that certain homes were very likely to lead to increased behavioural problems among young people, including running away. There were certain units that social workers tried to avoid placing young people in at all. As one social worker explained, referring to a particular unit: 'If you put a troubled youngster in there they will rapidly go downhill.'

Patterns were different for these short and long stay units. In both the long stay units one or two young people were responsible for half of all absences. In the two short stay units many different young people went missing during the course of the year, 29 in total from Pearl and 23 from Opal. This may be due in part to the fact that a short stay unit is likely to have a greater number of young people passing through it. Nevertheless, the fact that so many different young people went missing suggests that aspects of the home itself are likely to have played a part, including the unsettling effects of the short term nature of the placement. Residential workers thought it was difficult for short stay units to provide any structure as young people were reluctant to accept anything the homes had to offer, knowing they would have to move on. As one residential worker put it:

> They know they're not staying there so they don't buy into anything. So it's just the culture.

As we saw in the previous chapter, some of the young people in our study had established a pattern of running away from home, while others may have established a pattern of going missing in earlier placements. Clearly, it is likely that some young people will arrive in new placements predisposed to go missing again. In addition, all of the young people had young-person-centred or family-centred reasons for going missing, so placements cannot be seen as entirely responsible for their absences. What is at issue here is how placements make going missing more or less likely. 'Pull' factors deriving from young people's histories, family relationships and peer networks outside the placement may be reinforced or inhibited by the experience of living in particular placements. At one extreme, placement factors may provoke young people to start going missing for the first time while, at the other extreme, placements may discourage those with a history of going missing from continuing this pattern, or may at least reduce its frequency.

In order to understand more clearly what it is about residential placements that may reinforce or inhibit going missing, we examined two placements with low rates of going missing and two where this was a more serious problem. One home in each authority stood out as particularly well regarded by staff, social workers and young people alike and both had relatively low rates of running away. Perhaps it was no coincidence that we were advised to select these homes for our focus groups, so as well as individual case material we have drawn on focus group interviews with residential staff and young people in the discussion that follows.

Amber, in City East, had a manager who had been in post for many years and had imbued the unit with her particular ethos, that 'you've got to show young people that you care about them 100%'. Her philosophy and her methods of demonstrating her commitment to young people appeared to be shared by other staff and she was prepared to work directly with young people. In addition, staff worked well together as a fairly cohesive team. One young person explained that this was the only one of the four units he had been in that he had not run away from:

> Well the staff here they turn round and tell you that they care about you . . . you think twice. You run away and you think of them and you think, well they do care and they are bothered. And it's – why are you running away? But in another kids' home where they don't care – you don't think twice, you just go out and have a good time when you run away.

Even Curtis, a persistent runaway and persistent offender, told us that he had liked this unit so much that he had run away less often during his past placement there.

Jade, in City West, a home that had been chaotic in the past and where bullying had been rife, had recently been turned around by a new manager. She tried to establish greater control over admissions in order to establish a more settled group of young people. She also encouraged open staff discussion about different approaches to working with young people, which led to greater cohesiveness in the staff team, more planned work with young people and a more consistent approach. Consultation with young people about the day-to-day affairs of the home was also introduced. In these two homes there was strong leadership by managers with a clear view as to the aims of the home and how they might be achieved. Although staff felt there were problems in achieving a consistent approach, there appeared to be greater cohesiveness among these staff teams than in many of the other homes.

In both homes, despite the regular crises that occurred, staff morale appeared to be high relative to most other units. The homes with high staff morale also had reasonably positive peer cultures among the young people. In our focus group with young people from Amber it became clear that, beneath the usual daily tensions and conflicts, relationships between residents were generally friendly. There was a shared regard for staff, a feeling that staff were angry or upset every time anyone went missing because they genuinely cared about them. They explained that because they felt the norms of behaviour the staff were trying to establish arose from a genuine commitment to them, they accepted them and did make an effort to behave differently (with varying degrees of success). Staff in this home monitored the peer cultures, intervening to fragment groups that showed signs of developing an 'us' and 'them' mentality. In Jade, the regime introduced by the new manager and the improvement in staff morale had been accompanied by changes in the previously negative, disruptive peer culture among young people in the unit:

> Before, morale used to be zero with staff and nobody expected anything and nothing was expected of the young people, so therefore they didn't do anything. Expectations have been raised, you do have to behave in a reasonable manner to get on with people. So a lot of the young people have responded to a certain extent to that. And it has improved and staff morale has improved because they feel they're doing something. (residential worker)

Staff had clear expectations of the young people and responses to misbehaviour involved individual discussion rather than universal sanctions. Young people were drawn into making decisions in the unit and appeared to have developed a greater investment in it. Staff morale and the more positive peer culture among residents appeared to be mutually reinforcing. Also, once this culture had been established it worked to dissuade new residents from misbehaviour, as a residential worker explained: 'because they come in and eventually the peer pressure works and the other young people say "don't do that"'. Staff were aware, however, that children's homes do not normally remain in a steady state for long and that this more positive culture among young people was fragile. The dynamics within the group could easily change with a new arrival:

> It only takes one and you've had it. We've had people in the past . . . just forget it. They destroy anything in their sight, other young people around them, staff, it's horrible.

Also, it was clear that even in a more positive residential environment the 'pull' of the unit to inhibit going missing could be counterbalanced by the 'pull' of others on the outside. When Karl was first placed at Jade it was chaotic and unstable. He sometimes ran away to escape bullying and sometimes in order to be with his father. When he returned to the unit after a period elsewhere, the climate of the home had changed. Bullying was now under control in the unit and he felt he had to settle down and improve his behaviour in order to fit in with the other residents. However, Karl still felt anxious, guilty and protective towards his father and when his father got in touch with him his behaviour would deteriorate and he would go missing in order to be with him, putting himself very much at risk when he returned home.

In both the homes described, the leadership of the head of home was an important factor. Similarly, research on residential establishments has found that the leadership style of the head of home influences the nature of the regime and its effectiveness in dealing with difficult behaviour (Sinclair 1971; Berridge and Brodie 1998; Sinclair and Gibbs 1998). Berridge and Brodie found that a head of home's ability to define a specific theoretical/therapeutic orientation or methods of work was the factor most strongly linked to quality of care, although the head's ability to keep to the home's main objectives was also very important. The head of home's clear views as to the appropriate regime has also been linked to staff agreement with the aims of the home and the philosophy of the regime (Brown et al 1998; Sinclair and Gibbs 1998).

Consistency between staff is clearly a key issue for residential care. In his study of probation hostels, Sinclair found that agreement between senior staff of the hostels over the way they should be run was associated with low absconding rates (Sinclair 1971). A more recent study of children's homes found that agreement between staff as to the home's aims and philosophy was strongly associated with positive resident cultures and low running away and conviction rates. Small homes where heads of home felt they had adequate autonomy to get on with their job and where staff and management agreed on what the home was about were found to be more likely to produce acceptable behaviour among residents, including lower rates of running away (Sinclair and Gibbs 1998). Similarly, Berridge and Brodie (1998) found a strong relationship between quality of care and the extent to which the head of home and staff were in agreement on issues of policy and practice. Consistent with this, another study of nine children's homes found that homes provided better quality care where there was concordance between societal goals for looked after young people, as expressed in legislation, the formal goals of heads of homes and the underlying beliefs and values of staff, and where there was a strong staff culture that supported the aims and objectives of the home (Brown et al 1998).

Staff in all the homes in our study felt that consistency was difficult to achieve, and was hindered by high staff turnover and the use of agency staff. The larger homes with large staff teams said they found consistency particularly difficult to achieve. Where a large home had three or four staff teams, staff felt that consistency of approach was possible within teams but less likely to occur across teams. This particular difficulty with achieving consistency in large homes may be one of the reasons why other research has found smaller homes to be more successful. In terms of running away and other problematic behaviour, two residential workers explained that some staff focused on managing the behaviour, while others did not attempt this but focused solely on addressing the underlying reasons for that behaviour. Some residential staff spoke of feeling undermined by colleagues who took a different approach. Young people were aware of differences of approach between staff and sometimes adjusted their behaviour according to the known level of tolerance of whichever staff were on duty, or played staff off against each other.

Research on residential care has also found a strong relationship between staff morale and overall quality of care in homes (Berridge and Brodie 1998). Perhaps not surprisingly, staff morale appeared to be low in those homes with particularly high rates of going missing and these homes appeared to have other problems as well. High levels of stress meant that staff turnover was high, some staff were on long term sick leave and agency staff were often used – so from the point of view of young people, staff were going missing too. All of this made a stable environment and consistent approach to young people difficult to achieve. Staff morale was very low both in units with high numbers of unauthorised absences and in units containing a high proportion of offenders. Although committed, the staff appeared to be overwhelmed by a sense of fatalism about their inability to control the behaviour of residents. Staff felt powerless to intervene effectively with young people:

> I think there's a culture of, you know, you can be attacked and injured and you just keep quiet about it and you put up with it . . . verbal abuse as well. I think if people just stopped and thought about what they were doing then it would be worse. I think they just get on with the job without thinking because that's the only way to survive. (residential worker)

> The staff get so used to (running away and truancy) happening that they can't be as worried as they used to be, it's easy for everybody to get a bit blasé. (social worker)

Staff in these units felt unsupported and unprotected by senior management in their authorities, who they felt placed young people inappropriately with them due to a lack of resources for more appropriate placements. In units such as these control appeared to have broken down and going missing was almost a routine occurrence.

The management of homes with many incidents of absence did appear to be important. The home with the highest rate of absences in City East, Agate, had had no permanent senior management team for four years. A new head of home and deputy had recently been appointed and were trying to deal with divisions within the staff team. Another home, Jet, which was universally regarded as 'horrendous', 'scary' and 'bleak' by social workers, and which even one of its own staff described as suitable only for those aged 17 and over, had only recently appointed a new manager. This home, together with the home in City West with the highest number of absences, had long standing problems with an entrenched culture of offending among residents.

These three homes which had serious problems with going missing and offending were not helped by their buildings, all of which were large and rambling, making it hard to control bullying and intimidation. This highlights a dilemma for residential care, as there is a tension between giving young people privacy and allowing them the freedom of unsupervised space, and exercising sufficient surveillance and control of buildings to enable staff to protect residents from one another.

Peer Cultures

Homes containing young people involved in prostitution or a high proportion of offenders were notable for the negative peer cultures which directly encouraged going missing. Other recent studies of residential care have found little evidence of peer cultures in children's homes (Berridge and Brodie 1998; Brown et al 1998). Brown and colleagues felt that resident cultures did not exist because the young people rarely acted cohesively. However, it is perhaps the definition of culture employed – a group acting cohesively – which has led to this dismissal of the importance of resident cultures. If culture is defined differently we may see it as a set of attitudes, norms and values which are inscribed in certain practices (du Gay 1996). These expressed attitudes may not be internalised by individuals, they may simply be expressed within the group as a form of superficial solidarity. This aspiration to solidarity with the group through expressing certain attitudes and engaging in certain practices – such as going missing or offending – may be closely linked to power relations within groups of young people. Bullying and intimidation were rife within certain units and, as we have seen earlier, some young people with no previous history of going missing or offending felt pressurised into joining in these activities in order to gain acceptance by the group.

Resident cultures and sub-cultures were not stable, but were closely linked to the changing pecking order in homes. Patterns of dominance within the group could shift over time as young people joined or left the unit and as the bullied went on to intimidate others. These power relations within peer cultures may have a more powerful effect on individual young people's behaviour than the interventions of staff. Failure to conform to staff expectations brings few effective sanctions, whereas failure to conform to the norms of the peer group in a residential institution can make life very unpleasant indeed. In an earlier study of children's homes, Whitaker and colleagues found that many children felt compelled to adopt a tough persona and aggressive attitude, simply in order to survive, and did not feel sufficiently protected by staff (Whitaker et al 1984). In these circumstances, the peer culture in certain units led young people to adopt public identities considered acceptable by the group. Peer cultures were therefore closely linked to the adoption or reinforcement of certain aspects of identity by young people – as anti-authority, or a runaway, or an offender. In other cases, some young people who had not gone missing prior to being accommodated were encouraged by individual peers to go missing with them, even in units where negative peer cultures were not operating.

These were very clear environmental effects which can go some way towards explaining higher rates of absences from certain units. Sinclair and Gibbs (1998) found that environmental effects on behaviour are often transitory. Identities adopted in order to conform to the expectations of one group may shift when a young person moves to a new placement. In one home, Amber, we found evidence of a generally positive peer culture, as described above, where the particular group of young people in residence at the time we carried out the research largely accepted the norms that staff were trying to establish, even though their behaviour did always not conform to staff expectations. At the other extreme, in another home which contained a concentration of offenders there appeared to be an entrenched delinquent culture and high levels of intimidation and, as both we and others have found, young offenders have a very high rate of running away (Sinclair and Gibbs 1998). It was hard for new admissions to the home to avoid being drawn into this culture while in the home:

> You start getting picked on and get hit if you don't join in with them . . . there's a group of five lads. And you want to stay out of it, but you just get bullied if you don't join in with them. (young person)

In a similar vein, the Utting report has highlighted the way in which the mix of 'fearsome' children and vulnerable children can amount to abuse by the system that is supposed to give protection (Utting 1997). Some peer sub-cultures were clearly linked to networks outside the home, for example where at least one girl involved in prostitution pressurised and intimidated others to join her, as she herself was under pressure from her pimp and clients. Equally, delinquent sub-cultures within certain homes sometimes had strong links with 'street' sub-cultures outside them, which reinforced patterns of going missing. Similarly, Sinclair and Gibbs found that issues of order and behaviour within children's homes are linked to behaviour outside the home, particularly offending. As we have seen, for those who went missing often this behaviour was frequently linked with persistent offending. Another study of children's homes found that where sub-cultures did exist these tended to operate more in relation to social networks outside the home, often involving groups of care leavers who lived locally (Berridge and Brodie 1998).

Also, a culture in children's homes of non-attendance at school could be another aspect of peer cultures which had a bearing on going missing. As a social worker explained:

> Once a kid gets into a children's home they see very clearly that there's a pecking order and all kids don't go to school most of the time.

In units where none of the residents went to school regularly there was a pervasive sense of boredom and listlessness, and where this was the case young people often spent much of the day in bed despite staff attempts to rouse them. With no structure to their day and an absence of more positive social networks outside the home, young people could be more easily drawn into seeing going missing overnight as an exciting activity which would enliven their day-to-day existence. The key worker of a 13 year old excluded from school who had been waiting a long time for an assessment for a special school described the effects of a lack of structured daily activities:

> It's not as if he's wandering off from the unit because he doesn't want to be here. But I think at times he's going missing because he's not getting what he needs, he's not stimulated enough, he's not involved, he's not busy enough and he's bored.

Professionals' Views

Many social workers and residential workers felt that, although some children's homes provided excellent care, on the whole most local community homes were offering a generalist service that could not meet the particular needs of many of the young people who lived in them. Both social workers and residential staff alike felt that many young people entering residential care today are those for whom preventive work or foster placements have failed and are consequently far more damaged, and have far more complex needs, than those placed in children's homes in the past. Berridge and Brodie's research supports this view, as they found that children's homes are now sheltering a more complex and problematic group of residents than they were 10 years ago (Berridge and Brodie 1998). Some demoralised residential staff felt they could offer little more than containment, as one worker at a unit where going missing was a frequent occurrence commented:

> It (residential care) just seems to be like a holding pen for a holding situation. Containment until they're ready to be released into the community at 16.

Several social workers and residential staff observed that what these young people needed was more structure and security, with specialist therapeutic help on site in children's homes. Unfortunately, it was felt that community homes did not have the resources to provide this and local authorities could not afford to pay for specialist therapeutic placements outside the authority for more than a minority. However, there has been little published research on private registered children's homes. A recent comparison of a sample of private registered children's homes, the majority of which described themselves as 'therapeutic communities', with local authority homes found that these homes had a population with particularly severe behavioural difficulties and were more concerned with treatment (Sinclair and Gibbs, forthcoming 1998).

The above study found that residents in the specialist private homes were distanced from their local peer networks and felt less exposed to outside temptations and pressures than those in local authority homes, which made it easier for staff to control them without resorting to unacceptable methods of discipline. Also, young people and staff were more committed to the ethos of the home. As the specialist homes offered greater provision of education on the premises, residents were more likely to be at school. However, the disadvantages were that they saw their families less frequently and it was harder to integrate the care they received in the homes into an overall plan which also addressed changes in the environment to which they would return. The local authority homes in the above study were best adapted to providing close contact between residents and their families, but there was no evidence that this advantage was exploited.

This comparative study suggests that specialist therapeutic homes which are out of authority might indeed, as social workers in our authorities felt, be better able to meet the needs of those showing the greatest detachment, including those who went missing very often. However, Sinclair and Gibbs' study points out that resident improvements while in a home do not predict successful outcomes once they leave and longer term success depends on the nature of the subsequent environment. The specialist homes were less able than local authority homes to intervene in the family and school environment to which a young person might eventually return.

The Utting Report has shown how the contraction in the residential sector in recent years has meant that it is no longer diverse enough to cater for specialist needs. As a result, many children are placed in homes unsuited to their particular needs because there is too little choice and too little planning (Utting 1997). Whether provision is in the residential sector or in foster care, there appears to be a need for specialist provision to meet the needs of those whose behaviour puts them seriously at risk. Locally based services are needed to meet these specialist needs wherever possible, to enable an integrated approach which intervenes in young people's family and in other local networks. However, for those young people showing the greatest detachment from placements and school or where wider networks have drawn them into prostitution or persistent offending, specialist placements outside the authority may be more appropriate.

FOSTER PLACEMENTS

Eight of the young people we interviewed were in foster placements at the time of our study but seven others had been in foster placements in the past. The reasons that young people went missing from foster placements included their unhappiness in the placement or dislike of foster carers, their inability to accept the boundaries, restrictions and routines of a family environment and the difficulty they experienced in coping with the intensity of family life. Family life brought particular problems such as rivalry with the carers' own children. Here we consider those broader aspects of the organisation of foster care which have a bearing on young people going missing.

Questions about the ability or willingness of foster carers to cope with serious behaviour problems such as going missing were raised by a number of social workers. Some foster carers said they were simply not prepared to accept young people with a history of running away, offending or drug misuse. For some of the young people we interviewed who had previously lived with foster carers, going missing had contributed to placement breakdown and had led to their placement in residential care. School issues were important too, as social workers explained that most foster carers would not accept young people who were either excluded from school or not attending. It was generally agreed that young people had to establish a settled pattern of school attendance before a foster placement would be feasible. Yet, as we have seen, some residential placements had the effect of reinforcing patterns of non-attendance, making it even less likely that a foster placement might become viable.

Other research has found that where young people have serious behaviour problems, foster placements are more likely to break down (Triseliotis et al 1995b; Berridge 1997). Breakdown rates for foster care are generally high, as around half of planned long term placements break down within three to five years and one in five intermediate term placements (which are often professional foster placements for teenagers) break down within the first year (Berridge 1994). It has long been known that foster placements for teenagers are particularly prone to breaking down (Rowe et al 1989). Social workers in our focus groups felt that foster carers were rarely willing to hold on to young people who went missing:

> We are tending to concentrate absconders in residential homes because if they are in foster homes they tend to abscond once, maybe twice, but then they get thrown out. It's very hard work for foster parents.
>
> I think foster carers don't cope so well with habitual absconders, so we do tend to get a concentration of habitual absconders in residential care.

This raises the question of whether foster carers for teenagers have adequate ongoing support to help them work with young people who go missing. Several foster carers commented on their sense of isolation, feeling that they had to take responsibility for dealing with very difficult behaviour with little support from social services. As in other studies, some of the foster carers we spoke to felt undervalued and unsupported (Bebbington and Miles 1990; ADSS 1996). As one foster carer demanded:

> What happens when it's eight o'clock at night and you want to talk to someone and the young person is still missing? Who do you turn to then? Do you wait for the next day? You need someone when the problem's there, not 12 hours later.

Given the complexity of the task facing the foster carers of young people who go missing and who perhaps have other behaviour problems too, this lack of ongoing support is likely to reinforce carers' reluctance to accept the placement of these young people or to continue working with those who go missing. Equally, recognition of the difficulty of coping with teenagers whose behaviour causes concern raises questions about the need for greater investment in the development of professional fostering services for this group (ADSS 1996).

Another key issue was the lack of appropriate placements. Several social workers in both authorities commented on the lack of choice of foster placements, so that placement decisions were based on what was available rather than what was most appropriate. This made matching impossible. Placements were often made in a crisis rather than being planned, so that social workers had to place young people wherever there was a bed available. Even where placements were planned, the child's needs were rarely matched with an appropriate foster carer as lack of resources meant that there were too few specialist carers for teenagers and there was no choice available. In addition, some social workers complained that they had been obliged to place young people who needed a foster placement in residential care due to a shortage of experienced foster carers who could cope with their going missing. None of this is surprising in the light of recent investigations of fostering, which have mentioned the difficulty of securing appropriate placements due to placement shortages and have found that foster carers are often pressurised to accept children outside their remit (Social Services Inspectorate 1995; ADSS 1996). A recent study of fostering outcomes in five local authorities also found that matching was often hasty or minimal and that only 10% of young people said they were offered a choice of placements by social workers. This study found that pre-placement matching and contracting was important in order to clarify the expectations of both parties and ensure that they share similar aims for the placement (Hill et al 1996). A young person in our care leavers' focus group made a similar point:

> Before you actually go into the placement, instead of just getting to know the family you need to get to know the family rules as well. Because if you can't live to those rules then you're going to run off anyway.

If young people are not appropriately matched with foster carers there is a greater likelihood that they will fail to settle and may demonstrate their unhappiness with the placement by going missing. If foster carers are not offered adequate support when they need it, many will find it hard to continue caring for those young people who go missing.

Young people may have underlying reasons for going missing that derive from their individual biographies or may be influenced by their social networks outside placements. These are issues that may require skilled direct work by social workers and residential or foster carers on an individual basis. However, as we have seen, the cultures and contexts of residential care and foster care also represent important influences on young people's decisions to go missing. Simply working with individual young people is therefore not enough, as these issues of organisation and culture must be addressed at the level of the placement and the agency.

SUMMARY

Young people in residential care are likely to have started going missing at an earlier age and to have gone missing more often in the past than those in foster care.

Children's homes in City East and City West were mostly large and staff found it difficult to manage large numbers of adolescents. Other research has shown that smaller homes can provide better quality care. The mix of young people and unplanned admissions also caused problems.

There were variations between local authorities and between children's homes in the extent of going missing, indicating that there are environmental effects on patterns of going missing. Particular placements may reinforce or inhibit patterns of going missing. 'Pull' factors deriving from young people's histories, family relationships and peer networks outside the placement may be reinforced or inhibited by the experience of living in particular placements.

Children's homes where going missing was a less frequent occurrence had managers with a clear idea of what they were trying to achieve, and who managed to exert some control over admissions to the unit. Staff teams were reasonably cohesive and staff morale was relatively high. Managers and staff demonstrated their clear commitment to the young people, had clear expectations of their behaviour and involved them in decisions about day-to-day affairs within the home. Action was taken to deal with bullying and attempts were made to promote a positive culture among the young people. However, even these homes experienced serious crises and the 'pull' of the home to inhibit going missing could be counterbalanced by the 'pull' of others outside the home.

In homes where going missing occurred more often, staff had no control over admissions or the mix of children. Senior management teams were not stable and did not appear to offer clear leadership. There were high levels of stress and staff appeared to be overwhelmed by a sense of fatalism about their inability to control children. These homes tended to have negative peer cultures where bullying and intimidation were rife.

Negative peer cultures appeared to operate in homes containing a high proportion of offenders. Bullying, and a desire to be accepted by an intimidating group, led some young people into going missing, offending or not attending school. Peer cultures were sometimes linked to networks outside the home which encouraged prostitution or offending. A general culture of non-attendance at school in certain homes made it easier for young people to be drawn into going missing by their peers.

There was a shortage of foster placements in both City East and City West. There was also a shortage of professional foster parents with sufficient training, support and pay to enable them to cope with difficult teenagers. The lack of sufficient and appropriate foster placements meant that pre-placement matching was often impossible. Foster carers often felt unsupported in dealing with going missing and many were not prepared to accept young people with a history of running away or who were not attending school regularly.

The organisation and practice of residential and foster care can have an impact on young people's decisions to go missing. These issues require attention at the level of the placement and the agency.

12

THE BROADER SOCIAL WORK CONTEXT

The preceding chapter showed how placement contexts can influence young people's decisions to go missing. The wider agency and inter-agency contexts in which social work takes place are also influential in shaping young people's experiences while they are looked after and so have a bearing on their decisions to go missing. This chapter considers young people's experience of social work practice and the impact of the resource context on their care careers and histories of going missing. Finally, it considers the inter-agency context and discusses the impact of other agencies' responses to school attendance and exclusion, health problems and offending on patterns of going missing.

SOCIAL WORK PRACTICE

The shift towards a case management approach by social workers, involving a greater emphasis on the planning and coordination of services and a concomitant reduction in direct work with young people, was evident in our interview sample. Some social workers interviewed were involved in direct work with young people, helping them to work through issues surrounding rejection or abuse as well as liaising closely with residential or foster carers, families and other professionals. Although they did not necessarily respond to every incident of going missing, they did discuss this with the young people and with residential staff or foster carers. Their direct involvement in working with young people was valued both by the young people and by those caring for them.

Others, however, adopted a more 'hands off' approach, visiting young people infrequently and not concerning themselves with day-to-day incidents. Both residential workers and young people in our focus groups agreed that it is common for social workers to withdraw from direct involvement in work with young people once they have been placed in residential or foster care, limiting contact largely to attendance at planning meetings and reviews. Residential workers were critical of this but understood that this was partly due to workload pressures on field social workers and the prioritisation of child protection work.

Social workers with less direct involvement with young people were seen by residential staff as more concerned with fulfilling the bureaucratic requirements of their role, ensuring that forms were filled and files were kept up to date and, in some cases, that services were coordinated. Others have argued that the increasing bureaucratisation of social work, which has come about partly as a result of social policy and management drives for efficiency and accountability, has constituted an attack on the communicative practice whereby worker and client interact to create a mutual understanding of problems and solutions (Blaug 1995). These social workers saw their role as supervising reviews and planning for the young person, while responding directly to going missing was seen as the province of residential or foster carers. Several social workers themselves expressed regret at the case management role that workload pressures and agency policy had obliged them to adopt. They also bemoaned the fact that their work was almost entirely crisis driven and that they had little time either for preventive work or for ongoing direct work with looked after children:

> You're told 'We can't take referrals for support.' It's things like direct work with children . . . to help people have a voice and express what they're feeling, they're the rewards for social work. And we don't see those very often. (social worker, City West)

> We're lacking the ability to do preventive work, it's all about filling bloody forms in. I think in real terms our role has changed. I think it's become more a paper exercise. (social worker, City East)

Some young people and residential workers commented wryly that although social workers had the power to make decisions in planning meetings, those social workers adopting a more distant case management role had little direct knowledge of the young people they were planning for. However, the particular social work role adopted did not appear to be linked to the nature of planning for young people, as the social workers who made clear plans included both those doing direct work with young people on a regular basis and those operating largely as case managers. Approaches to planning were variable. There were a number of cases where clear plans were made for and with young people and were regularly re-evaluated. This was not always easy, as plans could be overtaken by events and crises, such as young people going missing. In some cases social workers found it difficult to implement plans as young people were missing so often that it was difficult for anyone to do any work with them.

There was also evidence in a few cases of 'planning blight', which was directly related to running away, where young people were drifting in substitute care without any clear plans for their medium to long term future. Once an immediate crisis had been resolved by accommodating a young person, social workers appeared to give little priority to planning what would happen next. These workers tended to operate on a 'wait and see' basis, reacting to events as they occurred rather than assessing the young person's needs and planning the best way to meet them. Given no indication about what was likely to happen to them, a few young people fantasised that if they ran away often enough social services would become exasperated by them and allow them to return home. The failure of some social workers to plan for young people and to involve them in decision-making raises questions about the adequacy of management supervision. In addition, review procedures could not always be relied upon to ensure that planning took place, as in one authority reviews were delayed because a district reviewing officer post had been frozen as a result of budget cuts.

Where no clear planning was taking place, social workers did not appear to have consulted young people as to their own views about their future. In a few cases short term plans were made for a move to another placement, but with no consultation with young people and no discussion as to how this would fit into a longer term plan for continuing care or rehabilitation. Some young people were left in limbo as a result of these processes, either uninformed of decisions that had been taken or unaware of what might happen in the future because no serious consideration had been given to this. This left them confused and unsettled:

> They decide your life. They tell you where you're moving and where you're not moving and you just get so confused. (young person, City West)

In other cases, young people knew that social workers hoped to move them to a different placement but there were long delays due to a shortage of appropriate local placements or a shortage of resources for specialist placements. These, too, drifted for many months at a time with no knowledge of where and when they were likely to move. In these circumstances, it was perhaps not surprising that a few young people took matters into their own hands, running home in the hope of being allowed to stay or going missing to exert some control over their own lives.

The shift towards a case management role for field social workers has been linked to a move away from therapeutic models of social work. Social workers are required less and less to draw on therapeutic skills in direct work with children and families and are expected, instead, to assess need and risk and then to operationalise and monitor packages of care (Parton 1997). Utting has also pointed to a 'general decay in the understanding of social work responsibilities for looked after children due in part to gaps opening between case management and "therapeutic" social work' (Utting 1997). Yet where social workers adopt this more distant case management role it is unlikely that one of the key principles of the Children Act 1989, requiring that the wishes and feelings of the child are ascertained, can be put into practice. Consulting young people is unlikely to be more than a token exercise if carried out in the formal setting of reviews or by distant professionals who young people do not know very well (Fletcher 1993).

In addition, Parton argues that the case management model has reconstituted casework as counselling, which is expected to be bought in as part of an overall package of care. Yet, as we found, the young people in our study who were referred to psychologists or psychiatrists were often reluctant to attend appointments with professionals they hardly knew, so it may be that this is not an appropriate model for this group. Other studies have also found that young people either could not see the point of psychological or psychiatric assessments or complained that they simply did not 'get on' with the health professionals concerned (Triseliotis et al 1995a; Sinclair et al 1995). Sinclair and colleagues argue that, given their turbulent histories and often chaotic lifestyles, it is perhaps not surprising that the take-up of appointments is low.

In our study, some young people had social workers who saw them regularly and carried out direct work with them, but others could turn only to those caring for them on a day-to-day basis for help in resolving the often deep rooted and complex problems that they faced. As foster carers and most residential workers do not have professional training, these young people were unlikely to receive the skilled therapeutic help they needed. Also, if they were unhappy in their placements, they might have no one external to turn to. The contemporary practice of social work, therefore, with its varying degrees of direct work with young people, variable planning and its failure to provide therapeutic help to many looked after young people who may need it, also has a bearing on going missing from care placements.

THE RESOURCE CONTEXT

The resource context in which substitute care, education and health services are provided was a central issue underlying going missing. In both authorities the principal concerns of staff were the same: the lack of resources, the lack of choice of placements, and the ability of local children's homes to meet the complex needs of young people who are being looked after. The reorganisations which are endemic to social services were viewed with a degree of cynicism by staff, who saw them as being effected in order to solve their authority's acute financial problems rather than to improve service delivery.

Many social workers and residential staff described the ways in which cuts year after year had meant that basic services have been pared to the bone. The Association of Directors of Social Services has stated that nationally, expenditure on social services was cut by over £250 million in 1997–8, leading to unprecedented service cuts (Eaton 1998). In one of our authorities, expenditure cuts resulted in a failure to allocate social workers to nearly a fifth of the children on its child protection register. Given the prioritisation of child protection, the implications for the funding of residential and foster care and of field social work support to looked after children are even more serious. Many social workers felt that severe staff cuts and their expanding workloads meant that they were failing children. They felt they could not do the work with children in substitute care that needed to be done and that they were failing children in need, who were unlikely to receive a service until their situation reached crisis point. As a social worker in City East observed:

> We're supposed to be taking more cases and more work and covering bigger areas, there's an expectation that we can do all things. But we can't do all things and we will fail kids, because there's stacks of referrals on shelves awaiting allocation and the stacks are getting bigger.

This has major implications, not only for the refocusing debate but also for the issue of going missing. If resource cuts lead to a low priority for preventive work, young people running away from home or experiencing other problems are unlikely to receive more than a minimal service until their situation has become so severe that accommodation by the local authority cannot be avoided. By this stage, patterns of running away, non-attendance or offending may be entrenched and all the more difficult to resolve once young people are in substitute care. Indeed, as we have seen, certain placements may have the effect of reinforcing these patterns.

We interviewed several looked after young people who had experienced long delays in the allocation of field social workers and one who had had no social worker for over a year. This had the effect of causing major delays in the planning process as well as denying these young people the safeguard of having a professional outside the placement to whom they could turn if they were unhappy with residential staff or foster carers. For example, an emergency placement was made in a residential unit for a 15 year old girl, but no social worker was allocated for several months. By the time we interviewed her she had remained at the unit for 15 months. Her recently allocated social worker felt that if she had been given a social worker from the start she would by then have been back at home or, failing that, in a foster placement. Ironically, the long delay in allocating a social worker might actually have cost the authority far more than effective and immediate intervention to return the young person home or arrange a foster placement might have done.

We have already considered the connection between going missing and a lack of sufficient foster placements which made matching difficult. This shortage of foster placements was a big issue in both City East and City West, which social workers felt led to inappropriate placements being made, increasing the risk of placement breakdown. There were also a number of cases where social workers had to place young people who they felt would benefit from fostering in children's homes instead due to a lack of foster placements. Social workers in both cities agreed that a bigger investment needed to be made in a professional fostering service, which would pay foster carers a sufficient wage and offer adequate support to encourage them to work with difficult teenagers. This would avoid the need to place many young people in residential care by default, where the placement context might itself encourage or reinforce running away and other behaviour problems.

Of those in residential care, the majority were considered by their social workers to be in inappropriate placements due to resource shortages. Apart from those who social workers felt should be in foster placements if any were available, there were eight young people who had been placed in units because they had the only residential bed available in the city at the time, even though they were felt to be entirely inappropriate or even damaging. In these circumstances, social workers felt they had no choice and any consideration of matching services to needs had to be set aside, at least in the short term:

> I don't want to put him there, but it's there or on the street.

> They (management) say there's nowhere else for them to go.

> It wasn't the right place for him because he was a black child in a white environment. He did have a lot of racial abuse from the children. He was smaller, younger, he got a lot of bullying . . . The system just fails them.

Inappropriate placements due to a lack of in-house residential resources had a number of consequences. Residential staff complained that the pressure on bed spaces meant that young people who had sexually abused others were placed with children who had been abused. The number of placement moves was increased for some as they were moved on from inappropriate placements when alternatives became available.

Some remained in short stay units for many months where, as we have seen, going missing was a particularly common occurrence. Others in inappropriate placements simply walked out. According to one residential worker: 'They just up and leave after about two days.' As Utting (1997) has commented, 'Assessments, plans and reviews are a mockery if a reasonable range of services are not available to fulfil their purposes.'

There were also nine young people with serious emotional or behavioural problems, all of whom had gone missing often from their placements, who social workers felt needed specialist outside placements that could provide skilled therapeutic help and greater control and protection. However, social workers in both authorities complained that these were very expensive and it was now extremely difficult to get funding for these specialist placements. One social worker complained that she had to demonstrate that a particularly damaged young person had 'broken down' in every local community home before funding for the specialist therapeutic placement she felt he needed would be considered, due to the severe financial problems of the local authority. Another explained that the budget for outside placements had been exhausted so she would have to wait five months until the next financial year before she could apply for the resource she needed for a young person, with damaging consequences. Other social workers argued that cuts in the use of specialist outside placements had led to a concentration of young people with severe behaviour problems in community homes, which were unable to contain them or to meet their needs. Many social workers and residential staff felt that the inability to fund the specialist outside placements was causing untold damage to young people, with long term consequences:

> I mean you need expert help on some things which costs money, and we haven't got it. They might need a specialist outside placement somewhere and there isn't the money to fund that, so it's put here and you contain it, unfortunately, until they're 16 or 17, and you find them a place to move out to and you set them up to fail.

THE INTER-AGENCY CONTEXT

The resource context meant that a number of young people experienced long delays in receiving a service from other agencies too. Chapter 4 has already described the long delays in providing schooling for those who had been excluded, with young people waiting many months for an assessment to be carried out or for a place at a specialist unit to be made available. Non-attenders and those who had been excluded sometimes attended pupil referral units, but only for a few hours a week due to the shortage of places. The Audit Commission has found that over a third of children in residential care are not receiving an education (Utting 1997). As we saw in Chapter 9, non-attendance is closely associated with both offending and going missing often, so long delays in educational assessment and provision – which are often resource driven – can have an influence on patterns of going missing from substitute care.

Rapid reintegration into school life is clearly vital for these young people, but this rarely happened. Administrative delays, poor liaison, lengthy and cumbersome referral and assessment procedures for specialist units and resource shortages contributed to the problem. Indeed, the administrative delays built into the education department's referral and assessment procedures appeared to be at least partly due to these very resource shortages and also designed as a means of rationing scarce resources by delaying access to them by those in need. Some social workers in City West felt that the education authority had little commitment to providing a service for looked after children with severe problems: 'When it's our children they don't want to know.'

The experiences of Ricky, a 13 year old with emotional and behavioural difficulties, were not untypical. After leaving his special school two years earlier because he was about to be excluded, mainstream schools refused to take him because the education authority could not provide a support teacher. He attacked the educational psychologist who tried to assess him, after which the assessment process was abandoned. Although his social worker had argued strongly that he needed a placement in a residential special school, he was referred to a day school for children with emotional and behavioural difficulties. However, due to poor inter-agency liaison and administrative delays built into the admissions system, the place that was eventually offered was not to be available for nine months and by this time Ricky would have been out of school for two and a half years. All but three specialist schools of this kind in City West had been closed down as a result of expenditure cuts in the city, so waiting lists were very long. As the exasperated social worker complained: 'You know, they'd have his parents in court if they weren't sending him. But it's Education that aren't providing any schooling for him.'

Changes in the nature of residential provision in recent years have meant that those young people who would formerly have been accommodated in community homes with education are now living in children's homes in the midst of communities and have become the responsibility of the mainstream education service (Berridge and Brodie 1998). At the same time, and perhaps to some extent associated with these changes, there has been an increase in the numbers of young people looked after who are non-attenders or excluded from school, yet joint policies between education and social services are frequently absent (Brodie and Berridge 1996; Berridge and Brodie 1998). We found little evidence that education authorities were responding to this changing situation by providing adequate specialist provision for these young people. As we have seen, young people in children's homes who had little structure to their daily lives because they were not in school sometimes drifted into a pattern of going missing. There is clearly a need for closer coordination between these two agencies and a corporate approach to meeting the needs of looked after children.

There were also difficulties in gaining access to health services. Staff in both authorities complained of a lack of community-based therapeutic resources for young people and of delays in gaining access to those that existed. The profile of the young people in this study showed that many had serious behaviour problems or were struggling to cope with their experiences of abuse or rejection. However, few were receiving help which aimed to address these issues, either within or outside their placements. There has been little research which has taken the mental health needs of children who are looked after as its principal focus (Koprowska and Stein, forthcoming). One study of young people in children's homes discovered that 4 in 10 had considered killing themselves in the past month (Sinclair and Gibbs 1998). Another study of all adolescents being looked after in one county found that two thirds had a psychiatric disorder of some kind, including nearly a quarter of the sample who had a major depressive disorder (McCann et al 1996). In addition, submissions to the Utting review estimated that 75% of children looked after had mental health problems and that this group had serious health needs requiring expert attention from community paediatricians and psychiatrists (Utting 1997).

Yet several studies have found that therapeutic interventions are unlikely to be provided from within the care system. Reiterating the findings of the Warner Inquiry, Berridge and Brodie found that therapeutic methods were seldom used in children's homes (Berridge and Brodie 1998). Similarly, a study of sexually abused and abusing children found that over half of those who had been abused had had no opportunity to talk about the abuse in a therapeutic setting and only one abuser was offered work on that behaviour (Farmer and Pollock 1997). In this study, we identified a number of young people with severe behavioural and emotional problems being looked after in ordinary community homes which did not have staff with specialist skills. In the light of this, and of the other research findings cited, there does appear to be a need for specialist help to be provided by local health authorities. However, this appeared to be in short supply. In both City East and City West social workers complained that there were four to six month waiting lists for child psychological and adolescent psychiatric services. Several social workers complained both of a lack of local therapeutic resources for children and teenagers and of difficulty in finding out what might be available locally. Others, too, have found that children who are looked after rarely have access to counselling or other expert therapeutic help, despite the serious emotional and behavioural difficulties that many have experienced (Berridge and Brodie 1998).

We have discussed above the reluctance of some young people in our study and others to take up those psychological or psychiatric services that were offered, so some consideration may be needed as to the most effective way to deliver these services. Farmer and Pollock found, for example, that the best outcomes were achieved for the sexually abused or abusing young people they studied when outside therapeutic help was linked to opportunities to talk about past experiences in the context of their daily lives in their placements (Farmer and Pollock 1997). Within social services, the use of the Looking After Children Assessment and Action Records in care planning may help to ensure that consideration is given to the best ways of meeting the wider health and therapeutic needs of young people who are looked after, and can also be used to produce aggregated information on health needs for planning purposes (Quinton 1996). In an inter-agency context, there is a need for closer joint working between health authorities and social services to plan services for young people, as both the Audit Commission and the Utting Report have recommended. These services need to be both acceptable to young people and adequately resourced (Audit Commission 1994; Utting 1997).

The clear association between offending and going missing often has been a recurring theme in this study, yet we were not alone in finding little evidence of work being undertaken directly to address offending behaviour while young people were looked after (Berridge and Brodie 1998). As with provision for education and health needs, effective ways of tackling offending by looked after young people need to be developed in partnership with other agencies. The Audit Commission has criticised the inefficiency of current attempts to deal with criminality by young people and has recommended closer joint working between agencies and the development of coordinated programmes to prevent youth crime (Audit Commission 1996). Both the Audit Commission and a major Home Office study have recommended a focus on programmes to prevent the onset of offending or to limit its development (Graham and Bowling 1995).

As persistent offending and persistent running away are so closely linked, there may be little that children's homes can do once these patterns have become entrenched. Since other young people who have not previously gone missing or committed offences may be drawn in by persistent offenders, often through intimidation, it may be unwise to mix persistent offenders with other vulnerable young people in children's homes. For this reason, Sinclair and Gibbs have argued for the use of remand foster placements, bail support schemes and specialist residential facilities for young people remanded to the care of the local authority (Sinclair and Gibbs 1998). For looked after young people who have committed few offences, coordination of social services, education, local voluntary projects and the youth service to tackle offending at an early stage may be helpful, a strategy that others have suggested for young people at low risk of reoffending (Graham and Bowling 1995; Audit Commission 1996). For example, a coordinated approach by social services and education authorities to ensure that non-attenders or young people excluded from school do not spend long periods of time without any structured educational provision may be helpful in reducing incentives both to offend and to go missing from placements.

Overall, there is clearly a need for going missing, and some of the underlying issues that contribute to it, to be addressed at an inter-agency level. However, the slower pace at which health and education authorities deliver services can cause problems to young people (Sinclair et al 1995). These delays may be due in part to the same resource shortages that social services are contending with, but also arise from poor coordination between agencies. Joint planning is needed to develop partnerships between different agencies to address the education and health needs of young people who are looked after and tackle offending behaviour, all of which may make some contribution to reducing the extent of going missing from substitute care.

The experiences of Gary provide a good illustration of the ways in which the social services context, the resource context and the inter-agency context can conspire to fail young people and indirectly encourage, rather than inhibit, going missing. Gary, a 13 year old, had a history of sexual abuse and had gone on to abuse others. He had also tortured and almost killed a small child over a period of several days. Despite his severely disturbed behaviour, he was on a six month waiting list for a psychiatric assessment and his social worker had been told that he would not receive a service after this assessment until he was in a settled placement. This seemed unlikely to happen for some time. Two applications for funding specialist therapeutic placements had been turned down due to the authority's funding crisis. Although all concerned felt that the next best option would be a foster placement, no placements with childless carers were available in the authority. By the time we interviewed him he had remained in the authority's emergency residential unit for eight months. While he was there he had stopped attending school and had started going missing, in order to gain acceptance by other residents. He continued offending, which he had begun pre-care, and was eventually moved to a chaotic unit which contained a concentration of young offenders, in which his career was likely to worsen. In his case, the lack of resource options, combined with delays in accessing therapeutic help, had conspired to compound rather than remedy Gary's problems. The prospect for Gary looked bleak and the long term costs to society may be high.

SUMMARY

Some social workers worked directly with young people but others employed a case management approach and had little direct involvement, adopting a 'hands off' approach once young people were accommodated. Where a case management approach was employed, residential and foster carers were left to deal with going missing and young people did not have a trusted professional they knew well enough to turn to if they were unhappy in their placements. Also, this group of young people were not receiving direct intervention to address their problems and were unlikely to receive counselling from other agencies.

Workload pressures meant that little time could be devoted to preventive work with families, so that patterns of going missing were sometimes entrenched by the time a young person was accommodated. Social work planning was sometimes poor and 'planning blight' could sometimes have the indirect effect of encouraging young people to go missing.

Staff felt that cuts in social services expenditure had serious consequences with respect to going missing. Funding was often unavailable for the specialist therapeutic placements that staff felt some very damaged and out of control young people needed and there was little choice of in-house placements due to resource shortages. Young people were thought to be in inappropriate placements due to resource shortages. There were also a number of cases where looked after young people had not been allocated a social worker for many months, which meant that planning was delayed.

The inter-agency context also failed to meet the needs of many who went missing. There were long delays in the assessment of those excluded from school and in the provision of specialist help with education, so that young people drifted for months at a time with no structure to their lives. Little work appeared to be taking place to address offending directly. Despite the serious emotional and behavioural problems of many of the young people in our sample, there were long delays in the provision of community psychological and psychiatric services.

13

DEVELOPING A COORDINATED RESPONSE

The statutes and guidance that help to provide a framework for professional responses to young people who go missing were outlined in Chapter 2. In this chapter we will look more closely at their operation on the ground. We will examine the degree to which caregivers and social workers were aware of the policies, procedures and guidance that existed in their authorities and the extent to which they followed them in practice. In particular, we will explore recording and monitoring practices and will suggest that the development of an effective response to going missing will require more work to be done in these areas. Finally, the relationship between social services and the police in these authorities will be scrutinised. Although these relationships were mostly positive, closer cooperation and procedures that facilitate joint working aimed at the protection of young people are likely to be necessary.

POLICIES AND PROCEDURES IN PRACTICE

The regulations and guidance accompanying the Children Act 1989 with regard to procedures for those absent from placements without permission include a duty to circulate to all staff and young people written procedures to be followed when a young person goes missing. These should be included in the Statement of Purpose and Function of all children's homes (Department of Health 1991c). A recent study of children's homes found these Statements were frequently lacking and, where they did exist, there was a tendency for them to be bland, and to lack guiding principles and information about methods of working (Berridge and Brodie 1998).

Looking across all four of the authorities, we also found considerable variance in the degree to which these requirements had been met. Only one authority had included guidance on reporting procedures in the official handbooks available to both residential and fieldwork staff, one authority operated on 'custom and practice' and another, while having authority wide procedures, had failed to update them since the Act's implementation. None had as yet produced written guidance for young people or foster carers. Similar variance was found in relation to Statements of Purpose. In most cases the emphasis was placed upon the discharge of legal responsibilities, and guidance to staff about how to respond to an unauthorised absence if faced with it and how to manage the process of return was much less common.

Awareness of Procedures Amongst Staff

Given these variations it is perhaps not surprising that, in City East and City West, some confusion amongst social workers, residential staff and foster carers was apparent on the ground. Children's homes had worked out their own procedures for reporting unauthorised absences, usually based on the limited guidance provided by the Department, and quite often these took the form of basic administrative tasks. Normal practice involved reporting the absence to the police and arranging for a missing person's form to be completed. The timing of reports tended to vary with age and perceived vulnerability but there existed a clear policy to report by midnight at the latest. Other tasks centred on informing the social worker at the earliest opportunity, recording the absence and return in the daily log and, where possible, notifying parents. Although some homes were attempting to develop a closer working relationship with the police, a consensus about what extra steps could be taken when young people were missing and about managing the return process, these developments were not universal.

While residential staff operated within these unit guidelines, questions about the existence of any wider Departmental guidance often left them nonplussed, as the following comments indicate:

> To be totally honest, I'm not sure about the Departmental procedures or anything. As a unit . . . we inform the police, fill out a missing person's form . . . and, if they're missing for a period of time, inform parents, . . . social workers first chance, and that's about it. But whereas the Department policy, I'm not quite sure about that to be honest. Is there one? (City East)

> All I know is the internal policy. That's like a policy that affects all the units. I've never seen anything written down, but I'm sure the managers must know. That's quite interesting that. (City West)

Procedures for foster carers were considerably more *ad hoc*. The lack of written guidance meant that they were dependent on what was told to them by social workers and fostering support workers. Although many social workers were aware of basic reporting procedures and had conveyed these to carers, some were less clear. Generally it was expected that carers would contact the social worker or, if the absence was at night, which was more commonly the case, the Emergency Duty Team. Police and parents would then be notified after a brief discussion about the incident. However, there were a number of problems for anxious foster carers in practice. Some had received neither written nor verbal information about these procedures and, not surprisingly, acted more out of an instinct for self-protection and concern for the child: 'it's probably more instinct than anything' to ring the police. A few, more critically, felt that the absence of written guidance was symptomatic of a more general lack of support and protection for carers: some therefore felt that the burden of responsibility weighed heavily upon them. Social workers and the Emergency Duty Service were difficult to contact and, at a time of genuine anxiety, they often felt isolated and bereft of appropriate support.

The existence of clear written procedures circulated to all those likely to be affected by unauthorised absences, including young people themselves, represents an important first step in the protection of both young people and practitioners. It should help those charged with the care and protection of young people to feel more confident in the steps to be taken and, providing the procedures are followed, greater reassurance that their actions will be supported by the Department. Broader Departmental guidance on managing absences and the process of return, based on a clear philosophy and underpinned by good practice principles, is also likely to be helpful to residential staff, foster carers and social workers alike. Many felt keenly the lack of such guidance. In these areas our findings suggest that considerably more work needs to be done to meet the requirements of the Children Act.

Recording and Monitoring

The Children Act regulations specify that all unauthorised absences should be recorded in the confidential files of children missing from children's homes (Department of Health 1991c). However, the guidance makes no mention of the duties of field social workers and foster carers in this regard. Across our four authorities recording practices were variable. All children's homes met their obligations to record all absences, although the degree of detail varied between homes. As we have seen, extracting information from young people about the reasons for their absence, where they stayed and the risks associated with it was not always easy to obtain and, in consequence, was sometimes not recorded. From our observations these are likely to represent the only records of young people's careers of going missing that have any degree of accuracy.

Foster carers rarely recorded young people's absences and, as we have previously noted, all attempts to obtain central information about the numbers and types of young people missing from foster placements defeated us. Foster carers notified social workers of absences and, understandably, responsibility for maintaining a record was usually left to them. Recording by social workers appeared hit and miss. It was more likely if an unauthorised absence was a rare event and much less likely if it became a frequent occurrence. When frequent, or when social workers were perceived as operating in an overall case management role, they were sometimes not informed by children's homes of all absences. More commonly, social workers simply did nothing about the reports they were given.

These are not merely academic concerns. Where young people move between one residential home and another there would appear to be a chance that some documented history of their careers of going missing would travel with them, provided the material is in their files and not merely in a daily log that remains at the unit. However, we know that young people frequently move between foster and residential placements and that social workers come and go. If fieldwork case files do not carry a complete record of absences, the reasons for them, the risks associated and the kinds of responses attempted, it is highly likely that information important to protecting and planning the support of that young person will be lost to future caregivers and social workers.

The traumatic events surrounding the case of Frederic and Rosemary West highlighted, *in extremis*, the tragic fate that some young people who go missing can suffer. The review of case files in Gloucestershire undertaken by the Bridge Child Care Development Service (1996), as a result of this case, pointed both to the loss of records over time and the lack of clearly ordered factual histories for these young people in case files. Later attempts to reconstruct why young people had gone missing and what action had been taken therefore proved difficult. Other reports on runaways have also found similar difficulties in relation to police missing persons' reports (Abrahams and Mungall 1992; Local Government Association 1997). Improvements in recording information, shared between social workers, caregivers and the police, are therefore likely to help them plan consistent preventive interventions and appropriate responses to young people when they do go missing.

Procedures for monitoring the absences of young people did not extend beyond the level of individual cases and, even then, these procedures were patchy. Recent advice from the Association of Directors of Social Services suggested that regular reports on young people missing from placements should be directed to a senior manager with responsibility for monitoring these cases (Brian Waller, personal communication). Our authorities had such arrangements but the degree of time young people needed to be missing before these procedures were triggered ranged from two to eight or more days. Absences of shorter duration were normally dealt with under the procedures identified earlier. Evidence from City East and City West suggested that these procedures were not always followed in practice, especially where young people were routinely missing for several days at a time. Some social workers felt they were too pressured to complete the required notification forms or forgot to do them. One mentioned that, for foster placements, the potential disruption to payments that might ensue acted as a disincentive. Some others were unaware of the procedures and, especially if work with young people going missing was a rarity, relied upon management supervision to monitor their practice.

None of the authorities attempted to monitor patterns of absences across the authority. Although children's homes kept records these were not collated centrally and no data was routinely recorded or collected for those missing from foster placements. These authorities therefore had little idea of the scale of the problem nor of where pockets of high absence existed. Adequate monitoring is essential to identify areas of weakness, not least since running away can be an indicator of significant difficulties for young people in placements, but is also central to the forward planning of effective services. As we have seen, some children's homes were much less effective than others at managing unauthorised absences and, without adequate monitoring, it is difficult to see how homes in difficulty can be readily identified by senior managers and structured assistance be provided to help staff teams resolve these difficulties. Such procedures are given added importance by recent recommendations concerning the need for improved safeguards for looked after young people (Utting 1997).

In response to the West case, Gloucestershire Social Services have implemented procedures for monitoring absences from residential placements. Each unit is required to prepare monthly reports for external line managers that include the number of incidents, concerns about individuals, the length of and reasons for absences and actions that have been or need to be taken (Bridge Child Care Development Service 1996). While such developments are to be welcomed and provide a basis for monitoring patterns, they need to be extended to foster placements, about which very little is known. Given that two thirds of young people accommodated are now in foster placements (Department of Health 1996a), a failure to gather data about absences in this area would represent a serious omission.

A recent joint review of procedures for young people missing from substitute care by the Local Government Association and the Association of Chief Police Officers also recommended that data on absences from all types of placement, including those in the independent sector, should be collated and centrally monitored in all local authorities. Monitoring should form part of authority wide protocols between social service departments and the police and the data gathered be made available to regular joint meetings at management level and an annual strategic review. It also recommended that an assessment of patterns of absence should be included in the inspection procedures of local authority inspection units and, at a national level, in those of the Home Office and Social Services Inspectorates (Local Government Association 1997). The findings from this study further reinforce the appropriateness of these recommendations.

THE ROLE OF THE POLICE

Virtually all of the young people included in the main survey (97%) had been reported missing to the police. Although missing overnight or reported missing represented the two criteria for inclusion in the survey, the level of reporting related to the Departmental policies in the four authorities that, where young people failed to return, they should be reported by midnight at the latest. This was, as we have seen, the usual procedure in City East and City West, but where there were concerns about the age or vulnerability of the young person reports were often made sooner.

Relationships with the Police

Two recent studies of children's homes found that, out of all relationships external to the home, including those with field social workers, those with the police were amongst the most positive and created few difficulties (Berridge and Brodie 1998; Sinclair and Gibbs 1998). By and large this was true for caregivers and social workers in this study. There was considerable sympathy for the strain on police time and resources that going missing from substitute care could cause and recognition of the police role in attempting to trace and return vulnerable young people.

Returning to the main survey, while 52% of the young people returned voluntarily on the occasion reported, of those who did not, two thirds were brought back by the police. In the interview sample, some young people would report to the police themselves for a lift back, others were traced to addresses provided by caregivers and some were picked up on the streets, occasionally linked to offences that had been committed. In many instances returns were negotiated with good humour, even if young people were soon to return to the streets after 'safe and well' interviews had been conducted:

> They have to do their job. They know I (will) go back out after. They drove past me once on my way back down but they never spoke or anything. They knew that I were going back down whatever they did.

In other cases, often linked to offending, relationships were more adversarial: 'What can they do to me? They can only bring me back.' While many young people resented the intrusion of police or caregivers into their activities, some saw it as a sign of concern and appreciated it as such: 'But 'cos they care and, you know, want to help you, they get the police to look for you.'

Almost inevitably, on both sides, there were frustrations linked to variations in the level of police response. A recent review has highlighted, from a police perspective, the immense strain on time and resources that can be attributed to following up absences from substitute care and suggested that, without some prioritisation, responses could be generally downgraded (Local Government Association 1997). Evidence from the main survey pointed to variations in the level of response. In over one third of cases, action was limited to recording the young people's details from the placement. At the other end of the spectrum, in a quarter of the cases known addresses were checked and just under one fifth of the young people were located by the police.

Many caregivers and social workers expressed concern that young people missing from substitute care were not treated as seriously as those missing from the family home, even though they were often aware that the numbers going missing presented the police with real dilemmas. Where young people went missing often, it was commonly felt that the response was downgraded:

> She's actually what they call a regular missing so she's not on their priority list.

> If they know that (a young person) is likely to be back on the street as soon as he is returned to placement, they think, what's the point?

Responses were most positive where young people were considered vulnerable through age, disability, high risk associations or where they had been missing longer. However, even for those in the younger age range, there were complaints that the police response was delayed until late at night. It also helped when this sense of urgency was communicated clearly at the time of reporting:

> Because they prioritise it depending on the level of risk . . . and when it reaches a certain stage they've got to treat it like they treat everyone else.

Police frustrations tended to centre on the indiscriminate nature of reporting, irrespective of whether young people were likely to be at greater or lesser risk (Local Government Association 1997), and the apparent inability of caregivers to exercise greater control and protection. Difficulties in liaison could also arise where young people were known to be with their families or friends and the police were called upon to retrieve them. Even though, as we have seen, practitioners often had genuine concerns about the safety of young people in these circumstances, their requests could be met with some resistance. These problems could be compounded where young people were accommodated rather than subject to court orders. Where accommodated, recovery orders could not be obtained and the police often had difficulties gaining access to the parental home if parents were harbouring young people. Although, as we have said, relations overall tended to be quite positive and harmonious, the difficulties identified here point to the need for formal joint procedures to be developed, founded on child protection principles, that will promote a more effective coordinated response to young people who go missing.

Developing a Coordinated Approach

Previous studies of runaways have commented upon the lack of effective joint working arrangements between social services, the police and voluntary agencies in this area and compared the situation unfavourably to those that exist in child protection (Abrahams and Mungall 1992; Barter 1996). In this study, a few children's homes were attempting to improve liaison with the police, occasionally in response to crises that had emerged in these relationships. In some instances, links had been made with local community police officers. A number of advantages were perceived by some staff. Officers were able to get to know young people on a more informal basis and, through this, have some leverage in dissuading young people from going missing. Where young people persistently went missing, it was felt their involvement in planning meetings could improve communication and create an understanding of the problems that young people and staff were encountering. Relationships of this kind could therefore lead to a more consistent police response to absences and 'safe and well' interviews had more meaning if conducted by someone the young person already knew quite well.

These developments, however, tended to be ad hoc and informal, often dependent upon the initiative of individual homes or workers within them. One model worthy of further consideration has emerged in one West Midlands authority. Here, a police officer has been seconded to provide liaison with all children's homes in that authority. This officer collates all information, coordinates responses and conducts interviews with young people. The informal nature of this brief appears to have had a beneficial effect on the numbers of young people reported missing (Local Government Association 1997).

In City East and City West attempts to develop a strategic multi-agency response to the problems associated with going missing had, as yet, been limited in scope. As we have seen, some practitioners concerned about the vulnerability of young people were attempting to trace addresses and contacts and would pass these to the police for further investigation. Child protection teams were attempting to collate information at a broader level. However, it is likely that, without authority wide joint working agreements between social services, the police and voluntary agencies involved with runaways, these developments will remain fragmented and piecemeal. The Association of Directors of Social Services (Brian Waller, personal communication) and a number of recent reviews of procedures have recommended the formation of local joint protocols to plan strategic responses (Bridge Child Care Development Service 1996; Local Government Association 1997).

Effective joint working is not without problems and is likely to require some shift in organisational cultures. Voluntary agencies that work with runaways tend to be young person centred and to operate with high levels of confidentiality (Stein et al 1994). In relation to the one agency operating in our authorities, although some practitioners felt its existence could encourage young people to stay away longer, communication and liaison with children's homes and foster carers was generally positive. Caregivers often appreciated the confidential advice given to young people and felt its role could enhance young people's safety while away.

For those at risk of sexual exploitation, especially where young people are drawn into organised networks, the perspectives and traditional methodologies of both police and social services may be inadequate (Kelly et al 1995). Protection for these young people, as for all who go missing, needs to be consistent with child protection principles. To punish through prosecution can only create further damage and the kinds of investigation, evidence gathering and support that young people may need is likely to require close collaboration and the development of a more imaginative practice framework. The limited protection afforded to these young people is, perhaps, one of the most worrying findings of this and other recent studies (Farmer and Pollock 1997).

Joint working is also likely to require caregivers and social workers to grapple with the difficult issue of risk assessment. Findings from the survey have suggested that there can be few guarantees in this area. Young people may be at risk on any occasion they go missing, even if past absences have not appeared risky, and predicting risk in advance is likely to be shrouded in uncertainty. Nonetheless, the survey did point to some categories of young people who appeared to be at greater immediate and longer term risk than others; for example, those whose absences tended to fit a *runaways* profile as compared to those more closely approximating a *friends/family* profile. As we have also seen, assessment of likely risks was taking place informally on the ground. Reporting procedures did vary according to the known age and vulnerability of young people, even if that flexibility tended to end at midnight. In addition, as we shall see in the next chapter, in the search for more flexible ways of working with older teenagers, calculated risks were being taken. The problem is that these initiatives were unstructured and offered at best limited protection for individual caregivers and social workers attempting to manage risk. This is only likely to be enhanced through local protocols, agreed at senior management level in all relevant agencies, that establish clear criteria for determining risk and link these to an appropriate level of police response.

Model agreements are being developed in some local authorities and these can help this process (see Local Government Association 1997). In addition to reporting and response procedures, they can help the development of an integrated practice framework and provide a basis for monitoring and reviewing absences from all types of placement. However, such arrangements need to be extended beyond those in substitute care and include an improved response framework for those who go missing from the family home. Evidence from this study has suggested that one half of those missing from substitute care had first gone missing from their families and that, where these patterns had become set prior to being looked after, later attempts to intervene were less likely to be successful. The provision of preventive services to teenagers and their families has been identified as an area of weakness for social services (Sinclair et al 1995; Triseliotis et al 1995a; Department of Health 1996c) and the development of an integrated perspective will require greater attention to be given to services at this stage. Those who go missing from home rarely do so for pleasure and constitute part of the population of children in need. The provision of a multi-agency framework for addressing these needs should therefore be incorporated into the children's services plans of local authorities.

SUMMARY

Across the four authorities considerable variations were identified in the content and dissemination of policies and procedures to guide the responses of staff when young people go missing. Despite the statutes and guidance provided by the Children Act, not all these requirements were being met. While reporting procedures for children's homes were usually clear, only one authority had included advice and guidance in the handbooks available to both residential and fieldwork staff and none of the authorities had produced written guidance for foster carers and young people. Written procedures in the Statements of Purpose of children's homes often only covered the administrative tasks of reporting, and advice about how to manage absences and the process of return was much less common. In consequence, caregivers and social workers were often confused about whether broader Departmental guidance existed or what its contents might be.

Clear written procedures to all those affected, including young people, and guidance on managing the processes associated with going missing represent an important first step in the protection of young people. Many caregivers, especially foster carers, felt isolated, unsupported and anxious. Clear guidance can create confidence in the steps to be followed and, once followed, greater reassurance that the Department will support those actions.

Recording practices were also variable. The records kept by children's homes are likely to be the only ones containing any degree of accuracy. Foster carers rarely recorded absences and record keeping by social workers was extremely patchy. Reviews stemming from the West case have highlighted the importance of case files containing a clearly ordered factual history of absences, including the reasons for them, the risks associated and the responses attempted. Without such a record, it is highly likely that information important to the protection and support of young people will be lost to future caregivers and social workers.

Monitoring of absences was not undertaken beyond the level of individual cases and, even then, the operation of these procedures was often inconsistent. No attempts were being made to monitor absences across the authority. Children's homes records were not collated and no data was routinely collected on absences from foster care. The authorities therefore had no central knowledge of the scale of the problem nor of where pockets of high absence existed. Such knowledge is crucial to the forward planning of effective services, to identify placements in difficulty and to organise management-led assistance to resolve problems within them.

The collection of data on patterns of absence should include all types of placement, including those in the independent sector, and be subject to review at joint meetings of all agencies with an interest in planning a strategic response to unauthorised absences at the local level. At a national level, assessment of patterns of absence should also be included in the inspection procedures of the Home Office and Social Services Inspectorates.

The police role in relation to missing persons gives them a central place in negotiations about a more effective response. Although relations between social services personnel and the police were broadly positive, some frustrations were apparent on both sides. Attempts were being made to improve liaison but these tended to be *ad hoc* and dependent on the initiative of individuals or children's homes. Greater cooperation is likely to be facilitated through formal written agreements incorporating social services, the police and voluntary agencies working with young runaways. Local protocols of this type can help to establish clear reporting and response procedures, assist the development of an integrated practice framework, consistent with child protection principles, and provide a basis for monitoring and reviewing absences. Such agreements are likely to require some shift in organisational cultures and social work staff to grapple with the difficult issue of risk assessment.

14

WORKING WITH YOUNG PEOPLE

There can be little doubt that when young people go missing from their placements it causes considerable anxiety to those charged with responsibility for their care and control. Residential staff, foster carers and social workers not only worry about what may be happening to their young person, and the risks to which they may be exposed, but are also faced with a number of difficult dilemmas. Could their absence have been prevented? What steps might be taken while they are missing? How should they respond when and if the young person returns? In the longer term, what kinds of strategies might help to dissuade them from going missing again? At all these levels the professional responses offered to young people in our interview sample, and those factors which inhibited an effective response, will form the substance of this chapter.

IMMEDIATE RESPONSES TO YOUNG PEOPLE

The responsibilities placed upon caregivers and social workers as substitute parents involve a necessity to provide consistent care, protection and firm boundaries to help young people structure their lives. These are complex tasks when working with young people who may have lacked these in the past. Preventing young people leaving and placing themselves at risk proved an intractable problem to many practitioners.

Control and Protection

Pervasive amongst caregivers and social workers was a sense of real difficulty, even powerlessness, when confronted by young people determined to leave the placement. These perceptions, while particularly acute in homes where a negative peer culture had formed, were also common to residential staff, foster carers and social workers more generally and could affect the morale and confidence of staff teams. Most felt they lacked sufficient power and authority to protect young people adequately in the context of open placements, as the following comments suggest:

> You can restrain them and stop them going out if you think they're going to be at risk and arrested. And if that's the case, we could stand at the front door all day 'cos they're all at risk when they go out that front door, aren't they? (residential social worker)

> You see these kids, once they're in care, they know the worst you can do is shout at them, really, and you shout at them so often it goes straight in one ear and out the other. (foster carer)

Feeling unable to contain and protect young people often left carers feeling distressed at the ambiguous messages it gave them:

> 'Cos in their heads they must be thinking you don't care about me. You know what I'm doing and you're going to let me go through that door, and we can't physically stop them going through the door. (residential workers' focus group)

A number of factors seemed to influence these perceptions. The Department of Health's *Guidance on Permissible Forms of Control* in residential settings was felt, by many, to be ineffective when confronted by teenagers determined to leave. The *Guidance* itself acknowledges the limits of its advice with regard to teenagers when it points to the 'practical limitations on (staff's) ability to prevent young people running away from an open children's home' (Department of Health 1993, Section 4.4). Some felt that the Children Act had shifted the balance of power too much towards children, although there was less certainty about what powers had in effect been lost or were needed. In addition, further limits appeared to be inherent in the process of substitute parenting itself. Caregivers often felt that they lacked the moral authority that birth parents had in relation to influencing young people's behaviour. Even for young people who had previously experienced abuse, neglect or a lack of boundaries in their own families, it was commonly felt that parents retained a greater influence upon them. This view was sometimes endorsed by young people and carers could be confronted with comments such as 'you're not my parents' or 'you're paid to do this job' when attempting to impose discipline. Other studies have pointed to the continuing resonance of and search for reconciliation with parents amongst looked after young people, even for those severely rejected (Biehal et al 1995).

Where absences were frequent, placements disorganised or practitioners felt overwhelmed by the pressures of their work, going missing could become accepted as a normal feature of everyday life. Acceptance of going missing tended to inhibit an early preventive response and could have damaging implications as young people's careers continued unchecked:

> I think the whole thing could be taken more seriously. It's such a frequent thing that it's very much part of the routine . . . and we're so busy . . . We don't always prevent them from going missing and I think (it) will come over to the kid that maybe they're not valued enough. (social worker)

Young people were often themselves aware of this lack of control by caregivers:

> There's nothing they can do, is there? They can't lock us up for ages 'cos, if they lock us up, I'm going to do more damage. (fostered male)

> There was nothing they could do. Nothing they could say, 'cos I wouldn't have listened in the first place. I was going to do whatever I wanted to do anyway. (residential female)

For young people with deeply entrenched careers of going missing, as was the case with these two young people, preventing their absences did seem an intractable problem. However, other young people felt a greater ambivalence and, perhaps, more tightly drawn boundaries or a positive intervention would have enhanced their sense of security. Some rued the fact that there was no discipline imposed upon them. One female, heavily involved in prostitution and the violent underworld associated with it, when viewing her life from the vantage point of a secure placement, felt action of this nature should have happened sooner. She was aware she had been out of control and, although reluctant to cooperate at the time, felt some control should have been taken from her. Another young male, seriously bullied and reluctantly involved in peer absences linked to offending, was followed and stopped by a staff member on one occasion and was 'glad he did it'. Rather than it remaining an isolated incident in a troubled career, it could have provided a cue for a more positive attempt to tackle his underlying difficulties.

Berridge and Brodie's (1998) study of children's homes also found a lack of staff belief in their ability to impose firm boundaries with teenagers when it really mattered, especially in relation to leaving without permission. Although day-to-day order in the homes was good and successfully negotiated by staff and young people, there appeared less certainty about transferring these successes to situations where young people might be at serious risk. Loss of confidence in the ability to intervene effectively, however difficult, carries a risk that young people's careers will continue to escalate and, as we have seen, the longer the career the more difficult later intervention is likely to be.

Many caregivers had attempted to intervene, often repeatedly, although not always with success. Standing in the doorway, holding young people by the arm or following them out and reasoning with them sometimes bore fruit, although more usually with those ambivalent about leaving. As one earlier quote suggests, in the context of a children's home these strategies are often quite difficult to implement consistently, given the likelihood of other events or crises occurring simultaneously. Some had tried temporarily locking young people in or removing shoes or items of clothing but, if sufficiently determined, such strategies merely presented a further challenge. One private home, in an extreme bid to prevent residents leaving or boyfriends arriving, had barred all the windows. While it had some effect it was at a severe cost to the feel of the home. One keyworker, desperate to contain a 12 year old boy who was out of control and very vulnerable, described the extreme measures that had been attempted:

> We would take him back and he'd be gone an hour later. We'd bring him
> back here and he would walk round these walls looking for a way out . . .
> This turned into a mini-secure unit for a time. We locked everything, and
> everywhere he went we'd be with him to try and break the habit. And he'd
> go with no shoes or clothing on, whatever.

However, not all young people were so determined to leave and some were attempting to escape the pain and distress in their lives or problems they were experiencing in the placement itself. In these circumstances, although never easy, positive preventive intervention should be possible to organise. As we saw in some detail in Chapter 11, recent research in residential care has identified a range of factors associated with good quality care in children's homes. We also highlighted how, for at least two children's homes in this study, firm leadership based on a clear philosophy of care had led to improvements in the morale and confidence of staff and a greater consensus between staff and young people about appropriate standards of behaviour. Although these developments remained fragile and open to disruption, they do point to a framework that may help to reinforce the belief of staff in their ability to influence young people's behaviour and to intervene when necessary to protect them. In addition, more adequate monitoring of absences, as we have seen, should help senior managers to identify those placements experiencing difficulties and plan a structured programme of support to help staff turn that situation around. Residential staff commonly felt that they were too isolated from senior managers and insufficiently supported.

Responses While Missing

Beyond reporting absences to the police, a number of caregivers and social workers attempted to locate the whereabouts of missing young people and this was usually linked to broader strategies aimed at bringing about a change in their behaviour. Attempts were made to trace them through known addresses of family and friends or contacts that caregivers were aware of and were either followed up directly or passed to the police. Occasionally, where young people had stayed with friends for a while, caregivers would visit and negotiate a return, sometimes responding to difficulties young people had been experiencing within the placement as part of that package. As we will see, such an approach could prove effective in the longer term. Attempts were also made to search the streets for young people and sometimes involved direct intervention where young people were staying at the homes of adults known to have past convictions for sexual offfences against children, or where they were in contact with drug dealers on the street. Such strategies took caregivers beyond the boundary of their professional role and could involve risks to themselves:

> We've actually put ourselves at risk, which we shouldn't be doing. But we've done it because we care about the kids we work with. (residential worker)

Often these risks could be mitigated through joint actions with the police to retrieve young people from dangerous situations. Although not always successful, as some young people simply refused to return, and not to be officially recommended, it did demonstrate the level of commitment some caregivers had to the young people in their care. What could be done, however, was limited by the level of staffing in units, especially at night, and by foster carers' responsibilities to other children in their homes. It was often simply not possible to do much at all except wait.

Not all practitioners appeared to show similar levels of concern. Where young people went missing frequently or where, in a minority of children's homes, daily absences had become normalised as part of everyday life, responses could be muted. This could also be the case for social workers who had less direct involvement with young people and caregivers. One social worker was aware of the frustration this could cause to foster carers:

> When a (carer) rings me up and says, 'Well, (he's) missing again', and I say, 'Oh, right then, have you rung the police? Well, let me know when he comes back' . . . I know it's quite shocking . . . (and) . . . people think you must be able to do something, but of course you can't.

A number of foster carers felt isolated and unsupported in such circumstances and, even if practical action was genuinely difficult to organise, would have appreciated some advice and reassurance about how to manage these situations in their own right.

Inconsistent responses within staff teams were generally unhelpful. Young people were readily able to identify differing levels of concern, stronger or weaker staff, and were therefore able to exploit the opportunities this afforded. Some timed their absences or returns according to which particular staff were on duty or, if phoning in, felt able to mislead some staff concerning their whereabouts if they felt no follow-up would take place.

More generally, young people's views about strategies to locate them were mixed. Some resented their freedom being curbed but others more readily accepted that attempts to find them, whether directly or through the police, were part of the responsibilities that carers had to promote their welfare. Some even appreciated it. Where young people had previously lacked consistent care and concern or firm boundaries to guide their behaviour, these actions could prompt confusing or ambivalent feelings. More detached young people might remain unconcerned while, for others, demonstrations of concern could provoke quite complex emotions, as was the case for one young female. For her, the worst thing about being missing was:

> Thinking nobody cared. That was the most depressing thing about it . . . (but) . . . when they did look for me, I used to get a bit upset 'cos I didn't want them to look for me. I didn't want 'em to care.

Actions that demonstrate care may therefore open up a space for emotional exploration with a young person that may, in the long term, have a beneficial effect. Although many resented the intrusion at the time, young people did often value it when, as they saw it, staff stepped beyond their professional brief and showed a genuine commitment to them as individuals. In short, while inaction can never be helpful, any safe steps that can be taken may serve to protect young people, strengthen relationships and provide greater leverage to influence change in their behaviour.

Responses upon Return

Whether young people return voluntarily or are brought back, the initial response made to them tends to set the tone for everything that follows. Accumulated wisdom from research on runaways has suggested the need for a warm welcome and sensitive follow-up directed towards identifying and resolving any underlying difficulties that may have prompted the action (Newman 1989; Abrahams and Mungall 1992; Rees 1993; Bridge Child Care Development Service 1996). Studies of residential settings in the 1970s also suggested that accepting young people back and maintaining the placement tended to have a beneficial effect on subsequent rates of running away (Sinclair 1971; Millham et al 1977a).

In broad terms these messages had been incorporated into the practice of most caregivers although, as we have already seen, repeat bouts of going missing tended to test the security of foster placements and the reserves of many residential staff. A typical approach was to offer young people a warm welcome, make initial checks to ensure they had not been harmed, especially if they had been away some time and returned dishevelled, offer some food and then allow them to sleep off the effects. Attempts would then be made, usually the next day, to follow up the incident in an effort to identify why they had gone, where they had been, who they had been involved with and whether they had been at risk.

Initial responses sometimes varied according to the degree to which caregivers had an understanding of the young person involved. Where a positive relationship with the young person existed, and where it was felt young people might accept it, the response of caregivers might be strong. Demonstrations of anger, worry and parental concern could sometimes prove effective and be appreciated by young people:

> The staff shout at you and tell you how much they've missed you, and they worry about you and that.

> If they didn't care they wouldn't be angry about it. But you can tell which ones do care, 'cos they're the ones that get at you most.

Knowing young people could also guide a different response. Where they had difficulty coping with anger and criticism, the follow-up was often conducted more calmly and at the young person's pace in an attempt to prise information from them. Caregivers would often engage the young person in general conversation, look for an opening and avoid any scent of interrogation. While neither strategy necessarily brought immediate rewards, they could help to reinforce longer term relationships that might.

Following up young people's absences could often prove difficult. Where young people had problems with attachment, had little respect for their caregivers, were new to placement or substitute care or heavily committed to their course of action, they were sometimes unconcerned about any response. In these circumstances young people might refuse to say anything or lie or ignore advice offered about the risks to which they were exposing themselves. For some, the pull of their lives outside was simply too great. Some young people who had been bullied and reluctantly drawn into peer-led absences were afraid to tell. Yet others wanted to keep addresses of family, friends or other contacts secret. A few young people were concerned about the confidentiality of what was told. While they may have wanted to confide in their keyworkers, they held back because they knew this information would be shared with other members of the staff team. Finally, where young people went missing often or where the authority of staff in units with negative peer cultures was being undermined, young people were aware of its attritional effect. Following up could take the form of a routine ritual to be ignored, as the following comment by a young person suggests:

> They don't say nothing. They bring you in the staff room and say, 'right, tell me where you were, what you were doing . . . Get your wash and if you're going out, go out but come back at a certain time.'

Given the importance of information about young people's whereabouts to their future protection, responses like this were unfortunate to say the least.

In general terms, young people felt that a warm welcome and sensitive questioning showed positive concern and, if they were going missing due to problems they were experiencing, could lead to a resolution:

> That's how you know that people care, 'cos they talk to you and say 'what's your problems, tell me about it' and so on. (young people's focus group)

Punitive and negative responses were seen as undesirable and likely to reinforce a tendency to run away. One young female had experienced both types of response in two children's homes. On both occasions her running away was linked to bullying. In one home she was sent to her room and grounded on return. Feeling locked in and afraid of further bullying she left by the window and remained away for several weeks. On the second occasion, she went to stay with a friend. She eventually phoned the unit, her keyworker visited her and negotiated her return by helping her to make a formal complaint. Her fears allayed, she was able to gradually build relationships with staff and young people and, although she still stayed out late occasionally, she no longer ran away. For some young people, physically abused in the past, harsh responses held few fears:

> They used to argue with me all the time and shout at me, but I weren't really bothered . . . 'cos I've been hit all through me life anyway, so they couldn't hurt me very much.

Previous research on runaways has also pointed to the importance of young people having access to someone independent of the placement when they return (Newman 1989; Abrahams and Mungall 1992; Bridge Child Care Development Service 1996). Whether this requirement can be adequately met by the police, social workers or a voluntary agency has been the focus of some debate (Rees 1993). In our authorities, although many caregivers welcomed, even depended upon, such interventions, responses were patchy. Not all social workers visited young people upon return, a source of frustration to some carers, and their relationships with young people could be fraught in any case. In some cases young people carried resentment about their separation from their families or, given the social worker's role *with the family*, had concerns about confidentiality. So while this arrangement worked well in some cases it could not offer a universal service. Similar problems were apparent in the police response. While many did interview young people, this was by no means universal, nor were the young people always happy about it. They were sometimes seen as too lenient or insensitive in approach and encounters could become ritualised, with young people meeting their warnings in stony silence. However, where it did work well, especially with those at an early point in their careers, it could prove effective.

However authorities choose to organise this service, and it may be that a strong case can be made for the role of a voluntary agency, a children's rights service or an independent visitors scheme, offering young people access to someone independent, is important. Whoever performs this task needs to be capable of listening carefully, evaluating the evidence young people offer, and to have sufficient influence to be able to act effectively in their best interests (Bridge Child Care Development Service 1996).

The Use of Sanctions

Previous research on running away from residential care has been pessimistic about the use of institutional controls by themselves, including sanctions, having much positive effect on young people's behaviour (Clarke and Martin 1971; Sinclair 1971; Millham et al 1977a). Since going missing is rarely based on rational calculation, sanctions may carry the risk of reinforcing their behaviour. Attitudes to the use of sanctions amongst residential workers and foster carers in this study were mixed. Some children's homes had a policy of not applying sanctions, viewing them as ineffective and counterproductive. A number of young people concurred with this perspective, 'it just gets people wound up and they just do worse things'. Others seemed to accept them with some resignation and a few felt that some sanction on their behaviour was appropriate.

By and large those who had used them were not optimistic about their effect and, in most instances, they were quite limited in scope. Young people may be grounded, lose pocket money for the time they were away, be expected to go to bed early or miss organised trips. Some felt they had to be used selectively and that, where young people were at an early stage of their careers and had no other sources of income, legitimate or illegitimate, they could prove useful:

> You'll find that if you're sanctioning children too much then it spoils the effect of sanctions, because then they've nothing to lose.

Grounding was rarely viewed as a punishment *per se*, rather as an opportunity to offer immediate protection and some space for discussion with young people. However, where young people were determined to leave it was unlikely to prove effective, as one exasperated foster carer complained:

> Well, what have you got? You've only got a grounding and if you can't enforce the grounding, you've got absolutely nothing.

Some caregivers felt their powers were too limited and compared them unfavourably to those of birth parents. Short of locking the doors and staying in with young people, a strategy not available to children's homes and that usually appeared ineffective in foster homes, it was by no means clear what these alternatives might look like and how they might work. Most accepted that influencing change in young people depended upon longer term strategies based upon a stable placement experience and a strengthening relationship.

LONGER TERM STRATEGIES

By almost universal consent the key to working effectively with young people around going missing lay in the formation of close relationships based on trust and mutual respect. Relationships took time to form, sometimes were unachievable, and proved particularly difficult where young people's careers were unstable, involving successive placement moves, or where they were in short term residential or foster placements. Where it proved possible, attempts were made to divert young people through constructive activities or through attempts to resolve underlying difficulties that were influencing their behaviour. In some instances, where young people were regularly visiting friends or families, flexible negotiated solutions were sought. Alongside these initiatives, or where all else failed, emphasis was given to harm minimisation. Without wishing to paint a rosy picture, as successful outcomes were at best partial and often non-existent, these findings do point to positive steps that can be taken to bring about change.

Building Relationships and the Need for Staying Power

Given the lack of explicit controls to prevent young people going missing, a common perception amongst caregivers and social workers was that their principal leverage with young people lay in the formation of a close and trusting relationship, and that this outweighed the merits of any particular technique:

> It's about trust, it's about them having someone they can trust, someone they can depend on, rather than any specific technique to work with them. (residential worker)

Without this it was felt that their ability to influence change was severely curtailed. In virtually all the cases where some positive change had been achieved in young people's patterns of going missing, this had been an ingredient. The provision of a stable placement experience was an important precondition for attachment to grow over time although, in some instances, change had been effected through a move to an alternative placement where young people felt greater safety and security. Usually this had occurred where young people had been quite heavily implicated in high risk absences, involving offending or prostitution, and the need for separation from peer influences had coincided with the possibility of an alternative placement.

In the early stages of a placement, an intensive period of relationship building could form part of a preventive approach:

> We have to get better skills at engaging and building relationships with young people before they start to look at the alternatives. (residential worker)

Understanding young people as individuals, being aware of what made them 'tick', was considered important to devising appropriate structures of support. Without an emotional toehold, other forms of control were likely to be ineffective:

> If a young person is completely determined (to go missing) they will succeed, because short of being insecure you cannot hold them. If emotionally you've lost it, physical restraint, physical barriers . . . there's nothing you can do to stop them. (social worker)

Although a precondition for effective support, building a close relationship was rarely sufficient in itself and usually coincided with more direct forms of intervention. Where young people had extensive careers of going missing prior to being looked after, where going missing often had acted to destabilise the structure of their lives or where the influence of peer groups and weakened staff authority came together, it often had only a minimal influence over their careers.

Attempts to make young people's homes safe, secure and comfortable could help to assuage anxiety and provide greater security. Although more difficult to achieve in some children's homes, such an approach had been effective in enabling young people to settle and in limiting the absences of a few young people. One foster carer laid claim to an 'old fashioned' strategy that, as part of a package of support, had helped to turn around one young male with an extensive career of going missing:

> First of all I try to get him into a routine, and feed him . . . breakfast, dinner, tea, supper. Keep him clean . . . make him look nice. Build his confidence up. Get his hair cut. Buy him some new clothes. You know, 'cos it takes time.

Building relationships, offering stability, comfort and security and working on young people's sense of self-esteem could therefore provide time and space in which more underlying issues could be explored. Equally important for one young female was the continued reassurance from her foster carer and social worker that, despite her absences, her placement remained a secure home for her. The closeness of her relationship with her carer proved protective of further disruption.

Successful work with young people who went missing demanded considerable staying power. Caregivers had to be resourceful and resilient to cope with disruption to their routines and the levels of anxiety that young people's behaviour could cause. Where young people had lacked consistent care in the past, they would often anticipate rejection and severely test the patience of caregivers:

> There'll still be people who will test that out . . . (to) see how bothered they are and test out the rejection. See how many times they have to go missing before they'll be moved. (residential worker)

The following example provides a good illustration of the level of commitment that might be required to influence change in a young person with an extensive career of going missing in the context of a foster placement.

Paul (aged 12) came from a disorganised family that had a chaotic lifestyle and had known neither consistent care nor firm boundaries. He had gone missing from home for a few hours at a time as a release from pressure and to be with his friends. This pattern continued once looked after and several foster placements had broken down through running away. His career accelerated with his move to a children's home and he was involved in daily peer-based absences. His 18 months at his present foster placement had been his first experience of stability and, although he still stayed out occasionally with his friends, he no longer went missing regularly, nor for long periods. According to his social worker this change had been achieved through the consistent care and commitment shown by his carer. She was older and very experienced, having cared for troubled teenagers for 20 years. Her approach was to make her home safe, comfortable and secure for him, a place he would want to be. She quickly tried to establish a rapport and identify the kinds of responses that might work with him. She rarely scolded him for his absences, since he was unable to take criticism and this was likely to reinforce his behaviour. However, she demonstrated her commitment by searching for him at his usual haunts and bringing him home. She was flexible in her routines, was able to accept disruption and his testing out behaviour and strove to reassure him that this was his home. Together with his social worker, she attempted to separate him from his former peers. They approached his former unit and got agreement from them to refuse him entry. They had also persuaded him to return to school part-time in an effort to provide greater structure to his days.

The apparent vulnerability of foster placements to break down when young people go missing needs to be understood against the size of the task that is described here. The ability to be philosophical, maintain unconditional acceptance and tolerate disruption were attributes that Paul's social worker had rarely experienced in other placements:

> She'll deal with the episode and move on. But I think a lot of foster carers are not able to do that.

As we have suggested, foster placements seemed to operate best where young people presented few behavioural difficulties and where absences were a rare event. However, even where young people had not gone missing often, in two cases their placements appeared to be in some jeopardy. Lisa's absence to be with her mother was her first from her current placement. Although her social worker felt that, if reassured, they would stick with her this time, her concerns for the future were apparent:

> She hasn't broken a great deal or stolen or been using drugs or bringing trouble to the house . . . It's just this episode now that's causing a problem. So I think we can probably work it through providing the other behaviours don't come along with it.

These signs of fragility suggest that young people with more extensive careers are only likely to access foster placements in any numbers if moves towards a properly remunerated, professionalised fostering service for teenagers are extended. Some research evidence suggests that specialist fostering schemes for more challenging teenagers can have some success (Hazel 1981; Berridge 1997).

Diversion Strategies

Attempts were made to offer greater structure to young people's lives through involvement in a range of positive recreational activities. It was hoped that organised social activities would prove more attractive to young people than the dubious pleasures associated with going missing and would offer quality space for cementing relationships. Sometimes trips out were viewed as rewards for positive behaviour and formed part of basic behaviour modification programmes. Placements that were well structured, with a positive ethos linked to school attendance and appropriate behaviour standards, appeared to do somewhat better in this regard.

However, diversion strategies did not always work. Where they formed part of an early preventive approach or an immediate response to signs that young people were at risk of going missing, they were more likely to be successful. Where young people had established a pattern of going missing they were much less likely to work. If young people had access to money while away, through offending or prostitution, were strongly drawn to peer or street cultures or their absences were linked to unresolved problems they were experiencing within the placement, the attraction of other activities was often limited. This was also sometimes the case where the pull exerted on young people was to be with their families.

Where caregivers could organise quality individual time with young people it appeared to be helpful. This was less likely to happen in children's homes that were disorganised and affected by staff turnover and sickness. For example, one keyworker had plans to do this with one young male, but it had yet to come to fruition for these reasons. The social worker was aware of these constraints: 'So even though this plan is there in theory, putting it into practice is very hard.'

Staff in some children's homes had come to the conclusion that the emphasis on organised group trips was undesirable. A key problem for looked after young people was their tendency to stick together, a tendency reinforced by group activities. Damaging past experiences often lowered young people's self-image and left them lacking in confidence and could be reinforced by the stigma associated with being in 'care'. Staying together, while it could be positive, also tended to reinforce negative behaviours and limit opportunities for making new friends:

> They're not going to achieve anything (by) just going out *en bloc* every time they go out of the unit, 'cos they're going to stay together. They're not going to meet new friends.

In these placements concerted efforts were made to link young people in with outside activities and, in at least one children's home, identifying young people's needs and leisure interests had been formally built into the assessment process on entry. Strategies for promoting outside interests were then built into individual child care plans and progress could be monitored using the Looking After Children schedules (Parker et al 1991; Ward 1995).

Negotiated Approaches

Evidence from the main survey suggested that, where the absences of young people closely approximated the profile of the *family/friends* group, a more flexible, negotiated approach may help to lessen their need to go missing. These young people were likely to be older, from foster settings and to have gone missing less often in the past. Although tending to be away longer, their absences tended to be less problem focused, they were less likely to be involved in offending and more likely to return voluntarily. Although, as we have also seen from the survey, young people could be at equal risk on *any* occasion they went missing, these young people tended to be at less risk than those who fitted the *runaways* profile.

Evidence from the interview sample suggests that some caregivers and social workers were attempting to adopt this kind of approach with some teenagers. In a few instances it was enforced and in others was part of a proactive strategy to limit their absences and appeared to be having some success. Enforced flexibility tended to occur where young people had chosen to place themselves elsewhere and refused to conform to the requirements of a placement. In such circumstances, caregivers and social workers were often left with little choice but to negotiate and fulfil an arms-length protection role. However, some flexibility could also represent a more positive option.

In one children's home in particular, Jade, as part of the broader reorganisation of their work with young people that was earlier discussed in some depth, attempts were being made to adopt such an approach. The need for a more flexible response was leading them away from the Department's explicit policy that all young people who had not returned by midnight were to be reported missing. Instead, if older young people occasionally wanted to stay out late or stay with friends or family, provided this was agreed in advance, and staff were reasonably certain that they would be safe and that they could reach them, then this could be sanctioned. If these procedures were not followed or were abused, young people would be reported in the usual way.

For two of the young people in our sample, taking them and picking them up late at night from family or boyfriend, which the staff viewed as an appropriate parental role, had lessened their need to go missing. For a third, a 16 year old male wanting greater independence to be with family or friends, a negotiated approach had reduced the need to report him missing. Despite Neil having had an extensive career of going missing, much of which fitted a *runaways* profile, and continuing concerns about his involvement in offending, his growing maturity had enabled a different response from his keyworker:

> All I say to him is if you're going to stay out late, all you've got to do is give us a phone call. If you're not coming back to the unit just tell us where you're staying. I try and work it that way. Try and break down these barriers that come up.

Although this strategy involved calculated risks, could be stressful and did require reporting him on occasion, Neil's keyworker felt that, as the quality of relationship and trust between them grew, it was paying dividends. Neil was becoming more responsible, aware that he had choices he could make and more cooperative about informing staff of his movements. When he did test the boundaries of acceptable behaviour, his keyworker was now confident about stepping in to reinforce them. Neil's mother and sister, with whom he often stayed, had the home's number and would maintain contact and, if Neil wanted to stay with a friend, his keyworker would check through them if this would be safe for him.

In general terms, the bureaucratic procedures for approving overnight stays were felt to be a considerable barrier to this approach; young people often would not wait. Social workers, who had the ultimate authority, could take a week to complete these procedures and young people were often exposed to considerable embarrassment. In order to speed things up and undertake checks with greater sensitivity, staff were trying to visit themselves and report back to social workers.

In the context of children's homes, such a strategy requires a level of organisation and consensus not apparent in all placements. Staff routines need to be flexible to accommodate the needs of individual young people, firm leadership and consistency amongst the staff team are likely to be essential, as are negotiated agreements between staff and young people about the acceptable boundaries of behaviour. In Jade some problems remained. Not all staff were comfortable with this approach and not all operated it consistently. It does involve staff undertaking risk assessments and, as we have seen, there are few guarantees concerning the safety of young people while they are away. As a strategy, it clearly would not be appropriate for all young people who go missing, nor perhaps for the majority, but for some it may help to mitigate the risk of detachment that we have identified with going missing often. To offer staff greater protection, it perhaps needs to be more formalised, agreed with senior managers, communicated to social workers and families and written into local agreements between social services and the police as part of a more formal coordinated response to young people going missing.

Attempts to Resolve Underlying Difficulties

In Chapter 10 we saw that young people's motivations for going missing could be complex, multi-layered and shift over time. Whether the primary motivation lay in family problems, placement contexts or deeper personal difficulties related to past experiences, help to resolve young people's underlying problems proved difficult to organise effectively without a period of stability in which relationships could form. The destabilising effects of frequently going missing sometimes presented an insurmountable barrier. Young people might simply not be around to work with. Developing an appropriate response was also harder if no discernible reason could be identified for absences, as one frustrated foster carer explained:

> If there's a reason for him to do it, then you can work on that reason and you can sort it out, but when it's (because) he's just felt like it, and there's no reason for it, then you've got nothing to work with to change it.

Where young people's motivations were linked to rejection, separation from their families or concerns about parents who were unable to care for themselves, signs of successful longer term intervention appeared limited. Problems often proved irresolvable, some families refused cooperation and, as we have seen, could actively undermine attempts to support young people by manipulating their emotions or harbouring them when missing:

> What little bit of power she's got is through (her daughter) coming to her and her saying, 'Yeah, you can stay with me. At least I've got you for a while.' None of it surprises me. (social worker)

Attempts were made to structure visits to parents or receive them in children's homes but, especially where parents had problems with alcohol or drug misuse, these could be *ad hoc* and a failure to keep appointments could leave young people in greater distress. Even where such arrangements had some success, the desire of young people to be with their families often remained too strong.

Where, as in Neil's case, cooperation could be engendered, it could prove fruitful. Not least because even quite neglectful parents continued to exercise some moral authority over their children. Young people often felt that their parents were more likely to worry about them than their carers and were most concerned about their parents finding out about their absences. They did not want to worry them, were afraid it would confirm parental impressions of them and might worsen already shaky relationships. Persistent attempts to incorporate parents could bring rewards. In one case, a concerted joint effort by keyworker and social worker to plan regular visits to a mother, gain her cooperation in informing when her son arrived without permission and to reinforce consistent messages, had some effect in reducing the scale of his absences:

> When we've had contact with his mother we've had that as . . . a positive carrot, so he's not run away so much . . . and (he's) not stayed away overnight. Obviously he's still running away, but . . . he knows that if he stays away longer, he's worried about what his mum's reaction will be and whether . . . he will miss contact with her. (It's) an incentive to go back and at least try to toe the line a bit. (social worker)

For young people in children's homes whose absences were more context driven, attempts to separate them from the influence of their peers also met with varying degrees of success. Peer influence could be through coercion or enticement and, as we saw in Chapter 11, some homes were more successful than others at dealing with these problems. Many young people recognised the need to tackle bullying as part of a strategy to limit running away:

> If they sorted out the problems, then that would stop some of the running away. So if you're having problems or you're getting bullied and they stopped the bullying, then I don't think you'd run away. (young people's focus group)

Two children's homes identified in Chapter 11 had attempted to tackle these issues at a broad level, through changes to the ethos and organisation of the homes. In this context, both staff and young people were more able to agree codes of conduct and influence the behaviour of others positively. In children's homes that were more disorganised and with weaker staff authority, attempts to tackle placement difficulties such as bullying met with little success. Young people enticed or reluctantly drawn into peer-based absences were rarely protected effectively and their careers of going missing were at risk of escalation.

If caught early, attempts were made by keyworkers to separate young people from negative influences and could meet with some success. Where young people were reluctantly or marginally involved, quality time spent with staff or diversion through constructive activities helped. In some instances, young people were only able to settle through a change of placement or, in two cases of young females caught up in the fringes of prostitution, through those influencing them being sent to secure accommodation. Our findings, together with those of other recent studies (Farmer and Pollock 1997; Sinclair and Gibbs 1998), question the merits of mixing together in children's homes those with histories of offending or involvement in prostitution with other groups of vulnerable young people requiring protection. The influence of one upon the other is such that effective change is difficult to achieve.

Going missing could often form part of a cluster of problems that needed to be addressed in an integrated way.

Tiffany, aged 16, had been abandoned by her mother at an early age and raised in an emotionally cold environment provided by private foster carers. Her pain at rejection, reinforced by infrequent and hostile contact with her mother, led her to run away regularly. While away she had been raped and abused, was heavily involved in drugs, engaged in unprotected sexual encounters and self harmed. Over two years at her children's home, her growing attachment to staff enabled her gradually to appreciate their genuine concern for her safety: 'I know them better, I understand them.' Shouting made her withdraw, so a core group of staff planned a consistent calm response, despite the worry her absences caused. Gradually they persuaded her to give up drugs and her social worker arranged a counselling group linked to self-harming behaviour which gave her more confidence to discuss her feelings. The commitment shown to her over time lessened her fears of further rejection, increased her self-esteem and, at the time we interviewed her, she had not been missing for six months.

Despite similar strategies being tried with other young people, such successes were rare. Longer term strategic approaches were less likely to work where young people's careers of going missing had become entrenched unless, like Tiffany, young people themselves recognised the need for change. Even where some resolution had been achieved, other pull factors, such as the excitement of being out with friends, could still be seductive. They were certainly unlikely to work where caregivers and social workers had become demoralised and pessimistic about the possibility of stimulating change, a perception that was sadly quite common and, as we have seen, often linked to a lack of options and specialist resources to help them in their work.

Some caregivers and social workers clearly felt out of their depth, lacking the skills and knowledge to meet the often complex needs of young people. This was particularly evident where young people exhibited behaviour that was quite deeply disturbing or where they were heavily involved in offending or prostitution as part of going missing. Fear of entering this ground could lead to paralysis, as was the case with one badly abused male who was also an abuser. Everyone agreed his placement in a children's home was wrong for all concerned and, although he had been there six months, his social worker had been unable to access therapeutic help or an alternative placement. His keyworker was nervous about intervening: 'I think if it's handled wrong it could make the situation worse.' Yet, in effect, fear of making things worse meant that this young person was drifting and his pattern of going missing deteriorating. No plans were in place to tackle this aspect of his behaviour, as his social worker's comment made clear:

We don't tend to plan around that. We don't make provisions, we don't . . . have a strategy for dealing with (going missing).

Harm Minimisation

Alongside these other strategies, or where all else had failed, caregivers and social workers offered advice and support aimed at minimising the harm to which young people might be exposed. Considerable effort was devoted to reasoning with young people about the risks associated with going missing and, prior to them leaving, attempts made to get them to tell where they were going, leave phone numbers or ring if they were going to be late back. Where possible, some caregivers would pick up young people or arrangements could be made in advance for a taxi back late at night. As we have seen, when allied to other strategies, such measures could bring about gradual change and reduce the need to report young people missing. However, when other measures were absent or had failed, it could leave young people in control of high risk patterns of behaviour and practitioners floundering in their wake as they attempted to obtain the names and addresses of contacts with whom they were involved:

> We're trying to go where (he) leads us and trying to keep it as safe as possible. You know he is going to doss around. Let's know about these people, let's at least check them out, because he's going to go there whether we say no or yes to them. (social worker)

As we have seen, broader health issues were another major concern, especially where young people were at risk of sexual exploitation, including prostitution. Advice about safe sex and substance misuse and the provision of condoms were not uncommon and, upon return, appointments arranged at doctors, dentists or clinics. Where young people were missing less frequently or prepared to cooperate with this type of assistance, while it may not have reduced their absences or the immediate risks of such encounters, could be vital to the promotion of their longer term health. However, going missing often could result in the breakdown of even the most basic health care.

The Benefits of Joint Working

It is perhaps not surprising that most of the examples of positive practice that have been described in this chapter have involved quite close collaboration between caregivers, social workers, young people and, where possible, parents. Accumulated research on residential and foster care tends to suggest that working in partnership can have a beneficial effect on the duration of placements and the ability of young people to settle within them (Millham et al 1986; Berridge and Cleaver 1987; Triseliotis et al 1995b). The close involvement of social workers was appreciated by young people and caregivers. It offered an independent ear external to the placement and the possibility for mediation and advocacy on behalf of the young person in relation to placement or family. For foster carers, in particular, it could help to assuage their sense of isolation and responsibility when confronted by, at times, quite seriously challenging behaviour. It could prove protective of further placement disruption and, when plans and strategies were jointly drawn up as part of the child care planning and review cycle, with a clear division of roles and tasks, give a greater focus to the work of all parties. Where relationships were positive, it could have a galvanising effect and young people clearly valued time spent with social workers and their attempts to repair or improve relationships with their families.

Where social workers were distant, perhaps engaged only in a case management role, levels of satisfaction dipped sharply. As we have seen, responses to young people going missing could become muted or non-existent and some caregivers and parents became intensely frustrated at this lack of support. In relation to going missing, a few social workers appeared to have abdicated all responsibility:

> I don't do anything about it. They deal with the day to day care. The (unit) phones the police. The (unit) are the ones who will discuss it with her in depth when she comes back.

For a number of young people in the sample, a lack of clear planning and of a strategic response to their careers of going missing appeared to be hastening their decline. They seemed to be held in a kind of limbo and, as their detachment increased, the chances of successful intervention at a later point was diminishing.

SUMMARY

Preventing absences: A pervasive sense of powerlessness about how to prevent young people going missing was apparent amongst caregivers and social workers and, in consequence, their morale and confidence was often affected. Loss of confidence in the ability to intervene, however difficult, ran the risk of young people's careers escalating and making later intervention yet more difficult. Where children's homes were well organised, with strong leadership allied to the creation of positive staff and peer cultures, there was some evidence that this could raise staff morale and strengthen their belief in their ability to influence young people's behaviour and intervene when necessary to protect them.

Responses while missing: Beyond reporting young people missing, more direct efforts were sometimes made to trace them. However, where absences were accepted as inevitable, responses could be muted. These efforts were generally appreciated by young people as evidence of genuine concern, even if they resented it at the time, and such demonstrations of care could help to cement relationships and provide greater leverage for longer term change.

Responses upon return: A warm welcome was generally viewed as a positive response. Although some young people were unconcerned either way, most felt it showed concern and, if their absences were problem linked, patient questioning could lead to a resolution. Attempts to follow up absences were often difficult if young people were reluctant to tell. Punitive responses were likely to reinforce negative patterns of behaviour. As a safeguard for young people's welfare, the option to speak to someone independent of the placement was important. The role of social workers and the police in this respect was variable and it may be that, for some young people, access to a voluntary agency, children's rights officer or independent visitor may be more appropriate.

Sanctions: Views on sanctions were mixed. Some placements had policies not to employ them, viewing them as counterproductive. Some others felt that, if used selectively, they could prove effective for those at an early point in their careers. Overall there was little evidence that they worked for many young people. Most practitioners placed their faith in longer term strategies for change based on a stable placement experience and a strengthening relationship.

Building relationships: Given the lack of explicit controls, a strong consensus existed that a growing attachment based on mutual trust and respect represented the best chance for influencing change. In virtually all the cases where some positive change had been achieved in young people's patterns of going missing – and these were often marginal – this had been an ingredient. Placement security was important, although for a few young people greater security had only been achieved through a change of placement. Attempts to engage young people in the early phase of a placement formed part of a preventive strategy.

To achieve long term change, caregivers needed considerable staying power. They often had to be resourceful, sufficiently flexible to cope with disruptions to their routines and be able to maintain acceptance of young people in the face of quite challenging behaviour. These demands proved beyond the resources of most ordinary foster placements. Positive relationships in themselves were, however, rarely sufficient and were more helpful when allied to other strategies.

Diversion strategies: Attempts to provide greater structure to young people's lives through involvement in positive activities were helpful, as was the quality time that caregivers could spend with young people. These strategies were more likely to be successful in placements that were well organised and where they formed part of a preventive approach, linked to assessment and child care planning, or an immediate response to signs of young people going missing.

Negotiated approaches: Some attempts were being made to adopt a more flexible negotiated approach to older teenagers where the risks associated with their absences appeared low. In some instances this was enforced, usually when young people placed themselves elsewhere and there was little choice other than to negotiate a compromise; in others it represented a more positive option. Where young people were regularly visiting family or friends, attempts to informally assess risks and agree acceptable boundaries had some success in reducing their need to go missing. For such a strategy to work, children's homes needed a level of organisation and consensus not apparent in all placements and caregivers had to engage in the cautious management of risk.

Resolving underlying difficulties: Although young people's relationships with parents were often poor, wherever it proved possible, especially for those whose absences were linked to family problems, a partnership approach that incorporated parents brought some rewards. For those young people whose absences were linked to placement difficulties, attempts to resolve these could reduce patterns of going missing. Separating young people from negative peer influences, if attempted early in their careers, could be helped through diversion strategies. For others, however, improvements only came through a placement change or the removal of young people who were influencing them. Where children's homes were disorganised there were few signs of success in this area. For those young people where going missing formed part of a cluster of problems, coordinated efforts to tackle these over time in a holistic way had some success.

Longer term strategies were generally less successful where patterns of going missing were entrenched, where practitioners had themselves become pessimistic about the possibilities for change or where specialist resources were not available to help their work.

Harm minimisation: Alongside other strategies, or where all else had failed, support was offered to minimise the harm to which young people were exposing themselves. When allied to other strategies this could help to bring about change, but where other measures were absent or had failed it could leave young people in control of high risk behaviours.

However, even in these circumstances, harm minimisation could prove important to the protection of their longer term health.

Joint working: Most examples of positive practice in this study involved close collaboration between caregivers, young people, social workers and, wherever possible, families. The close involvement of social workers tended to be valued by caregivers and young people and could provide an enhanced focus to the work of all parties. Where social workers were distant, levels of satisfaction dipped sharply. For a number of young people in the sample, a lack of clear planning and of a strategic response to their careers of going missing appeared to be hastening their decline.

15

CONCLUSION

Going missing from residential and foster care not only puts many young people at risk but also raises wider questions about services for children looked after by local authorities. Consideration of why, and in what circumstances, young people go missing also leads us into important debates concerning the care system: how far is behaviour determined by the care contexts in which young people are placed and how far is it shaped by young people's individual biographies and wider social networks? How far are interventions by individual professionals and by agencies able to bring about positive outcomes for young people and in what circumstances might they compound the problems that young people bring with them into care settings?

This study set out to understand the extent and nature of going missing from care placements and found that going missing from residential care is a widespread phenomenon. There were marked variations between authorities, ranging from 25% to 71%, in the proportions of young people in community homes who went missing during the course of a year. There were also variations between homes in the number of residents going missing. Going missing from foster care appeared to be less common, but its true extent was difficult to measure due to a lack of central monitoring by local authorities. These variations suggest that agency and placement contexts have a bearing on going missing, and this raises questions about the ways in which local agencies deliver services. A care system which fails to prevent so many young people going missing, and often putting themselves at considerable risk, is clearly not succeeding in its task of caring for and protecting them.

DIVERSITY

Young people who go missing are, however, a heterogeneous group, diverse in terms of individual characteristics, patterns of going missing and motivations for doing so. Although the majority in our surveys were in the 13–15 age group, a sixth were only 12 years or under and particularly vulnerable in view of their age. Females appeared to be as likely to go missing as males, although the females in our main survey tended to be older. Contrary to other studies, we found that black young people were no more likely to go missing than others and that, in one authority, the high number of black young people going missing was due to their over-representation among looked after children, which was particularly acute in residential care. Black young people did not go missing in different circumstances or for different reasons, except that for them bullying sometimes had the added dimension of racist abuse. Young people with emotional and behavioural difficulties were a substantial minority, accounting for around a sixth of the young people in our survey. For this group patterns were particularly extreme: they had gone missing more often, were more likely to have been excluded from school, were more likely to have previous convictions for criminal offences and were clearly at high risk of detachment.

Patterns of going missing were also diverse. Some absences involved young people going missing to be with friends or family, the vast majority with friends, while in other incidents young people were running away or staying out. Those in the *friends* group were likely to be older and were more likely to be in foster placements. Although they tended to stay away longer, they were more likely to return voluntarily. The young people in the *runaways* group were likely to be younger and were more likely to be in residential care. They tended to stay away for a shorter time but were more likely to sleep rough while away and were less likely to return voluntarily. They were also more likely to commit offences while missing and to have gone missing more often in the past than those in the *friends* group.

BIOGRAPHIES AND CONTEXTS

Young people's motivations for going missing derived both from their individual histories and from the care context in which they found themselves. Not surprisingly, histories of abuse, rejection and neglect continued to trouble the young people we interviewed and for some these functioned as underlying reasons for going missing. Also, half had previously run away from home and, where this had become an established pattern, it could be reinforced rather than weakened once they were accommodated. For those looked after, relationships outside placements, including family, friends and other associates, could operate as 'pull' factors motivating them directly or indirectly to go missing. For many young people, therefore, motivations for going missing were rooted in individual histories and in social relations outside placements. However, in most cases these did not provide the sole explanation for why young people went missing but were articulated with factors deriving from the placements in which they found themselves or their overall experience of being looked after.

Within placements, a number of factors were at play. First, peer influences were important, as young people were often enticed or coerced into going missing. Coercion could involve the bullying and intimidation of younger or otherwise more vulnerable young people, who sometimes went on to coerce others. Second, young people often felt unsettled or insecure in placements, especially if they had been there only a short time or had had several previous placement moves, and this made it difficult for them to develop attachments to caregivers. The rapid turnover of young people passing through units and, in particular, the intrinsically unsettled nature of short stay units, contributed to this.

Third, a general lack of confidence and sense of disempowerment among residential staff was also influential. We found that in those children's homes which appeared to be dealing more successfully with going missing, heads of homes gave clear leadership regarding the way in which staff should work with residents, there was a reasonable consensus among staff as to how to carry out their tasks and staff morale was relatively high. Staff felt reasonably confident in setting clear expectations for young people's behaviour, which contributed to a reduction in bullying, the promotion of a more positive peer culture among residents and a focused, individualised response to young people who went missing. Where children's homes were more disorganised and going missing was more frequent, staff authority tended to weaken. In these circumstances, negative peer cultures, including going missing, were able to flourish.

In relation to foster placements, we found that positive change in patterns of going missing was more likely where foster carers were highly experienced and fairly confident about their role and where they were prepared to persist in working with young people exhibiting difficult behaviour. Direct involvement by social workers, working closely to support foster carers in their task, was an ingredient of success.

While underlying reasons for going missing may need to be addressed through skilled intervention at the level of the individual, motivations that are placement centred call for attention to the placement and agency contexts in which they arise. The limited availability of well supported and adequately funded foster placements for teenagers needs to be addressed at agency level. Equally, the organisation and cultures of children's homes, which may permit or reinforce going missing, require a response at both placement and agency levels.

THE IMPLICATIONS OF GOING MISSING OFTEN

Going missing often was associated with a growing risk of detachment from some of the main centres of adult authority for teenagers. Those with more extensive careers of going missing tended to have had less settled care careers, were less likely to be attending school and were more likely to have involvement in offending and substance misuse. Once this pattern became established, opportunities for caregivers, social workers, teachers or youth justice workers to engage young people and respond to difficulties they were experiencing tended to lessen. Where these elements came together to destabilise young people's lives, the risks of longer term detachment were most acute.

However, some young people appeared to be at greater risk of detachment than others. Those whose absences closely approximated a *runaways* profile seemed at greater risk than those whose absences followed the contours of a *friends* profile. In addition, where young people had established a pattern of going missing from the family home and where this was associated with a growing detachment at that stage, it was more likely that these patterns would continue to be played out in a care setting.

THE COMPLEXITIES OF MANAGING RISK

Managing risk is inherent to social work practice and presents considerable challenges to those working with teenagers, with whom negotiation and compromise are likely to be the order of the day. Balancing young people's need for exploration *as teenagers* with the provision of a secure base and firm boundaries to guide their behaviour is likely to require some finesse.

The management of risk for young people who go missing is surrounded by doubt and uncertainty for a number of reasons. First, knowledge about the risks associated with young people's absences proved difficult to obtain in many cases, even after the event, and suggested that attempts to predict risk at the time young people went missing would pose genuine problems for practitioners. Second, we failed to identify a link between going missing often and absences necessarily becoming riskier or more protracted. In other words, there was no survey evidence to support the idea of a progression in which each successive absence involves greater risk. The absence of such a link suggested that young people may be equally at risk at any time they go missing and that, in consequence, similar levels of concern should be shown to all young people whenever they go missing, whether it be on the first or twenty-first occasion.

Evidence from the interview sample enabled greater depth and complexity to be given to these findings. When young people's careers of going missing were viewed over time, it was apparent that what mattered when considering risks was not how many times young people had gone missing but what they did while they were away. Not all young people's absences involved similar levels of risk, regardless of how many times they had gone missing. Some young people tended to do the same things each time they went missing, for example visiting the same family members or friends, while for others, patterns degenerated or improved over time in response to changes in their lives.

Those young people whose absences tended to fit a *runaway* profile appeared to be at greater immediate and long term risk when compared to those whose absences fitted a *friends/family* profile. They tended to be younger, their absences were often more problem focused, they were more likely to offend and sleep rough and appeared to be at greater risk of detachment. Therefore, while caution should be exercised in relation to all absences, and lessening concern for those missing frequently is not justified, the assessment and management of risk needs to be grounded in a thorough knowledge of the young person. Although it is likely to remain an uncertain process, given the tendency for some young people to engage in different types of absence on different occasions, careful assessment of young people's past histories of going missing, their motivations for it, the types of places they go and the people they are in contact with, should help practitioners to gauge risks and appropriate responses with greater certainty. It is in this context that careful follow-up with young people once they return assumes such importance for their future protection.

Some calculated risks were being taken informally. Reporting procedures did vary according to the age and known vulnerability of young people and some attempts were being made to adopt a more flexible approach to older teenagers where the perceived risks associated with their absences seemed low. Local protocols between social services, the police and other agencies aimed at developing a coordinated response are also likely to require social services staff to grapple with this area. The advantage of agreements that clarify definitions and reporting procedures linked to appropriate levels of response is that, at a minimum, they can provide staff attempting to exercise some discretion with greater protection. Perhaps more importantly, they can help to provide a framework within which a greater consistency of response can be achieved, one that takes account of limited risk taking as a developmental phase, and that is likely to be beneficial to all young people

who go missing. Whether amongst the police or social services personnel, the tendency for responses to become muted when faced with persistent patterns of going missing represents a serious danger to the
well-being of young people.

POLICIES, PROCEDURES, RECORDING AND MONITORING

More effective management of risk also depends upon coherent social
services department policies and procedures that are clearly communicated to caregivers, social workers and young people. Written guidance
to all those likely to be affected, including foster carers and placement
providers in the independent sector, should include a detailed outline of
reporting procedures and the circumstances in which particular steps
should be taken. However, guidance should also embrace broader advice,
based on sound child care principles, about how to manage unauthorised
absences and the processes associated with return. Uncertainty in these
areas was not uncommon amongst practitioners. Variations within and
between the authorities in this study suggest that considerably more
work needs to be done to meet the requirements of the Children Act in
this respect.

Children's homes are required by statute to keep an accurate record of
unauthorised absences by all those resident and, from our observations,
these are likely to be the only accurate records that are kept. Foster carers
rarely recorded absences and the records of social workers were distinctly
hit and miss. The movement of young people in and out of care and
between residential and foster placements suggests that, unless accurate
records are maintained in the case files of social workers in a form that
makes later retrieval easy, information important to the future protection
and support of young people is likely to be lost. The importance of a
clearly ordered factual history that includes the reasons for absences, the
risks associated and the kinds of responses attempted has been highlighted by the review of the West case (Bridge Child Care Development
Service 1996).

Accurate records are also a precondition for monitoring patterns of
unauthorised absence across authorities. None of the authorities attempted to monitor patterns and, as a result, they had no grasp of the
scale of the problem nor of where pockets of high absence existed. Without such information it is difficult to see how strategic planning can take
place and, given that high rates of running away from particular children's homes could be indicative of quite serious problems, how

management-led strategies to resolve those problems could be implemented. Regular monitoring of absences from all types of placement should therefore be undertaken. This will require information to be centrally collated and made subject to review at senior level through regular joint meetings between social services, the police and voluntary agencies working with runaways. In addition, an assessment of patterns of absence should be included in the inspection procedures of the Home Office and Social Services Inspectorates.

INTER-AGENCY WORKING

The need for improved collaboration between agencies has been identified throughout this report. Apart from the need for joint strategies between social services, the police and voluntary agencies when young people do go missing, services for looked after children would benefit from improved coordination at a corporate level.

The links between going missing and school non-attendance marks this as an important area. The delays identified in referral and assessment procedures for those young people excluded from or refusing to attend mainstream school meant that young people could be out of school for very long periods and, even when a return was attempted, this was often part-time. Without a clear structure to their days, the attractions of going missing to relieve boredom were enhanced. Although these problems were in part resource driven, improved communication and joint planning between social services and education departments to meet the needs of this population more effectively could not only have a beneficial effect on their tendency to go missing but also prove crucial to their later transition to adulthood.

The strength of the relationship between going missing often and offending points to the need for more imaginative strategies to prevent or limit offending behaviour. There was little evidence of direct work being undertaken with young people in this area and, although such work was impeded where young people were rarely around, a more proactive approach is needed. The development of partnership approaches with other agencies – including the police, education, the youth service and voluntary agencies – are likely to be necessary and attempts to tackle offending may also help to reduce going missing.

Finally, difficulties have been identified in the provision of specialist therapeutic help to back up work being undertaken by caregivers and social workers. Some practitioners were uncertain what resources existed locally or whether they would be appropriate for young people. Differences in timescale between health and social service agencies in relation to assessment and the provision of a service often led to long delays, even for young people whose behaviour seemed seriously disturbed. Lack of action impeded planning and, in some cases, promoted drift. Some thought also needs to be given to how therapeutic services might be delivered more flexibly. Young people's lifestyles often made hospital or clinic attendance erratic and some rejected the limited options available. Perhaps closer collaboration that facilitates the integration of specialist help with that provided daily by caregivers could provide a more informal service to which young people would feel less resistant.

Given what we know about the implications of going missing often for young people's lives, the development of a more effective corporate approach to meeting young people's broader needs is likely to be most helpful when it is structured as part of a preventive programme of support.

THE IMPORTANCE OF PREVENTION

Services directed at preventing young people going missing need to address two populations – those resident in the family home and those entering substitute care. Half of the young people in this study had first gone missing from the family home and, where their careers were linked to a pattern of increasing detachment at this stage, there was a greater likelihood that once looked after these careers would continue unchecked. The vast majority were, initially at least, escaping difficulties they were experiencing in the family home and therefore constituted part of the population of children in need. Preventive services to teenagers and their families have been relatively neglected in the past and it is to be hoped that the requirement to include services for young runaways in children's services plans will lead to greater attention being given to this area. The stakes are high given that the factors associated with going missing often can only further destabilise young people's lives.

Once looked after, attention to the risk of going missing needs to be integrally linked to the child care planning and review cycle. The 'Looking After Children' Assessment and Action Records provide a basis for monitoring and reviewing the individual progress of young people in relation to broad areas of their welfare and development. Most of these dimensions – for example, behaviour, health, family, education, offending – influence and are influenced by going missing. Careful assessment and positive action in these areas is therefore likely to be helpful in developing a preventive approach with young people. While going missing is likely to be associated with poor outcomes across these dimensions, strategies designed to meet these needs in an integrated way are likely to prove protective.

RESPONSES TO GOING MISSING

There can be no simple prescriptions about how to respond once a young person has gone missing. The identification of appropriate strategies needs to be rooted in an understanding of them as individuals, their motivations for going missing and the patterns associated with their absences. The foundation for longer term intervention rests on providing young people with a stable experience in which relationships and attachments have an opportunity to grow. Without an emotional bond, it was evident that other more explicit forms of control were less likely to be effective. Where young people had established a pattern of going missing repeatedly, stability and attachment were more difficult to achieve. In these circumstances, bringing about longer term change required a considerable degree of staying power on the part of caregivers to cope with the level of disruption going missing could cause and this often proved beyond the resources of many ordinary foster placements.

The evidence from this study highlights the importance of an early response. Once a pattern of going missing becomes established, opportunities for intervention are likely to become more remote. As we have seen, going missing may already form part of a repertoire of responses to the pain and problems in a young person's life prior to being looked after. Where this is the case, solutions are likely to be found only in the longer term. Young people need to be offered a warm welcome upon return. Patient and sensitive follow-up, involving someone independent of the placement, can help to identify problems that may underpin absences. While such an approach can help to cement relationships and identify areas for work, it is unlikely to be sufficient unless more specific strategies to support young people are properly planned and coordinated. This was less likely to happen when caregivers or social workers felt overpowered by the scale of unauthorised absences and pessimistic about the possibility of bringing about change.

Where young people are at an early point in their careers of going missing or are more reluctantly involved, quality time spent with caregivers and social workers can facilitate the identification of needs and interests and provide a basis for diversion strategies. When addressed holistically as part of a wider planning to meet their needs, involvement in constructive educational and leisure activities, preferably outside of the placement, may prove helpful. It not only helps to give structure to their days but provides opportunities to meet new friends and may limit the influence of more negative peers.

Attempts to resolve underlying difficulties that have a bearing on young people's absences require longer term strategies. Especially, though not exclusively, for those whose pattern of going missing is linked to family problems, working in partnership with parents, incorporating them in the attempt to find solutions, can bring rewards. Although our findings were not very optimistic in this regard, as young people's relationships with parents were often poor and families seemed as likely to undermine as support the strategies of practitioners, where it did prove possible it did help to bring about some positive change. Another central issue for young people was the effects of bullying in children's homes. Bullying could lead young people to seek individual escape or involvement in peer-led absences in the attempt to find acceptance. Offering young people protection requires these issues to be tackled directly. Where this happened it often had a beneficial effect on their need to go missing.

The diversity we have identified amongst young people who go missing points to the need for differentiated responses to sub-groups within that population. For those whose absences closely fit a *friends/family* profile, mostly older teenagers spending lower risk time away with family or friends, a flexible negotiated response may lessen their need to go missing. To work successfully staff routines need to be flexible, since it may involve collecting young people at night. Informal checks on where young people go and who with are likely to be necessary and cooperation sought from them. A negotiated consensus between staff and young people that clearly delineates the boundaries of acceptable conduct will also be essential for such an approach to work. Finally, caregivers will inevitably enter the difficult terrain of risk assessment. However, given the longer term risks associated with going missing often, initiatives that can help to diminish unauthorised absences may be more protective in the long run.

Where patterns of going missing have become more entrenched, especially where they involve high risks, for example through involvement in prostitution or persistent offending, intensive and structured support will be necessary. While not very evident in this study, procedures consistent with a child protection approach are required. The organisation of case conferences that draw together the views of all parties can provide a forum in which a coherent way forward can be identified and roles and responsibilities allocated. If extreme risks are involved to self or others, quite radical steps may need to be taken in order to protect the young person and others whom they may influence. For a number of young people in our sample, some remission was only achieved through a move to a new placement or the removal of young people who had been exposing them to danger.

Having said all this, the signs of positive change for young people in this study were at best partial. Working with troubled and troublesome teenagers presents practitioners with genuine difficulties and, unless young people recognise that they are in difficulty and accept the need for change, negotiated solutions are likely to be hard to achieve.

PROVISION FOR LOOKED AFTER CHILDREN

The raising of the threshold for entry to care as a result of changes in child care policy over the last 20 years means that today those who are looked after are likely to have more severe difficulties than their predecessors. Residential placements, in particular, contain a greater concentration of children with long histories of abuse or neglect who have serious behaviour problems. At the same time, the contraction in the residential sector and the limited development of foster placements for teenagers has led to a reduction in placement choice, so that placement matching is often out of the question.

The accommodation of young people with serious behaviour problems in mainstream children's homes can cause serious control problems for staff. Ordinary community homes are now catering for some young people who only a decade ago might have been accommodated in more structured institutions with education on the premises, and the mix of young people in these homes may cause problems for those who do not already have an established pattern of going missing, non-attendance at school or offending. Young people in inappropriate placements may be unhappy or out of control, both of which make going missing more likely. The trend towards short term admissions can also make children's homes very unsettled places, making it harder for staff to engage young people.

In this context, some thought needs to be given to the development of a locally integrated service providing a range of placement options to meet the differing needs of individuals. Within this framework small, well managed children's homes operating to a clear brief would be available to work with those young people for whom foster placements are as yet unavailable or thought inappropriate. Some of this provision would either need to be specialist in nature, providing therapeutic help to young people with underlying difficulties arising from past experiences of abuse, rejection or neglect, or need to be able to draw upon outside specialists who could work alongside staff to provide this service. This strategy should also include provision for a well resourced and supported professional fostering service, with foster carers adequately trained in working with challenging teenagers. Without such a service, young people who go missing will continue to be denied access to substitute family care.

For those young people at high risk, through involvement in prostitution or persistent offending, separation from local networks may need to be considered both in order to protect them and to limit their potential impact on others. However, out-of-authority placements are not only expensive but can bring other problems, including reduced family contact. Where specialist outside placements are used, this needs to take place within the framework of an approach that links work in placement to work on the family and community environment to which the young person will eventually return.

The planning and coordination role undertaken by social workers is vital to the development of an effective response to going missing. Where child care planning was effective, it helped to prevent drift, sharpen responses and clarify the roles and responsibilities of all those involved. However, when planning and coordination become the social worker's principal task, as in the case management model, the concomitant reduction in direct work with looked after young people may make it harder for social workers to achieve a holistic understanding of their needs. This approach can also deprive looked after young people of the safeguard of having a familiar and trusted professional outside the placement with whom they can share concerns about the care they receive. It may also leave prime carers of children feeling insufficiently supported. Although the movement towards a case management model is in part linked to resource issues and in part to the separation of purchasers and providers in child care services, the implications of these developments for the practical support of young people is likely to need further thought.

In overall terms, this study has highlighted the diverse needs, motivations and behaviours associated with young people who go missing and the genuine difficulties this can present to practitioners charged with responsibility for their care. We have suggested that effective work with young people at risk of going missing needs to be situated along the spectrum of services provided to teenagers. These include the provision of preventive services both prior to and during the time young people are looked after, the provision of high quality accommodation options suited to young people's needs and, finally, a well coordinated inter-agency response to young people when they do go missing. While negotiation and compromise are always necessary in work with teenagers, young people need a secure and protective base from which they can explore the world in some safety. In this context, a failure to manage risk effectively is likely to have damaging consequences both for young people themselves and, in some circumstances, for wider society.

BIBLIOGRAPHY

Abrahams C and Mungall R (1992) *Runaways: Exploding the Myths*. NCH, London.

Ackland JW (1981) Institutional Reactions to Absconding. *British Journal of Social Work* 11: 171–87.

Aldgate J, Heath A, Colton M and Simm M (1993) Social work and the education of children in foster care. *Adoption and Fostering* 17(3): 25–34.

Association of Directors of Social Services (1996) *The Foster Care Market: A National Perspective*. ADSS, Bury St Edmunds.

Audit Commission (1994) *Seen But Not Heard*. HMSO, London.

Audit Commission (1996) *Misspent Youth, Young People and Crime*. Audit Commission Publications, Abingdon.

Barn R (1993) *Black Children in the Public Care System*. Batsford/BAAF, London.

Barn R, Sinclair R and Ferdinand D (1997) *Acting on Principle – an examination of race and ethnicity in social services provision for children and families*. BAAF, London.

Barter C (1996) *Nowhere to Hide: Giving Young Runaways a Voice*. Centrepoint/NSPCC, London.

Barter C, Keep G and Macleod M (1996) *Children at Crisis Point*. Childline, London.

Bebbington A and Miles J (1989) The background of children who enter local authority care. *British Journal of Social Work* 19: 349–68.

Bebbington A and Miles J (1990) The supply of foster families for children in care. *British Journal of Social Work* 20: 283–307.

Becker H (1967) Whose side are we on? *Social Problems* 14: 239–47.

Berridge D (1994) Foster and residential care reassessed: a research perspective. *Children and Society* 8: 132–50.

Berridge D (1997) *Foster Care: A Research Review*. HMSO, London.

Berridge D and Brodie I (1998) *Children's Homes Revisited*. Jessica Kingsley, London.

Berridge D and Cleaver H (1987) *Foster Home Breakdown*. Blackwell, Oxford.

Biehal N, Clayden J, Stein M and Wade J (1995) *Moving On: Young People and Leaving Care Schemes*. HMSO, London.

Blaug R (1995) Distortion of the face to face: Communicative reason and social work practice. *British Journal of Social Work* 25: 423–39.

Bourne J, Bridges L and Searle C (1994) *Outcast England: How Schools Exclude Black Children*. Institute for Race Relations, London.

Brennan T (1980) Mapping the diversity among runaways. *Journal of Family Issues* 1: 189–209.

Brennan T, Huizinga D and Elliott DS (1978) *Social Psychology of Runaways*. Lexington Books, Lexington, Massachusetts.

Bridge Child Care Development Service (1996) *In Care Contacts: The West Case*. Bridge Child Care Development Service/Gloucestershire County Council, London.

Brierley H and Jones HD (unpublished) *The absconding problem*. Report to Home Office.

Broad B (1994) *Leaving Care in the 1990s*. Royal Philanthropic Society, Westerham.

Brodie I and Berridge D (1996) *Exclusion from School: Research Themes and Issues*. University of Luton Press, Luton.

Brown E, Bullock R, Hobson C and Little M (1998) *Making Residential Care Work: Structure and Culture in Children's Homes*. Ashgate, Aldershot.

Bryman and Cramer D (1990) *Quantitative Data Analysis for Social Scientists*. Routledge, London.

Bullock R (1997) What we know from previous studies. *Young Runaways: Report of a National Seminar*. Dartington Social Research Unit.

Bullock R, Little M and Millham S (1993) *Residential Care for Children. A Review of the Research*. HMSO, London.

Cawson P (1987) The sexist social worker? Some gender issues in social work practice with adolescent girls. *Practice* 1: 39–52.

Clarke R and Martin D (1971) *Absconding from Approved Schools*. Home Office Research Study, Number 12, HMSO.

Cliffe D and Berridge D (1991) *Closing Children's Homes: an End to Residential Childcare?* National Children's Bureau, London.

Coffield F and Gofton L (1994) *Drugs and Young People*. IPPR, London.

Cohen E, Mackenzie RG and Yates GI (1991) HEADSS A psychosocial risk assessment instrument: implications for designing effective intervention programs for runaway youth. *Journal of Adolescent Health* 12: 539–44.

Cohen P (1997) *Rethinking the Youth Question. Education, Labour and Cultural Studies*. Macmillan, London.

Coleman JC (1997) The parenting of adolescents in Britain today. *Children and Society* 2: 44–52.

Cook R (1994) Are we helping foster care youth prepare for their future? *Children and Youth Services Review* 16: 213–29.

Davies M and Sinclair I (1971) Families, hostels and delinquents: an attempt to assess cause and effect. *British Journal of Criminology* 11: 213–29.

Denzin N (1970) *The Research Act in Sociology*. Aldine, Chicago.

Department for Education and Employment (1996) *Permanent Exclusions 1994–95 by Ethnicity*. Hansard 21 November 1996.

Department of Health (1985) *Social Work Decisions in Child Care*. HMSO, London.

Department of Health (1991a) *Children in Care of Local Authorities Year ending 31 March 1988*. Government Statistical Service.

Department of Health (Utting Report) (1991b) *Children in the Public Care: a Review of Residential Child Care*. Social Services Inspectorate, HMSO, London.

Department of Health (1991c) *The Children Act 1989 Guidance and Regulations Volume 4 Residential Care*. HMSO, London.

Department of Health (1991d) *Children's Homes Regulations 1991*. Statutory Instrument 1506.

Department of Health (1993) *Guidance on Permissible Forms of Control in Children's Residential Care*. Local Authority Circular LAC(93)13 Department of Health, London.

Department of Health (1996a) *Statistical Bulletin: Children Looked After by Local Authorities. Year Ending 31 March 1995*. Government Statistical Service.

Department of Health (1996b) *Children's Homes at 31 March 1995 England*. Government Statistical Service.

Department of Health (1996c) *Focus on Teenagers: Research into Practice*. HMSO, London.

Department of Health (1997) *Statistical Bulletin: Children Looked After by Local Authorities. Year ending 31 March 1996*. Government Statistical Service.

du Gay P (1996) Organizing identity: entrepreneurial governance and public management. In Hall S and du Gay P (eds) *Questions of Cultural Identity.* Sage, London.

Eaton L (1998) To the bone and deeper. *Community Care* 19–25 February: 18–19.

Farber ED, Kinast C, McCoard WD and Falkner D (1984) Violence in families of adolescent runaways. *Child Abuse and Neglect* 8: 295–9.

Farmer E and Parker RA (1991) *Trials and Tribulations.* HMSO, London.

Farmer E and Pollock S (1997) *Substitute Care for Sexually Abused and Abusing Children.* Report to the Department of Health, School for Policy Studies, Bristol.

Finkelhor D (1986) *A Sourcebook on Child Sexual Abuse.* Sage, London.

Fisher M, Marsh P, Phillips D with Sainsbury E (1986) *In and Out of Care: the experiences of children, parents and social workers.* Batsford/BAAF, London.

Fletcher B (1993) *Not Just a Name.* National Consumer Council, London.

Francis J (1994) 'In a drug fix'. *Community Care* 28 July–3 August.

Garnett L (1992) *Leaving Care and After.* National Children's Bureau, London.

Graham J and Bowling B (1995) *Young People and Crime.* Research Study 145, Home Office, London.

Hall S and du Gay P (1996) (eds) *Questions of Cultural Identity.* Sage, London.

Hammersley M and Atkinson P (1983) *Ethnography: Principles in Practice.* Tavistock, London.

Hazel N (1981) *A Bridge to Independence: The Kent Family Placement Project.* Blackwell, Oxford.

Heath A, Colton M and Aldgate J (1994) Failure to escape: a longitudinal study of foster children's educational attainment. *British Journal of Social Work* 24: 241–60.

Hier SJ, Korboot PJ and Schweitzer RD (1990) Social adjustment and symptomatology in two types of homeless adolescents: runaways and throwaways. *Adolescence* 25: 761–71.

Hill M, Triseliotis J, Borland M and Lambert L (1996) Fostering adolescents in Britain: outcomes and processes. *Community Alternatives* 8(1): 77–92.

Homer LE (1973) A community based resource for runaway girls. *Social Casework* 54: 473–9.

Hudson F and Ineichen B (1991) *Taking it Lying Down: Sexuality and Teenager Motherhood.* Macmillan, Basingstoke.

Hutson S and Liddiard M (1989) *Street Children in Wales.* University College Swansea.

Jackson S (1988/9) Residential care and education. *Children and Society* 4: 335–8.

Jamieson L and Corr H (1990) Earning your keep: self-reliance and family obligation. *ESRC 16–19 Initiative Occasional Paper 30.* SSRU, City University, London.

Janus MD, Burgess A and McCormack A (1987) Histories of sexual abuse in adolescent male runaways. *Adolescence* 22: 405–17.

Jesson J (1993) Understanding adolescent female prostitution: a literature review. *British Journal of Social Work* 23: 517–30.

Johnson R and Carter M (1980) Flight of the young: why children run away from their homes. *Adolescence* 15: 483–9.

Jones G and Wallace C (1992) *Youth, Family and Citizenship.* Open University Press, Buckingham.

Kelly L, Wingfield R, Burton S and Regan L (1995) *Splintered Lives.* Barnardos, Ilford.

Koprowska J and Stein M (forthcoming) The mental health of looked after children. In Aggleton P, Hurry J and Warwick I (eds) *Young People and Mental Health.* Wiley, Chichester.

Kufeldt K and Nimmo M (1987) Youth on the street: abuse and neglect in the eighties. *Child Abuse and Neglect* 11: 531–43.

Kurtz P (1991) Problems of maltreated runaway youth. *Adolescence* 103: 543–55.

Lawrenson F (1997) Runaway children: whose problem? *British Medical Journal* 314: 1064.

Lee M and O'Brien R (1995) *The Game's Up: Redefining Child Prostitution.* The Children's Society, London.

Local Government Association and the Association of Chief Police Officers (1997) *Missing from Care: Procedures and Practices in Caring for Missing Children.* Local Government Association, London.

Martin DN (1977) Disruptive behaviour and staff attitudes at the St Charles Youth Treatment Centre. *Child Psychology and Psychiatry* 18: 221–28.

Mason J (1994) Linking qualitative and quantitative data analysis. In Bryman A and Burgess R (eds) *Analyzing Qualitative Data.* Routledge, London.

Mason J (1996) *Qualitative Researching.* Sage, London.

McCann JB, James A, Wilson S and Dunn G (1996) Prevalence of psychiatric disorders in young people in the care system. *British Medical Journal* 313: 1529–30.

Millham S, Bullock R and Cherrett P (1975) *After Grace – Teeth: A Comparative Study of Eighteen Boys' Approved Schools.* Human Context Books, London.

Millham S, Bullock R, Hosie F and Frankenberg R (1977a) Absconding – part one. *Community Home Schools Gazette* 71: 280–91.

Millham S, Bullock R, Hosie F and Frankenberg R (1977b) Absconding – part two. *Community Home Schools Gazette* 71: 325–37.

Millham S, Bullock R and Hosie K (1978) *Locking up Children.* Saxon House, Farnborough.

Millham S, Bullock R, Hosie K and Haak M (1986) *Lost in Care.* Gower, Aldershot.

Newman C (1989) *Young Runaways.* The Children's Society, London.

Nye FI (1980) A theoretical perspective on running away. *Journal of Family Issues* 1: 274–99.

Opinion Research Corporation (1976) *National Statistical Survey of Runaway Youth.* Opinion Research Corporation, Princeton, New Jersey, USA.

Packman J and Hall C (1996) *Draft Report on the Implementation of Section 20 of the Children Act 1989.* Dartington Social Research Unit.

Packman J, Randall J and Jaques N (1986) *Who Needs Care?* Blackwell, Oxford.

Parker R, Wards H, Jackson S, Aldgate J and Wedge P (1991) *Looking After Children: Assessing Outcomes in Child Care.* HMSO, London.

Parton N (1997) Child protection and family support: current debates and future prospects. In Parton N (ed) *Child Protection and Family Support: Tensions, Contradictions and Possibilities.* Routledge, London.

Payne M (1995) Understanding 'going missing': issues for social work and social services. *British Journal of Social Work* 25: 333–48.

Pinchbeck I and Hewitt M (1973) *Children in English Society.* Routledge and Kegan Paul, London.

Pitts J (1988) *The Politics of Juvenile Crime.* Sage, London.

Pitts J (1991) Less harm or more good? Politics, research and practice with young people in crisis. In Dennington J and Pitts J *Developing Services for Young People in Crisis.* Longman, London.

Porteous MA and McLoughlin CS (1974) A comparison of absconders and non absconders from an assessment centre. *Community Schools Gazette* 67: 681–90.

Quinton D (1996) Emotional and behavioural development. In Jackson S and Kilroe S (eds) *Looking After Children: Good Parenting, Good Outcomes.* HMSO, London.

Rees G (1993) *Hidden Truths – Young People's Experiences of Running Away.* The Children's Society, London.

Rowe J, Hundleby M and Garnett L (1989) *Child Care Now.* British Agencies for Fostering and Adoption, London.

Shaw I, Butter I, Crowley A and Patel G (1996) *Pay the Price? Young People and Prostitution.* School of Social and Administrative Studies, University of Wales, Cardiff.

Shellow R, Schamp JR, Liebow E and Unger E (1967) Suburban runaways of the 1960s. *Monographs of the Society for Research in Child Development (Chicago)* 32(3): 28–33.

Simons R and Whitbeck L (1991) Running away during adolescence as a precursor to adult homelessness. *Social Services Review* June.

Sinclair I (1971) *Hostels for Probationers.* Home Office Research Study Number 6, HMSO, London.

Sinclair I and Clarke RV (1973) Acting-out behaviour and its significance for the residential treatment of delinquents. *Journal of Child Psychology* 14: 283–91.

Sinclair I and Gibbs I (1998) *Children's Homes: A Study in Diversity.* Wiley, Chichester.

Sinclair I and Gibbs I (forthcoming 1998) Private and local authority children's homes: a comparison. *Journal of Adolescence.*

Sinclair R, Garnett L and Berridge D (1995) *Social Work and Assessment with Adolescents.* National Children's Bureau, London.

Social Services Committee of the House of Commons (1984) *Children in Care (The Short Report).*

Social Services Inspectorate (1995) *Inspection of Local Authority Fostering 1994–5.* Department of Health, London.

Social Services Inspectorate/Ofsted (1995) *The Education of Children who are Looked After by Local Authorities.* Department of Health, London.

Social Services Inspectorate (1997) *The Control of Children in the Public Care: Interpretation of the Children Act 1989* CI(97)6.

Spatz C, Widom C and Ames MA (1994) Criminal consequences of childhood victimization. *Child Abuse and Neglect* 18(4): 303–17.

Stein M and Carey K (1986) *Leaving Care.* Blackwell, Oxford.

Stein M, Rees G and Frost N (1994) *Running – The Risk: Young People on the Streets of Britain Today.* The Children's Society, London.

Stiffman AR (1989) Physical and sexual abuse in runaway youths. *Child Abuse and Neglect* 13: 417–26.

Thoburn J, Murdoch A and O'Brien A (1986) *Permanence in Child Care.* Blackwell, Oxford.

Thompson A (1995) Running out of time. *Community Care* 7–13 December.

Triseliotis J, Borland M, Hill M and Lambert L (1995a) *Teenagers and the Social Work Services.* HMSO, London.

Triseliotis J, Sellick C and Short R (1995b) *Foster Care: Theory and Practice.* Batsford, London.

Tsunts M (1966) Dropouts on the run. *Atlas* 11: 158–60.

Utting W (1997) *People Like Us.* The Stationery Office, London.

Van der Ploeg J (1989) Homelessness: a multi dimensional problem. *Children and Youth Services Review* 11: 45–6.

Vernon J and Fruin D (1986) *A Study of Social Work Decision Making.* National Children's Bureau, London.

Ward H (ed) (1995) *Looking After Children: Research into Practice.* HMSO, London.

Whitbeck L and Simons R (1990) Life on the streets: the victimisation of runaway and homeless adolescents. *Youth and Society* 22: 108–25.

Whitaker DS, Cook J, Dunne C and Rockliffe S (1984) *The Experience of Residential Care from the Perspectives of Children, Parents and Care-givers.* Department of Social Policy and Social Work, University of York.

Whitaker D, Archer L and Hicks L (1998) *Working in Children's Homes: Challenges and Complexities.* Wiley, Chichester.

Who Cares? Trust (1993) *Not Just a Name: The Views of Young People in Foster and Residential Care*. National Consumer Council, London.

Wild N (1989) Prevalence of child sex rings. *Paediatrics* 83: 553–8.

Wilkins LT (unpublished) *Prediction methods in relation to approved school training*. Home Office Research Unit report.

LIST OF FIGURES AND TABLES

INDEX

Related titles of interest from Wiley...

From Hearing to Healing
Working with the Aftermath of Child Sexual Abuse, 2nd Edition
Anne Bannister
Published in association with the NSPCC
0-471-98298-9   216pp   1998   Paperback

Making Sense of the Children Act
Third Edition
Nicholas Allen
0-471-97831-0   304pp   1998   Paperback

Women Who Sexually Abuse Children
From Research to Clinical Practice
Jacqui Saradjian in association with Helga Hanks
Wiley Series in Child Care & Protection
0-471-96072-1   336pp   1996   Paperback

The Emotionally Abused and Neglected Child
Identification, Assessment and Intervention
Dorota Iwaniec
Wiley Series in Child Care & Protection
0-471-95579-5   222pp   1995   Paperback

Cycles of Child Maltreatment
Facts, Fallacies and Interventions
Ann Buchanan
Wiley Series in Child Care & Protection
0-471-95889-1   328pp   1996   Paperback

 ### Child Abuse Review
ISSN: 0952-9136

 ### Children & Society
Published in association with the National Children's Bureau
ISSN: 0951-0605